ESSAYS AND ADDRESSES

By the same Author

THE BACKGROUND OF ENGLISH LITERATURE :
AND OTHER ESSAYS AND ADDRESSES

CROSS CURRENTS IN ENGLISH LITERATURE OF
THE SEVENTEENTH CENTURY

Chatto & Windus

ESSAYS AND ADDRESSES

By

SIR HERBERT GRIERSON
LL.D., LITT.D., LITT. ET PHIL.D., F.B.A.

1940

CHATTO & WINDUS

LONDON

PUBLISHED BY
Chatto and Windus
LONDON
*
The Macmillan Company
of Canada, Limited
TORONTO

53182

To

MY OLD STUDENTS OF ABERDEEN
AND EDINBURGH

And in Memory of

THOSE OF THEM WHO HAVE PERISHED IN
THE HOLOCAUST OF WAR

1914–1940

CONTENTS

PAGE

PREFACE   ix

I ADDRESS AT THE PRESENTATION TO ABERDEEN GRAMMAR SCHOOL OF A STATUE OF LORD BYRON—1923   1

II PREFACE TO A COLLECTION OF ANCIENT CHINESE PARABLES—1924   19

III SCOTT AND CARLYLE (THE SUBSTANCE OF AN ADDRESS TO THE EDINBURGH SIR WALTER SCOTT CLUB—1927)   27

IV A NOTE UPON THE "SAMSON AGONISTES" OF JOHN MILTON AND "SAMSON OF HEILIGE WRAECK" BY JOOST VAN DEN VONDEL—1930   55

V CARLYLE AND HITLER (THE ADAMSON LECTURE IN THE UNIVERSITY OF MANCHESTER—1930)   65

VI ROBERT HENRYSON (AN ADDRESS TO THE SCOTTISH P.E.N. CLUB, AT A HENRYSON DINNER—1933)   105

VII LANG, LOCKHART, AND BIOGRAPHY (THE ANDREW LANG LECTURE IN THE UNIVERSITY OF ST. ANDREWS—1933)   119

VIII TWO DUTCH POETS (THE TAYLORIAN LECTURE IN THE UNIVERSITY OF OXFORD—1936)   153

IX THE UNIVERSITY AND A LIBERAL EDUCATION (THE RECTORIAL ADDRESS TO THE UNIVERSITY OF EDINBURGH—1937)   187

X A REVIEW OF "PASTORAL POETRY AND PASTORAL DRAMA", BY WALTER W. GREG—1908   211

vii

CONTENTS

PAGE

XI BACON'S POEM, "THE WORLD": ITS DATE AND
RELATION TO CERTAIN OTHER POEMS—1911   221

XII A REVIEW OF "THE LETTERS OF DOROTHY
OSBORNE TO WILLIAM TEMPLE", EDITED BY
G. C. MOORE SMITH—1929   239

XIII A REVIEW OF "LA JEUNESSE DE SWINBURNE",
BY GEORGES LAFOURCADE—1930   245

XIV A REVIEW OF "THE LATER WORDSWORTH", BY
EDITH C. BATHO—1934   261

Byron we know the worst there is to know, and we can judge him more temperately and tolerantly, conscious of two things —first, that everyone of us has the right to be judged as a whole, not by our failures but by our achievements, that we must remember not only Byron's unhappy marriage and separation, but the service which he rendered to the cause of liberty and humanity, and by the great fact that he did lay down his life for his fellow-men; and secondly, we can distinguish better between the man and the poet, the prophetic inspiration and the earthly vessel in which it was contained. The Byron whom we are celebrating to-day is not the individual about whom gossip raged, but the poet who in the greatest of his works, in the last cantos of *Childe Harold, Cain, Don Juan*, was the voice of England and Europe at an era of disaster and disillusionment not unlike that through which we ourselves are passing, champion in a double conflict which has raged ever since, and in which time reveals ever more steadily that Byron, with all his faults, was on the right side.

What those conflicts were I shall try to state briefly, but first I wish to say a word about Byron's debt to Aberdeen and Aberdeenshire, for that is my proper theme to-day, not Byron alone, but Byron and Aberdeen, what he owes to us, and why we should be proud of our connection with Byron.

Byron's inheritance from his Scottish ancestors was a strain of wild and passionate blood. If it was from his Byron ancestry that there came, as I should conjecture, the blackest drop in his blood, the impulse that made him, when his pride was wounded, capable of cruelty to those whom he loved, his own worst enemy; he certainly derived from his Gordon ancestry a tradition of almost insane turbulence and recklessness. It is a lurid chapter the history of the Gordons of Gight as told in Dr. John Malcolm Bulloch's admirable *The House of Gordon*, a story of feuds with surrounding families —Forbes, Keith, Mowat, Hay, Leask—involving cruel

3

murders, the raiding of houses and towns—Turriff, Aberdeen, Montrose—defiance of the law of every kind. William, the fifth laird, had murdered, while he was still a young man, William Leslie of Warthill and a Thomas Fraser, and when he succeeded, he murdered his sister's husband, John Keith, and was the principal in the murder of the bonny Earl of Murray. His son and successor, George, the sixth laird, took the lead in the sham trial and cruel murder of Francis Hay; and his attempts to coerce his mother-in-law, Lady Saltoun, and intimidate her agents, the Livingstones, form some of the liveliest reading in the Register of the Privy Council. The uncontrolled spirit of the man and his race is vividly expressed in his words to his wife when she would have calmed his spirit and thirst of revenge on those who had, he believed, wronged him: "Jean, I can tak' no rest. I know I will die upon a scaffold. Thair is an evill turn in my hand quhilk I avow to God presently to performe."

His brothers were men of the same spirit, as you may read in J. M. Bulloch's narrative, and so was his sister Elspeth. Her husband, James Cheyne of Pennan, having plundered the house of some unhappy man called Petrie, when the latter expostulated, the lady herself "conseiving ane heich offense againis him, in the hicht of hir distemperit passion . . . pat violent hand on him and schamfullie and unhonestlie strak and dang him with hir handis and feit in syndrie pairtis of his body, and left him for deid". Of George, the seventh laird, Dr. Bulloch says: "His career was almost as stormy as his father's", and the eighth, among other exploits, raided the town of Montrose and attempted to oust his father from his estates.

This was the blood which Byron inherited through his passionate and uncontrolled mother from the Aberdeenshire Gordons. If in the poet of *Childe Harold*, of *Prometheus*, of *Cain*, there is the indomitable pride of his Byron ancestry,

4

there is also at times the sense of *being possessed*, which his Gordon grandsire uttered in the words: "Jean, I cannot rest". So his descendant cries:

> I am as a weed
> Flung from the rock, on Ocean's foam to sail
> Where'er the surge may sweep, the tempest's breath prevail.

And again through Cain, for Cain is Byron:

> No;
> Nothing can calm me more. Calm! say I? Never
> Knew I what calm was in the soul, although
> I have seen the elements stilled.

> .   .   .   .

> That which I am, I am; I did not seek for life,
> Nor did I make myself.

But if Byron derived from his Gordon forebears the rest-lessness, the passionate inconstancy of his nature, he got also his splendid courage, and for the part he was to play, the battle he had to fight with Europe and with England, that courage was a great asset. Compared with Byron all the other poets of liberty and justice since Milton seem timid. Shelley's was perhaps a finer courage, but Shelley was never so much in the world's eye. Coleridge and Wordsworth show a bourgeois caution—Wordsworth writing but never publishing his letter to Bishop Watson, suppressing even *The Prelude* till his death, writing a generous poem on poor Burns and afraid to issue it till forty years later, printing only the tame and canting lines, *To the Sons of Burns*. Byron was the single-handed champion of European freedom in the days of the Triple Alliance; and he dared Mrs. Grundy at a time when her sway in England was almost at its zenith, when she was preparing to take her place on the English throne.

But Aberdeen gave Byron more than a turbulent ancestry.

To his years in Aberdeen he owes his earliest and some of his most enduring impressions. Little touches in his letters betray the vividness of his memories, for Byron's mind was tenacious as it was sensitive. Speaking of his tutors, he comes to one Paterson, and continues: "He was a rigid Presbyterian also. With him I began Latin in Ruddiman's Grammar, and continued till I went to the Grammar School (*Scotice* 'schule'—*Aberdonice* 'squeel'), where I threaded all the classes to the fourth." That little parenthesis is to me eloquent. Byron really knew the difference between Aberdeenshire and other Scots. I rather suspect that he spoke the Doric in his childhood, or could speak it. His mother could, his nurses, his teachers, his schoolfellows all spoke it. It is practically certain that he himself did. He left Scotland early enough to outgrow an accent, but I fancy his memory of the degree to which he had been a Scot accounts for his sensitiveness if anyone seemed to detect a flavour of it in his speech. "I never could learn anything by study, not even a language; it was all by rote, and ear, and memory. Rousseau had a bad memory; I *had*, at least, an excellent one."

But Aberdeen left other impressions on Byron than a memory of the Doric. The reference to Paterson and his Presbyterianism is also significant. It was here that Byron acquired that intimate knowledge of the Bible which he carried with him through life.

Send [he writes to Murray in 1821] a common Bible, of a good legible print. . .'. I have one; but as it was the last gift of my sister . . . I can only use it carefully, and less frequently, because I like to keep it in good order. Don't forget this, for I am a great reader and admirer of those books and had read them through and through before I was eight years old— that is to say, the Old Testament, for the New struck me as a task, but the other as a pleasure. I speak as a boy from the recollected impression of that period at Aberdeen in 1796.

There is no poet since Milton in whose poetry Bible history is more constantly an influence than Byron's. But it was not only to read the Bible that Byron learnt in Aberdeen. The Presbyterian, Calvinist doctrine of sin and retribution was impressed upon Byron's mind in a way he was never able to shake off. That doctrine, with its bearing on his own sense of wrong-doing, of guilt, lies at the heart of all his most passionate serious poems, *Childe Harold*, *Prometheus*, *Cain*. He felt its power, if he disputed its justice. But of this again.

And, lastly, it was in Aberdeen and Aberdeenshire that Byron acquired his deep feeling for two aspects of Nature—mountains and the sea. That came to him directly from his experience of our coasts and our Highlands:

> But I have loved thee, Ocean! and my joy
> Of youthful sports was on thy breast to be
> Borne, like thy bubbles onward: from a boy
> I wantoned with thy breakers—they to me
> Were a delight; and if the freshening sea
> Made them a terror, 'twas a pleasing fear.

> I live not in myself, but I become
> Portion of that around me; and to me
> High mountains are a feeling, but the hum
> Of human cities torture.

"From this period"—*i.e.* the Aberdeen period—he writes, "I date my love of mountainous country. I can never forget the effect, a few years afterwards in England, of the only thing I had long seen, even in miniature, of a mountain in the Malvern Hills. After I returned to Cheltenham I used to watch them every afternoon at sunset with a sensation which I cannot describe." But if Byron owed to Aberdeenshire his first impressions of mountains and the sea, it was to an Aberdeen professor, philosopher, and poet that he owed his introduction to the romantic and poetic feeling for Nature. Beattie's *The Minstrel* was one of the poems that Byron early knew by heart, and which became his model when he resolved to write his own *Childe Harold*, his own record of a poet's travels and his impressions, grave and gay. Beattie's *Minstrel* is the biography of a poet, a mild precursor of Wordsworth's *Prelude*, of Byron's *Childe Harold*, and of Shelley's *Alastor*—a description of the influences which shape a sensitive, poetic soul. Of these the chief is Nature, and not least her wilder aspects. The *Minstrel* seems very mild brew to us now, but one can imagine how the young Byron wandering by Lochnagar or on our stormy shore recited such verses as:

> And oft the craggy cliff he loved to climb,
> When all in mist the world below was lost,
> What dreadful pleasure there to stand sublime,
> Like ship-wreck'd mariner on desert coast,
> And view th' enormous waste of vapour, toss'd
> In billows, lengthening to the horizon round,
> Now scoop'd in gulfs, with mountains now emboss'd!
> And hear the voice of mirth and song rebound,
> Flocks, herds, and waterfalls, along the hoar profound.
>
> Oft when the winter storm had ceased to rave,
> He roam'd the snowy waste at even, to view
> The cloud stupendous, from th' Atlantic wave
> High-towering sail along the horizon blue;
> Where, 'mid the changeful scenery, ever new,
> Fancy a thousand wondrous forms descries
> More wildly great than ever pencil drew,
> Rocks, torrents, gulfs, and shapes of giant size,
> Sun glittering cliffs on cliffs, and fiery ramparts rise.

To Aberdeen and Aberdeenshire, then, Byron owed a troubled inheritance of passionate, reckless blood and some of the deepest impressions made upon his extraordinarily sensitive and extraordinarily retentive mind. The question remains, what does Aberdeen owe to Byron? Is he still a poet of such worth and eminence that it becomes us to erect

8

this enduring record of our early connection with the young boy? Well, if this statue had been erected and unveiled, say, sixty years ago, it would have been amid a more indiscriminating chorus of admiration of Byron's poetry than you will hear to-day; and if the date had been thirty years ago, it would have been accompanied, as I already hinted, by a considerable measure of thorough-going depreciation of Byron as a poet. To-day, I think, we can form a juster and more stable estimate. This is not the time for any elaborate criticism, and I will confine myself to indicating a few reasons why Aberdeen does well to remember and to put on record in an adequate form her connection with the youthful Byron.

The first is Byron's world-wide reputation, his enormous influence on the poetry and literature of Europe. There is nothing like it in the history of our great literature except the reputation and influence of Shakespeare, and even that has developed more gradually. The greatest of Byron's contemporaries, the most famous, except Byron himself, of European poets, Goethe, had no doubt of Byron's greatness.

> A character of such eminence has never existed before and probably will never come again. The beauty of *Cain* is such as we shall not see a second time in the world. . . . Byron issues from the sea-waves ever fresh. In *Helena* I could not make use of any man as the representative of the modern era except him, who is undoubtedly the greatest genius of our century.

Spain, Italy, France, Russia echoed the voice of Goethe and Germany. "What", says Castelar, "does Spain not owe to Byron. From his mouth came our hopes and fears. He has baptized us with his blood. There is no one with whom some song of his is not woven. His life is like a funeral torch over our graves." Mazzini bears the same witness for Italy. Elze, the German critic, ranks Byron among the four greatest English poets, and classes him as the intellectual parent of

9

Lamartine and Musset in France, of Espronceda in Spain, of Puschkin in Russia, of Heine in Germany, of Berchet and others in Italy. If you turn over the pages given to Byron in the British Museum catalogue you will find his works translated into every language of Europe, from Dutch and Scandinavian to Greek and Rumanian. In Cornell University I met this summer a young Icelander studying for his Ph.D., and he told me that his thesis was to be the influence of Byron on the Icelandic poetry of the nineteenth century.

That is a historical fact which cannot be ignored even if the enthusiasm has somewhat waned, and writers like M. Estève in France and Signor Farinelli in Italy speak of Byron's influence as a thing of the past; and their opinion is more representative of academic than popular taste. What was it, one asks, in Byron's poetry which gave this astounding power to excite and infect, and what of it still endures?

There are, I think, three things about Byron's poetry which made it a great historical event. The first is its passionate quality. The vehemence of Byron's temper gave the world, in Tennyson's words, "another heart and new pulses". Rousseau had already quickened men's sympathies and awakened humanitarian aspirations and enthusiasms, and Byron, with his vehement poetry, redoubled the effect, the longings, the loves and hates, the melancholy, the dreams of a period like that of the French Revolution. Passion has its dangers for the individual and for the community, and recent critics have been justly enough critical of many aspects and consequences of the movement to which Rousseau gave the first impetus. But we must not forget that every advance which humanity has made has originated in some such moving of the waters. The passion of the Jewish prophets, of the early Christians, of the humanitarian and revolutionary movement in which the eighteenth century closed, if they all produced many sore evils and bitter disappointments, were

10

also the sources of the most definite achievements which humanity has made in the quest of justice and purity and compassion.

But Byron not only quickened the pulses of poetry in Britain and in Europe, poured into it some of the reckless spirit of his Gordon ancestors, he was also a daring and generous fighter in the cause of liberty and humanity, even in his own strange way, the enemy, for he had little positive vision, of an unintelligent and narrow conception of Christianity, the enemy of the cynicism and cruelty of European diplomacy and war. What I mean will become clear if I may say a word or two on Byron's later poetry. The third canto of *Childe Harold* strikes a new note in Byron's poetry. All that had gone before that was not without freshness and influence, but it was essentially boyish and ephemeral. But between 1812 and 1816 Byron and Europe passed through a tremendous crisis; and if one part of a classical poem is that in it we hear the voice, not of an individual alone, but of a generation, Byron's *Childe Harold*, III and IV, might be styled the classical poem of Europe in the years immediately following 1815, when the long period of high hopes and fierce conflicts which the French Revolution inaugurated closed in shattering and complete disillusionment. Great men, great events, great cities, all tell the same tale, *vanitas vanitatum*. Only nature, only beauty endures. The Rhine, the Alps, Lake Thrasimene, and the Sea all speak of the transitoriness of human achievements, of a beauty and grandeur which outlives all the drums and tramplings of human conquests and empires; and yet human history too has its abiding values, not wars and conquests and empires, but heroism and love and art.

That is one side of the new *Childe Harold*, but there is another in which the poet's theme is not Europe after Waterloo, but Byron after the separation. Byron is the only

English romantic poet who has a sense of sin, and is, therefore, capable of a tragic view of life. A too facile optimism besets the romantics from Wordsworth and Shelley to Tennyson and Browning. But Byron had been driven from England in a tumult of contending emotions, at war not only with English society and English politics, but at war with his own soul, conscious of wrong done to those whom he loved, conscious of the waste of his great powers, his finer susceptibilities, his most generous impulses,

> The expense of spirit in a waste of shame.

And the most poignant stanzas in *Childe Harold*, the sombre and impressive poem *Prometheus*, *Manfred* and the greatest of his tragedies, *Cain*, are all the expression of the fierce conflict which raged in Byron's soul between his sense of sin, of guilt, which he never denied or ignored, like Shelley, and on the other hand what seemed to him the injustice of that conception of sin and retribution which he had learned in Calvinist Aberdeen and among the more emotional but less intellectual Evangelicals of England. In *Cain* he threw down the gauntlet to the unintelligent literalness with which the Bible was accepted in English pious circles, and presented with naked force the injustice of the conception of God's dealing with mankind which follows from such an unintelligent reading.

On all this I have not time to dwell, but wish just to emphasize this, that whatever we may think of Byron personally, the cause he was fighting is that which modern criticism and modern thought have vindicated. The work of great critics, like our own Robertson Smith, has been to teach us to read the Bible in a juster perspective and to regain for us a conception of Christianity, its teaching about sin and retribution, which is truer to the spirit of Christ and of humanity.

Byron's other great conflict in these later poems was with the spirit of European politics and diplomacy, the spirit which survived the Treaty of Vienna and begot the Holy Alliance, the spirit which for a time the growth of Liberalism appeared to be weakening and discrediting, but which Bismarck conjured into new life with the inevitable consequence of the Great War. This is the real significance of *Don Juan* and *The Vision of Judgment* and *The Age of Bronze*. *Don Juan* is, of course, not merely a satire on the governing classes of England and Europe, their immorality and frivolity, the careless cruelty of their endless game of war and intrigue. It is a strange medley of moods and scenes and incidents, and in the first cantos his chief aim is still, perhaps, to shock English respectability and morality, to force on their attention that side of life which they not only condemned but strove to ignore, and compelled the English novelist to ignore, so that the picture of life given by Thackeray and Dickens and Trollope is less complete than that of Fielding and Smollett. But the point of view from which the whole is seen in just perspective is that which Byron himself emphasized, a satire on higher society, the class that governed Europe, and ultimately a satire on human nature in that part of the business of life in which it has failed most conspicuously— the bungled, cruel business of government and war. "It is impossible", he told Kennedy, "you can believe the higher classes of society worse than they are in England, France, and Italy, for no language can sufficiently paint them." To paint them as he knew them, in all the external glitter of their life, intent upon the game of war and diplomacy, the pawns in which are the lives and fortunes of simple men, or diverting themselves in the sensual intrigues which the world calls love,—that is the motive of *Don Juan*, as it became the motive of the work of another great aristocratic artist, Count Tolstoi. Byron's work suffers by comparison with Tolstoi's because of its too uniformly cynical and mocking tone. The difference between *Don Juan* and *Anna Karenina* is the difference between the picture drawn by a satirist, a satirist like Jonathan Swift, one who is not wanting in heart, but seeks in gay mockery an escape from his outraged sensibilities, and a work which is moved by a great passion for humanity in all its weakness and a profound sense of man's need of God.

But do not forget that Byron's cynical, immoral, mundane poem, as it appears upon the surface, is inspired by the same idealism as Shelley's *Prometheus Unbound* and Tolstoi's *War and Peace*. He has the same hatred of war as Swift and Shelley and Tolstoi, of war and cruelty and injustice, and in that cause Byron laid down his life. Against all chatter about Byron's immorality and inconstancy I set always his words in Greece:

> I am come here not in search of adventures, but to assist the regeneration of a nation whose very debasement makes it more honourable to become their friend.

> Poverty is wretchedness; but it is perhaps to be preferred to the heartless, unmeaning dissipation of the higher orders. I am thankful I am now entirely clear of this, and my resolution to remain clear of it for the rest of my life is immutable.

And everything that Byron did in Greece showed the same unwearied patience, the same entire abdication of self, the same dauntless courage and power to inspire and to command.

For his last work Byron found a medium of which he had a more perfect command than any he had essayed. He is not a great and sustained artist. The last two cantos of *Childe Harold* are full of faults as well as beauties. The style and verse have something of the turbid flow of a lava stream, choked at times with the debris of imperfect phrasing and tormented rhythms; again flowing in a clear and strong if dark stream; and again growing incandescent in felicitous and magnificent lines and stanzas. For his last poems he found a measure in which he could write as spontaneously and easily as he conversed, whether by word of mouth or in

his letters. The result was a poem which for ease and buoy-
ancy and strength has no rival, and in its narrative passages,
the description of the shipwreck or of the Russo-Turkish
battle, comes nearer to the manner of Homer than any
English poem I know.

Of Byron's poetry, much has ceased to interest us to-day,
but some will always endure—the best of *Childe Harold*,
Prometheus, *Manfred*, *Sardanapalus*, *Cain*, the best of his personal
lyrics, *Beppo*, *The Vision of Judgment*, *Don Juan*, perhaps
Marino Faliero, *The Prisoner of Chillon*, and *The Island*. But
besides these remains the whole man and his whole work and
what it stands for in the history of Britain and Europe. That
is what we are memorializing to-day by the noble work of
art, and it is well to do so, for it is well to remind ourselves
of our ties with the larger world. Provinciality is not a bad
thing, a pride in ourselves and our local heroes, our Bards of
Bon-Accord; and Aberdeen provinciality is of a robust and
admirable type. No one who has known Aberdeen can fail
to conceive a profound respect and affection for its strong,
self-reliant, efficient people, and to admire its fine indifference to the criticism of outsiders. Nor is it really a narrow
provinciality, as the war and many other occasions have
proved. Still, provinciality of mind is a danger against which
we have ever to strive by an effort to expand and purify the
imagination. I have visited lately a great nation which in a
critical hour has failed to play a great part on the stage of
history from provinciality of mind. We are apt to think that
America's desertion of Europe after the close of the War was
deliberate and somewhat cynical. That is not the case.
One must visit America to realize how much it was due to the
provinciality of mind of the great mass of people, incapable—
perhaps naturally incapable—of seeing beyond the large yet
narrow limits of their own material welfare, and prize-fights,
and political and industrial problems. These things occupy

far more space in their papers than the problems and sufferings of Europe and Asia. I speak of the nation as a whole, not forgetting the generosity and humanity of individuals. America's failure has been due to provinciality of mind, but none the less history will reckon it a great failure. "A great empire and little minds go ill together." So with us, let us remember, and be proud of our local celebrities, our Beatties and Melvins and all the rest; but let us be still prouder of names like those of Byron and Clerk Maxwell and Robertson Smith, which link us with the larger world of history and science and thought.

And we have chosen a good time, as it proves, to recall the memory of Byron, for the cause for which he fought and for which he died is with us still in as acute a form as after the Napoleonic war. That is the cause of justice and humanity in the dealings of European nations with each other, and especially of greater with smaller nations. The spirit of Byron's poetry was the spirit in which Mr. Gladstone approached the problem of foreign politics in the famous Don Pacifico debate, when, like Burke and like Byron, he insisted that the relation between nations should be the same as that between individuals, and governed by a regard for justice and humanity. For some years after the collapse of the Holy Alliance that cause did make some progress. It was set back fatally by the rise of Prussia under Bismarck and his cynical doctrine of blood and iron. The outcome of that policy was the Great War. A shattered Europe looks round since that catastrophe for something to deliver it from the fatal wounds of cynical diplomacy and cruel war. The question is whether, deserted by America, Europe can find it. The League of Nations is the first feeble attempt to find a way out, how feeble recent events have shown, yet not altogether is it a failure. What Byron would have thought of the League it is easy to guess: the humane idealist would have welcomed the

16

conception, the cynical misanthropist would have doubted the success. He had hoped that Napoleon would give Europe freedom and union and he deplored his failure:

> Hear, hear Prometheus from his rock appeal
> To Earth-Air-Ocean—all that felt or feel
> His power and glory, all who yet shall hear
> A name eternal as the rolling year;
> He teaches them the lesson taught so long,
> So oft, so vainly—learn to do no wrong!
> A single step into the right had made
> This man, the Washington of worlds betray'd;
> A single step into the wrong has given
> His name a doubt to all the winds of heaven.

Well, the conflict to-day in each nation and in each individual bosom is the old one between cynical disbelief and impossible faith. Byron, despite the cynical temper of his mind, fought and died in the cause of the ideal, died a soldier of humanity. We do well to honour him at this time, even if we feel that the cause was hopeless then and seems more hopeless to-day, because it looks as though it were only the hopeless causes that it is worth while either to live or die for. At least, the success of that and every other worthy cause will depend upon the number of men who, like Byron and Mazzini and Gladstone, are willing to spend themselves and be spent in the cause of the right, however hopeless it may appear:

> They never fail who die
> In a great cause: the block may soak their gore:
> Their heads may sodden in the sun; their limbs
> Be strung to city gates and castle walls—
> But still their spirit walks abroad. Though years
> Elapse, and others share as dark a doom,
> They but augment the deep and sweeping thoughts
> Which overpower all others, and conduct
> The world at last to Freedom.

It is to Byron, a great poet, despite the faults in his art, a great man, despite the faults of his life, that we are to unveil this beautiful statue and to entrust it to the care of the authorities of the Grammar School and of the City of Aberdeen. May it remain a reminder of Aberdeen's connection with Byron, an inspiration to the students of this School, appealing to them to judge fairly and generously of their fellow-men, to estimate their lives not by their faults but by their achievements. It is a great thing to think that the name of a Grammar School boy is known to the whole world as the name of a great poet and a soldier in the cause of humanity.

II

Preface to a Collection
of Ancient Chinese Parables[1]—1924

I HAVE been asked by Dr. K. T. Sen to write a brief preface to this collection of ancient Chinese parables which
he has translated into excellent English. The responsibility
must rest with Dr. Sen, for I feel singularly ill-fitted for the
task; and, if I have consented, it is only as an expression of
the sincere respect which the character and ability of such
Chinese students as Dr. Sen and others, my acquaintances in
Aberdeen and in Edinburgh, have inspired in me. "To
know what it is that you know", says Confucius, "and to
know what it is that you do not know, that is true understanding." Well, the present writer knows that he knows
nothing of Chinese literature beyond the translations of
beautiful Chinese poems which we owe to Professor Giles,
Mr. Waley, and others—these and such glimpses of the spirit
of Confucius's wonderful teaching as have filtered through
many apertures into the European mind. Yet even so much
has been enough to deepen a feeling I have long entertained
that the world of the West to-day has much to learn from
China. That light from the East of which we often hear
may prove to be, unless China herself be involved in the dis-
solution which is threatening human civilization, a light
from the Far East, and not after all the mystical will-o'-the-
wisp which dances over the morass of Slavonic emotionalism

[1] *Ancient Chinese Parables.* Selected and edited by Yü Hsin Sen, and
translated by Dr. Kwei-Ting Sen. Shanghai, 1924.

nor the blue light of Buddhist and other theosophies. For what does the world want so deeply at the present moment as the light of common sense and common charity, as a morality *of the world*, not a worldly morality but a morality which is based on experience and claims no transcendent sanction, metaphysical or religious, beyond the fact of experience that we know God is, though we do not know what He is, but must interpret Him in the light of what is best in ourselves, for man lives by admiration, hope, and love:

> By love subsists
> All lasting grandeur, by pervading love;
> That gone, we are as dust.

Christian morality is other-worldly—that is at once its strength and its weakness. Its strength is seen in its saints, from St. Francis to Lord Shaftesbury, and in its power to convert, to change the heart by the expulsive power of a new affection, especially in the simple and lowly. Its weakness is that it gives to the ordinary, educated man of the world, who has not the making of an ascetic or a saint, nor is able to accept the mere guidance of his feelings, no clear "way", no reasonable discipline for everyday life in the world; and there ensues a hopeless contradiction between profession and practice: "Therefore I say unto you, take no thought for your life what ye shall eat or what ye shall drink, nor yet for your body what ye shall put on". That is the language of the teacher whose "way" we profess to follow. Truer to experience and to our practice is the word of Confucius: "If a man takes no thought for the morrow he will be sorry before to-day is out". And so to profess one rule and act upon another has become the most obvious characteristic of the average life of so-called Christian peoples as seen by others. Law's *Serious Call to the Unconverted* was a challenge to Christians to realize what Christianity demands of us.

The contrast between our profession and our practice is the burden of all the great satirists from Chaucer to Trollope. Fielding shows us in *Joseph Andrews* that anyone who like Parson Adams really tries to act on Christian principles is in the eyes of his fellows as mad as Don Quixote:

> Adams rebuked his wife for disputing his commands and quoted many texts of Scripture to prove that the husband is the head of the wife and she is to submit and obey. The wife answered that it was blasphemy to talk Scripture out of church; that such things were very proper to be said in the pulpit, but that it was profane to talk them in common discourse.

What Mrs. Adams says we all tend to think. Or listen next to Trollope:

> Had the Archdeacon been preaching about matrimony he would have recommended young men in taking wives to themselves especially to look for young women who feared the Lord. But in talking about his own son's wife no word as to her eligibility or non-eligibility in this respect escaped his lips. Had he talked on the subject till nightfall, no such word would have been spoken. Had any friend of his own, man or woman, in discussing such a matter with him, alluded to the fear of the Lord, the allusion would have been distasteful to him and would have smacked to his palate of hypocrisy.

Well, human nature will never live up to its ideals, Confucian or Christian. But that is not the whole matter. Christian ethics never were frankly a "way" of life for this world. Our life here was treated, in the early Church, as a short time of waiting for a new life, "when we which are alive and remain shall be caught up into the clouds"; in the Middle Ages, as a vale of tears through which each individual passes to the Day of Judgment. The judgment of the Middle Ages was quite definite. Only in a monastery or hermitage can the Christian life be led. The protestant, puritan attempt to enforce the Christian life on average men living in this world was a failure. It was a life, like the true monastic life, or more so, only for heroic spirits. With the world Christian ethics have had ever to compromise. The late Lord Salisbury found the ethics of Christ, of the Sermon on the Mount, incompatible with every human profession and calling. So we say the Sermon on the Mount must not be taken literally. The words of consecration in the Sacrament *must* be taken literally, but not "I say unto you, that ye resist not evil; but whosoever shall smite thee on thy right cheek, turn to him the other also". So Lord Hugh Cecil tells us. The one thing that Christian teaching has impressed on the Western mind, for good and for evil, is the virtue of following ideals, uncriticized ideals, knightly, ascetic, orthodox, patriotic, till the fanatic pursuit of ideals has become almost as destructive of human happiness as the abuses of commercial practice. The claim of a wise prudence and moderation has never received Christian sanction. Speaking of the resistance of the Irish extremists to their Free State brethren, and the destruction and bloodshed which has ensued, a writer in a very Christian paper declares, "The Irish have proved once again their power to die for an ideal". That is our attitude as shaped by Christ and the saints. That must be right for which we are prepared to die. But men will risk death to scale Mount Everest, to fly round the world, to win a bet by crossing the Atlantic in a ketch. The question the right-minded man has to ask himself is not "Am I prepared to die for an ideal?" Rather it should be: "How far am I justified in maiming, murdering, and destroying the happiness of others for the sake of my ideal?" For looked at in that light the ideal might reveal its true worth. It might be worth the tragic sacrifice of having to do these terrible things, and tragedy consists not in suffering but in being driven to do terrible things, and it might not. No ideal should have any authority which outrages common sense and common charity.

The energy of Christian thought has been expended on

dogma rather than ethics. It was quite otherwise with Confucianism. "With a highly practical people like the Chinese," says Professor Giles, "the acts of human beings have always been reckoned as of infinitely greater importance than their opinions. The value of morality has completely overshadowed any claim of belief; duty towards our neighbour has mostly taken the precedence of duty towards God." To separate belief and conduct entirely is perhaps a dangerous thing, apt to dry up ethics. But Confucius himself was no atheist. "There are three things," he says, "of which the superior man stands in awe. He stands in awe of the will of God. He stands in awe of great sages; and of inspired words which have been uttered by men." Yet, have not Western Christians something to learn from Confucianism here? The age of dogma is past. We shall never attempt these bold definitions and deductions. It is a shallow critic who would despise the history of dogma and wax witty about Homoousian and Homoiousian. But looking back we can see that the value of the Church's dogmatic definitions was negative. They ruled out dogmas from which more pernicious deductions might have been drawn. They lifted man's spirit above the sensible. But to-day what the Christian world needs to learn from Confucianism is that true religion begins and ends in ethics, and that man's duty to God is inseparable and indistinguishable from his duty to man, perhaps the deepest significance of the Incarnation:

> *God's wisdom and God's goodness!* Ay, but fools
> Mis-define these till God knows them no more.
> *Wisdom and goodness, they are God*—what schools
> Have yet so much as heard this simpler lore?
> This no saint preaches, and this no Church rules:
> 'Tis in the desert now and heretofore.

Well, Confucius was a saint of that school. Of duties to God other than duties to our fellow men—*tabus* like Catholic sacrilege and Protestant Sabbatarianism—he knew nothing. "When asked what constituted wisdom, Confucius replied: 'To cultivate earnestly our duty toward our neighbour, and to reverence spiritual beings while always maintaining a due reserve may be called wisdom'." The blessed words "a due reserve"! A due reserve about the origin and purpose of the Universe, the nature of God, of the atonement, of the world! It is a simple and yet a hard doctrine, as Confucius well knew. "Alas! for a very long time will only a very small portion of mankind be in a position to recognize the unchangeable law of the soul, and to draw from it the uttermost results"; and the religious history of China, as Professor Giles sketches it, is a series of invasions by more highly seasoned cults. Buddhism, Taoism, Christianity, Catholic and Protestant, have all made the appeal of subtler metaphysics, stronger appeals to emotion, more elaborate rites, extremer asceticisms—all so much more exciting than simply "to do justly, to love mercy, and to walk humbly with thy God". But that history reveals also the persistence and reassertion of Confucianism, the power of its "way" or "*tao*" to produce gentlemen and traders whose word is their bond, for whom war is barbaric, whose piety to parents and relations is perfect, whose courtesy is as delicate and as beautiful as their flowers and poems. Have Christian peoples nothing to learn? What is wanted, it seems to me, is that Christian feeling, as powerful to-day as ever it was, should be poured into the channels of conduct; and that Christian thought should face the problems of conduct in this world from which we cannot escape, for medieval escapes are for us logically absurd, and teach what is Christian duty as to war, or the stock-exchange, in the market and in politics, for this is the sphere of true religion, Christian or Confucian. The end of Confucius was to create "gentlemen", superior men, neither medieval saints nor Nietzschean supermen, for it was his

24

dream that all mankind should be composed of superior men governed by the laws which Confucius as well as Christ enunciated: "Do not unto others what you would not that they should do unto you!" "Love one another."

I may seem to have wandered far from the purpose of these little parables, some of which, Dr. Sen tells me, are presumably older than Confucius, for Confucius did not profess to originate but to renew and interpret. To me much of the interest of these tales is that they breathe the spirit of China which is made more articulate in Confucius and his great disciples. They are simple, yet withal sometimes subtle little tales told by a people curiously interested in experience and the problems of life and conduct, of prudence and justice, in the ways of men. In their dry simplicity lies their charm. Nor is the moral enforced always trite and obvious. In *Songs that Startle* the reply of the pleasure-loving prince silences Wu Chu and states a truth which Shakespeare put into the mouth of Prince Henry:

> If all the year were playing holidays,
> To sport would be as tedious as to work;
> But when they seldom come, they wish'd-for come,
> And nothing pleases but rare accidents.
> So, when this loose behaviour I throw off,
> And pay the debt I never promised,
> By how much better than my word I am,
> By so much shall I falsify men's hopes;
> And, like bright metal on a sullen ground,
> My reformation, glittering o'er my fault,
> Shall show more goodly and attract more eyes
> Than that which hath no foil to set it off.

In a charming lecture on Chinese character Dr. Sen dwelt on the unwillingness of a Chinese to give direct advice, his habit of indirect suggestion, his tendency "to hint a fault and hesitate dislike". A delightful instance of this is the story, a very good one, *Expecting Much for Little*; but one suspects

25

there are many more, that these innocent-looking little stories had political implications. *The Oven as an Emblem of Sovereignty* is another example of indirect suggestion. There are few that do not reveal more wisdom and morality the more they are reflected upon. The little sermon *The Old Paths* goes to the bottom of the matter. Morality is never altogether a thing of good impulse and right reasoning but always in large part of accepted usage, of established tradition. We may do more harm by weakening a prevailing sanction than any single action, however generous the impulse which prompted it, can do of good. "Remember the days of old, consider the years of many generations; ask thy father and he will show thee, thy elders and they will tell thee." But that is the very soul of Chinese and Confucian ethics, and to the Western world in the age of Ibsen, Shaw, D'Annunzio it is a principle that has no meaning. We have so broken up the power of tradition and convention that there is nothing left even to be witty about, and for the effects look round upon modern life as reflected in our novels and newspaper divorce columns. With tradition and convention, now sneered at as Victorian, have disappeared all principles and all decency. There is nothing real and fundamental but sexual impulse if our psychologists and greater novelists are to be believed. It is a pleasure to turn from these excesses to the dry light of the wisdom of a people who are very old and who reverence their own traditions, instead of considering them a butt for cheap and tedious wit, and who alike in poetry, art, and philosophy understand the value of suggestion, economy, "due reserve", the significant line, the well-chosen epithet, the simple but pregnant little tale. I can but hope that Dr. Sen, whom ability, scholarship, and refined appreciation of Chinese and Western character have prepared for such a task, will go on to give us more samples of Chinese wisdom and morality and delicate perception.

III

SCOTT AND CARLYLE

*The Substance of an Address
to the Edinburgh Sir Walter Scott Club—1927*

THE lives of the three greatest of Scottish imaginative writers—Burns, Scott, and Carlyle—overlapped in an interesting and, for each successor, an influential manner. Burns prepared the way for Scott's interpretation and popularization of Scottish character and history. Carlyle's *French Revolution* would not have been composed in the vivid dramatic manner it is but for the Waverley Novels, for "these historical novels have taught all men this truth, which looks like a truism, and yet was as good as unknown to writers of history and others till so taught: that the bygone ages of the world were actually filled by living men, not by protocols, state-papers, controversies, and abstractions of men . . . men in buff or other coats and breeches, with colour in their cheeks, with passions in their stomachs, and the idioms, features, and vitalities of very men. It is a little word this, inclusive of great meaning! History will henceforth have to take thought of it." And Carlyle before Macaulay took thought of it in composing his first and most vivid historical picture.

Scott was fifteen years old when Burns came to Edinburgh, and every one knows the story of their one meeting. He never wrote a study or biography of Burns, but his references to him in letters and journals, and in a short review of Cromek's *Reliques of Robert Burns* (1809), show a keen sense

27

of the poet's genius—"When I want to express a sentiment which I feel strongly I find the phrase in Shakespeare or thee". And in the review he supplies a more vivid glimpse of the poet's temperament and character than Scottish piety has always been willing to allow us.

> Robert Burns was the child of impulse and feeling. Of the steady principle which cleaves to that which is good, he was unfortunately divested by the violence of those passions which finally wrecked him. It is most affecting to add that while swimming, struggling, and finally yielding to the torrent, he never lost sight of the beacon which ought to have guided him to land, yet never profited by its light. The dignity, the spirit, the indignation of Burns was that of a plebeian—of a high-souled plebeian indeed—of a citizen of Rome or Athens; but still of a plebeian untinged with the slightest shade of that spirit of chivalry which since the feudal times has pervaded the higher ranks of society. This ardent and irritable temperament had its periods not merely of tranquillity, but of the most subduing tenderness. . . . It was in female society that his powers of expression displayed their utmost fascination. . . . The traits of sensibility which, told of another, would sound like instances of gross affectation were so native to the soul of this extra-ordinary man, and burst from him so involuntarily, that they not only obtained full credence as the genuine feelings of his own heart, but melted into unthought-of sympathy all who witnessed them.

The paragraphs from which these sentences are taken are worth all the *apologiae* of Burns that have ever been written. We see the man who wrote the few amazing poems and songs that alone are the real Burns. Carlyle, like Burns a high-souled plebeian, the son of laborious, serious, pious peasants, came to Edinburgh, a student fourteen years old, in 1809—the year between *Marmion* and *The Lady of the Lake*. In the year of *Waverley* he left college and began to look round for a profession, and during all the years that the novels were flowing from Scott's pen Carlyle was struggling to find a livelihood in or in the neighbourhood of Edinburgh, struggling with dyspepsia, poverty, "the condition of the country", which he viewed with other eyes than Scott, and the spiritual crisis which is described in *Sartor*. Of the novels and their author he says but little in contemporary letters and notes, and what he does is in the carping, contemptuous tone with which he generally spoke of contemporaries. Scott is the "literary restaurateur of Europe". "What are his novels—any of them? A bottle of champagne, claret, port, or even ale-drinking. Are we wiser, holier, stronger? No, we have been amused." The romantic career of Byron had more interest for the fundamentally romantic Carlyle; and in *Wilhelm Meister* he finds "more insight into the elements of human nature, and a more poetically perfect combining of them, than in all the other fictitious literature of our generation", though to Miss Welsh he has to admit a year later that *Wilhelm* is worth next to nothing as a novel.

But Carlyle *did* read the Waverley Novels and admire their treatment of history, and when the news of Scott's death reached him he spoke in more generous tones.

Sir Walter Scott died some days ago. Goethe at the spring equinox, Scott at the autumn one. A gifted spirit is wanting then from among men. Perhaps he died in good time, so far as his own reputation is concerned. He understood what history meant; this was his chief intellectual merit. As a thinker not feeble—rather strong and healthy, yet limited, almost mean and *kleinstädtisch*. I never spoke with Scott (had once some small epistolary intercourse with him on the part of Goethe, in which he behaved not very courteously I thought), have a hundred times seen him from of old, writing in the Courts, or hobbling with stout speed along the streets of Edinburgh, a large man; pale, shaggy face; fine, deep-browed, grey eyes; an expression of strong, homely intelligence, of humour and good humour, and perhaps (in later years), among the wrinkles, of sadness and weariness. A solid, well-built, effectual mind; the merits of which after all this delirious exaggeration is done, and the reaction thereof is also done, will not be forgotten. He has played his part, and left none like or second to him.—*Plaudite*.

Seven years later, when the twenty-three years of struggle and uncertainty were at last leading to some measure of competence and long-delayed recognition, Carlyle wrote his article on Scott for the *Westminster Review*. It is a remarkable study, not without insight and an element of justice in its implied protest against indiscriminate eulogy. The tone of the criticism is a blend of that of the early contemptuous references and the more generous tone of the note written when he heard of Scott's death. But the fact is, it was almost impossible for Carlyle to write of Scott with entire fairness, and that for reasons which throw light upon both Scott and Carlyle. It was always difficult for Carlyle to praise a contemporary whole-heartedly. In nothing did he differ more from Scott. Carlyle was a peasant, a great-souled plebeian, and had a measure of what is perhaps the besetting sin of his class and country—an inclination, I will not say to envy, for that implies malignity, a readiness to do injury, and that is not a common Scottish failing, and was certainly not Carlyle's, but a tendency to look with very critical eyes at a contemporary who has been more fortunate than ourselves, more prosperous, but especially more popular, a disposition to say with Cassius:

> and this man
> Is now become a god, and Cassius is
> A wretched creature, and must bend his body
> If Caesar carelessly but nod on him;

and Scott, ill and in trouble, omitted even to nod when Carlyle forwarded a letter from Goethe. The years of Scott's greatest prosperity and popularity had been those of

Carlyle's long-drawn-out suffering, poverty, ill-health, and spiritual conflicts. When in July 1821 Scott was setting out for London to attend the coronation, Carlyle was wrestling with the devil in Leith Walk, "toiling along the dirty little Rue St. Thomas de l'Enfer in a close atmosphere, and over pavements hot as Nebuchadnezzar's furnace"; and ten years later, when Scott passed through London, Carlyle was there, still unknown to all but a few, still given the cold shoulder by publishers. Scott could not but seem to him the embodiment of worldly prosperity—one at ease, not even in Zion but in Domdaniel.

> His life was worldly; his ambitions were worldly. There is nothing spiritual in him; all is economical, material, of the earth earthy. A love of the picturesque, of beautiful, vigorous, and graceful things; a genuine love, yet not more genuine than has dwelt in hundreds of men named minor poets; this is the highest quality to be discerned in him.

Scott's only aim is to amuse.

> The Genius of a faithless, sceptical age had said to himself: What man shall be the temporary comforter, or were it but the spiritual comfit-maker, of this my poor singular age, to solace its dead tedium and manifold sorrows a little? So had the Genius said, looking out over the world, What man? and found him walking the distant Outer Parliament House of Edinburgh with his advocate-gown on his back; and exclaimed, That is he!

But novels written to amuse and to make money must want serious interest, and so the Waverley Novels lack depth and reality of character as well as all philosophy of life.

> It were a long chapter to unfold the difference in drawing a character between a Scott, a Shakespeare, and a Goethe, yet it is a difference literally immense; they are of a different species; the value of the one is not to be counted in the coin of the other. We might say in a short word, which means a long matter, that your Shakespeare fashions his characters

from the heart outwards; your Scott fashions them from the skin inwards. The one set become living men and women; the others amount to little more than mechanical cases, deceptively painted automatons.

These famed books are altogether addressed to the everyday mind; there is next to no nourishment in them. Opinions, emotions, principles, doubts, beliefs, beyond what the intelligent country gentleman can carry along with him, are not to be found. It is orderly, customary, decent; nothing more.

The Waverley Novels "are not profitable for doctrine, for reproof, for edification, for building up or elevating in any shape". So speaks Carlyle, justifying what he said of himself to Jane Welsh, that there was a strange dark humour in him over which he had no control. His demon was—as many demons are—a conflict of unharmonized impulses. Like Byron, he was at war with himself, a passionate believer with no creed; censorious in his judgments, utterly kind-hearted in his actions; lover of solitude, yet miserable if for long cut off from intellectual companionship—the apostle of silence who wrote and spoke interminably, for even when alone he talks to himself in journals and notes. He must find expression for every thought and humour. But the tormented man is critical of the happy man, and if ever there was a happy man, despite some bitter and lifelong disappointments, it was Scott. He was one of those fortunate beings who, in the words of a psychologist and critic, "had achieved an ordered life, whose systems have developed clearing-houses by which the varying claims of different impulses are adjusted". Historian, antiquarian, happy in the country, and happy among his fellow-lawyers and literary friends in town, commercial adventurer, and great imaginative creator, and above all loving and loved by his fellow-men, even by dogs and cats and donkeys and pigs. Scott had endless interests and was happy in them all. We tend to love such persons for what they are. "The esteem and respect accorded to persons with the social virtues well developed is only in a small degree due to the use which we find we can make of them. It is much more a sense that their lives are rich and full."

We do not know enough of Shakespeare's life to be certain, but one suspects that his life had something of the same fulness—poet, actor, courtier, burgher of Stratford, the gentle Shakespeare whom even Jonson, a bit of a Carlyle in his censorious temper, loved "on this side idolatry". At any rate, one feels uncertain how Shakespeare would have fared at Carlyle's hand if he had lived in the nineteenth century, for much that Carlyle says of Scott applies immediately to Shakespeare. Did Scott "write daily with the ardour of a steam-engine that he might make £15,000 a year and buy upholstery with it"? Well, did not Shakespeare write plays, or cobble up old ones, at the rate of two a year that he might buy a spurious coat of arms, and become the owner of the best house in Stratford, and end his life as an influential burgher, leaving the editing of his plays to look after itself?

> Shakespeare (whom you and every play-house bill
> Call the divine, the matchless, what you will),
> For gain, not glory, winged his roving flight,
> And grew immortal in his own despite.

Did Scott write only to amuse? "If literature had no task but that of harmlessly amusing indolent, languid men, here was the very perfection of literature". Well, had Shakespeare any other conscious purpose? One may gather wisdom from his plays—and from Scott's novels—and critics, German and English, have discovered there much which would surprise Shakespeare. A candid student will, I think, come to the conclusion that more than any dramatist of his age, except Beaumont and Fletcher, Shakespeare accepted the rôle of a purveyor of amusement to Court and people, the rôle of "Master of Revels to Mankind" as Emerson calls him; that he wrote both comedy and tragedy with less of didactic purpose, genuine or assumed, than George Chapman or Ben Jonson or Webster or Cyril Tourneur, or even Philip Massinger, who all had, whatever we may think of it, their conception of the ways of God, of the Nemesis that follows crime, which they take trouble to enforce. Shakespeare tells his story and leaves it without comment for you to read as you may. There it is; the rest is silence.

But indeed Carlyle himself admits that Shakespeare had no other end in view than Scott's—to delight by his art.

> Since Shakespeare's time there has been no great speaker so unconscious of an aim in speaking as Walter Scott. Equally unconscious these two utterances; equally the sincere complete products of the minds they came from; and now if they were equally deep? Or if the one were living fire and the other was futile phosphorescence and mere resinous firework? It will depend on the relative worth of the minds, for both were equally spontaneous, both equally expressed themselves unencumbered by any ulterior aim. Beyond drawing audiences to the Globe theatre Shakespeare contemplated no result in these plays of his. Yet they have had results! Utter with free heart what thy own *daemon* gives thee; if fire from heaven it shall be well, if resinous fireworks it shall be as well as it could be, or better than otherwise.

The detachment of these two great artists could not be better put, if the implied censure of Scott was as short-sighted as ungenerous; and this brings us to the crucial indictment that Scott could only draw his characters from the skin inwards. Is it not the case that in this respect also there is a closer resemblance between Scott and Shakespeare than Carlyle is willing to admit; that Scott's method as an artist of character is Shakespeare's; and that if he is a less great dramatist and poet he did yet, for reasons not entirely

34

personal, portray some classes of men more generously, more sympathetically, more understandingly than Shakespeare?

If it is a matter of degree, if Carlyle meant only that the dramatist saw deeper and expressed more adequately the deeper passions of the heart, we need not question it. Shakespeare was a greater poet. Scott is a genuine but not a great poet. His poetic style is not of the highest order. As Adolphus pointed out, you will not find in Scott the marvellous phrases which only the great imaginative poet can strike out, lines like those of Shakespeare:

> Now . . .
> . . . creeping murmur and the poring dark
> Fills the wide vessel of the universe;

or those of Milton:

> The sounds and seas, with all their finny drove,
> Now to the moon in wandering morris move;

and where, describing the battle of the angels, he says that the war

> soaring on main wing
> Tormented all the air.

You will find them in Wordsworth:

> Newton with his prism and silent face,
> The marble index of a mind for ever
> Voyaging through strange seas of thought alone.

But whatever difference there may be in degree of insight and power, Scott's method of drawing his characters and Shakespeare's are the same. They both draw their characters from without inwards, inasmuch as they both make them reveal themselves by their actions and speeches as they mingle with other men. Their method is not that of Racine or Richardson. Even Shakespeare's soliloquies are not like those of the French dramatist, when the character speaks to himself or to a confidant. Shakespeare's are not revealing analyses of motive and character. They are outbursts in which the hero relieves his feelings, and generally reveal his character just as much or just as little as his dialogue with others or his actions. Hamlet's soliloquies betray the torture of his mind; they do not explain his delay, which Hamlet does not understand himself. Would it be fair to judge Brutus' motives for killing Caesar by his soliloquy just before the conspirators arrive? We must judge him by his conduct and words throughout the play, this puzzled, conscientious man, a kind of forecast of President Wilson. Neither Shakespeare nor Scott cared to play what Mr. Percy Lubbock calls the omniscient spectator behind their characters, revealing the hidden motives, the subtle secretions of the brain which determine conduct almost unknown to the actor himself. *Clarissa* and *Madame Bovary* are the work of a different order of artists. There is nothing in which Scott's debt to the Elizabethans is more obvious than his way of introducing his characters and gradually revealing them in dialogue. Compare the opening scenes in *Coriolanus* and *Julius Caesar* with the first scene in *The Heart of Midlothian*, when the crowd are dispersing after the reprieve of Porteous:

"An unco thing this, Mrs. Howden," said old Mr. Peter Plumdamas to his neighbour, the rouping wife . . . "to see the grit folk o' Lunnon set their face against law and gospel and let loose sic a reprobate as Porteous upon a peaceable town!"

"An' to think o' the weary walk they hae gien us," answered Mrs. Howden, with a groan; "and sic a comfortable window as I had gotten, too, just within a penny-stane cast of the scaffold—I could hae heard every word the minister said—and to pay twalpennies for my stand and a' for naething!"

"I am judging," said Mr. Plumdamas, "that this reprieve wadna stand guid in the auld Scots law when the kingdom *was* a kingdom."

"I dinna ken muckle about the law," answered Mrs. Howden; "but I ken when we had a king and a chancellor,

36

and parliamentmen o' our ain, we could ay peeble them wi'
stanes when they werena guid bairns—but naebody's nails can
reach the length o' Lunnon."

And so the scene develops, and through it emerge Bartoline
Saddletree and his wife, and Reuben Butler; and in their
wake come Davie Deans and Jeanie and Dumbiedykes,
none of whom are to be dismissed as "deceptively painted
automatons".

But Carlyle's charge may bear another significance. It
is true that some of Scott's characters, at least in single scenes,
are what the older dramatists called "humourists"—that the
externals of dress and archaisms, and the technical termin-
ology of hawking and hunting, make up nearly all we get.
The friar in *Ivanhoe* is a bundle of humours drawn from folk-
tales rather than either life or history. Even some of the
historical characters, as James in *The Fortunes of Nigel*, are
not much more. Cromwell is for Scott, as for many others,
somewhat of an enigma. It was one of Carlyle's services to
history to have made Cromwell more human, but Carlyle
could not quite bring himself to admit that the zealous
puritan and Machiavellian politician which revolution forced
Cromwell to become were not compatible; that Cromwell
used the language of religion to darken counsel because he
could not squarely tell his followers that England was not to
be ruled by the saints, that saints are not meant to rule the
world, that men must render unto Caesar the things that are
Caesar's and unto God the things that are God's. But was
Shakespeare really more successful than Scott with great
historical characters of whom we have more than some vague
traditional knowledge? Is Julius Caesar drawn from the
heart outwards? Moreover, it is with Scott as with Shakespeare. If a character is at first only a property or a
humourist, a frame on which to hang old clothes and manners
of speech, should the character begin to interest him, to

enter into the story, ten to one he will quickly become a vivid personality. It is so with Barnardine in *Measure for Measure*, as Sir Walter Raleigh points out in his delightful way (*Shakespeare*: pp. 148-9); and in Scott's case with, for example, Adam Woodcock in *The Monastery*. At his entry we think he is to be a piece of pure "tushery", as Stevenson calls it, a display of Scott's knowledge of falconry; but when Roland Græme is banished and encounters Adam, with whom he had quarrelled, lo! Adam becomes a real man, a rough but generous Englishman whom, with a certain malicious pleasure, Scott contrasts with the Scottish friend who has just thrown him over:

> "What now," said he, "Master Roland, do you, who are half an Englishman, think that I, who am a whole one, would keep up anger against you, and you in distress? That were like some of the Scots (my master's reverence always excepted) who can be fair and false, and wait their time, and keep their mind, as they say, to themselves, and touch pot and flagon with you, and after all, when time serves, pay off some old feud with the point of the dagger. Canny Yorkshire has no memory for such old sores";

and Adam becomes Roland's first friend and a living if minor character.

But a character of comedy. Scott's domain is comedy in a large sense of the word. Tragedy, says Professor Saintsbury, was certainly not Scott's *forte* to the same extent as were comedy and history. This is doubtless in the main true, and the fact gives support to Carlyle's sweeping judgment, for no doubt comedy presents a more superficial aspect of character than tragedy. It is in tragedy that a man's soul is laid bare. We do not know what is in a man, what is in ourselves, until we are involved in tragic or possibly tragic issues. "I write for general amusement", says Scott in the introduction to *The Fortunes of Nigel*, which is Carlyle's charge. But one must not

always take Scott's confessions at their face value. He be-
littled his own work as much as Wordsworth was disposed to
exalt his. He hated to make parade of his deeper feelings, or
to pose as teacher or author. He accepted, like Shakespeare,
the rôle of entertainer of the public, a public often interpreted
to him by James Ballantyne, who induced him to evade the
tragical issue in *St. Ronan's Well*. But he had a deeper motive
than to amuse and make money: his own delight in his work,
the thought of which was never absent from his mind; and he
knew that "amusement" is an inadequate word to describe
the satisfaction we derive from a great work of art, be it
drama or poem or novel or piece of music; even "pleasure" is
at least a misleading name for the satisfaction of some of our
deepest instincts which art may give and life deny us. And
tragedy is the source of the deepest satisfaction which literature can afford, as certainly as the greatest music is serious,
passionate, tragic. As his power developed Shakespeare
moved from comedy and romance to tragedy. *Othello* and
Lear are greater works than *Henry IV.* and *Twelfth Night*.
That Scott realized this may be gathered from his own work,
despite the preponderance in it of romance and comedy; for
leaving over for a moment his one pure tragedy, *The Bride of
Lammermoor*, in several, and those the best, of his novels the
tragic is the source of the intensest interest. The comedy
which relieves and supports the tragic is generally excellent,
but the romantic story of the hero and the heroine is not
infrequently the most insignificant part of the whole. What
are the fortunes of Edward Waverley and Rose Bradwardine
compared with the tragic fate of Fergus and Flora MacIvor
and Evan MacCombich? The only interesting thread in the
story of *Ivanhoe* is found in the fortunes and character of
Rebecca and the Templar; the rest is "tushery" and fun for
boys. The far finer comedy of *Redgauntlet* does not outweigh
the poignant tragedy of the last scene in the long drama of

the Stewarts or the death of poor Nanty Ewart. But what has not been sufficiently emphasized is that all that is really good in the novel in which Scott reached his highest level, *The Heart of Midlothian*, is tragedy of the purest kind. It hardly alters the fact that in the end Effie Deans is saved. That is an accident due to the caprice as much as the kindness of the Queen. Jeanie might have made her heroic journey and pleaded with all her native eloquence in vain. In the great trial scene Jeanie Deans makes a tragic choice as certainly as Antigone when she scattered dust upon her brother's body, and that whatever view we take of her conduct, whether with the author we feel that she did the right thing, or think with Mr. Bernard Shaw that she should have lied with equanimity. In the first case the tragedy is of the kind which Hegel thought the highest—a fatal conflict between two great principles, her duty to her sister and her duty to her fellow-men, the all in each of us that is the voice of conscience, or, if you like, between the love of her sister and the fear of God. If the other be the right view, if she was in bondage to a too scrupulous, superstitious conscience, then the tragedy is that which Aristotle defines. Through a noble error she dooms her sister, her father, and herself. The final issue and the remorse which it must have brought with it is evaded; but it is on the level of tragedy, supported rather than relieved by comedy, that the story moves from the Porteous Riots to the eloquent appeal of Jeanie to the Queen. Thereafter the novel loses all interest.

It will not do, therefore, to deny to Scott the capacity for poignant tragedy, whatever view we may take of his one story that is carried through to a tragic catastrophe. *The Bride of Lammermoor* has been very diversely judged. Professor Saintsbury condemned it, evoking a protest from Sir Henry Craik. My final feeling after repeated reading is that it is a great tragedy with some obvious faults. It suffers from rouse us if we are too much at our ease in Domdaniel, and to preach the duty of hard work and the virtue of being unhappy. But we also owe something to the artist who has gladdened life by adding to the stock of harmless pleasure. And one element in the pleasure we derive from the work of an artist like Shakespeare or Cervantes or Scott is the impression conveyed of his own personality. Everything in Scott's work, as he said with less truth of Beaumont and Fletcher, is set to a good tune. Wherever we feel his own presence in his life or his work we have the same impression of a large, generous nature, an angelic sweetness of disposition.

This is what one is always drawn to lay stress on when one hears criticism of Scott's style. Of the purity, beauty, and power of his style when he writes in the vernacular there is no longer any question. It is Scott's English style in the narrative body of his work that has provoked criticism from the time of Adolphus to our own day, and especially during the vogue of his young disciple and rival Robert Louis Stevenson. But it is necessary again to distinguish. There have always been two schools of stylists and critics of style, the exquisites, as one might call them, and those who possess or who value above everything, the creative touch. The greatest of French novelists, Balzac, has also been accused of writing a bad style. Flaubert is the idol of the exquisites, the precious stylists. But the late Professor Angellier, the biographer of Burns, was not of the same opinion.

Of a truth [he says] Flaubert has an expert understanding of the vocabulary. He has mastered the science of words. His style is beautiful, but it is always the same. What can be more regular, better ordered, more classical than his style? Yet he is an inferior artist, for he has never got beyond the words. His rhythm has no variety. He never understood that variety of movement is one of the artist's tools. It is the same with Leconte de Lisle. He understands only the science of the word. He is incapable of giving movement to a phrase.

He has no syntax. In a word, they are poor creatures, beggars, paupers, all these people when put beside Balzac. They have got a goffering iron and can turn out frills.

It is Shakespeare as well as Balzac whom Angellier was defending against the advocates of correctness. But with due distinction much of what he says can be extended to Scott. He too may lack correctness, and the studied effects of vowel and consonant music on which Stevenson and his admirers laid such stress; yet what flow and movement his style gathers in great scenes, and what an evocative power! Of the greater scenes you can say as Dryden said of Shakespeare, you do not only see what he describes, you feel it too. One would think that Scott had been in the streets of Edinburgh on the night of the Porteous Riots. Flow, vision, and the impress of a large and generous nature, these compensate for faults of carelessness that to a smaller writer would be fatal. Not even Shakespeare gives us such an impression of largeness and generosity and wisdom as Scott. The iron of a harder life than Scott's, a dishonoured calling, had entered deeper into his soul:

> O for my sake do you with Fortune chide
> The guilty Goddess of my harmful deeds,
> That did not better for my life provide
> Than public means which public manners breeds;

and

> 'Tis better to be vile than vile esteemed.

He had seen sides of human nature that made it hard for him not at times to hate human nature; known types of men and women he could not forgive. Moreover Shakespeare's sympathies were somewhat circumscribed by his Courtly and London audiences. For common people he has little sympathy. The common man has not yet emerged for polite literature. To learn something of his virtues we must turn not to the Elizabethan dramatists, but to Bunyan. The writer who gives me any impression of the same depth and range of sympathy as Scott is Cervantes, of whose great novel it has been said that of the six hundred odd characters introduced not one is wholly odious or despicable. Burns is the most fiery star in the heaven of Scottish letters, radiating laughter and love. Carlyle is a splendid erratic star, a comet with a glittering tail, who, like other comets, will return from time to time to startle and delight us. But Scott is the largest and most beneficent luminary. He has built the golden bridge that will for ever connect the Scotland of to-day with the Scotland of the past. In the actual course of events Scotland is turning away from her past, not only her feudal, but her religious past, with a startling, an alarming rapidity and recklessness. A modern industrial people, what has she to do with the past, whether Bruce and Kings and nobles, or Knox and Presbyterians and Covenanters. Her eyes are fixed upon the future. Her religious ardour is evoked by economics, not covenants. But Scott's work holds the past before her imagination, and appeals quite as much as Carlyle's to her soul, for the soul of man has more needs than are to be satisfied by puritanism. Chivalry, generosity, loyalty, honour, a sense of the beauty of nature, and the beauty of human nature in every class, a deep regard for right, a sober fear of God—all these things one may learn who reads Sir Walter, and all of them Scotland needs if she is to advance into the future without a moral disaster. Are all Carlyle's effusions over the Eternal Verities more 'doctrinal to a nation' or individual than the sober words in which Scott justifies himself for not assigning to Rebecca in *Ivanhoe* a happier fate?

A character of a highly virtuous and lofty stamp is degraded rather than exalted by an attempt to reward virtue with temporal prosperity. Such is not the recompense that Providence has deemed worthy of suffering merit. . . . A glance at the great picture of life will show that the duties of self-denial and the sacrifice of passion to principle are seldom thus remunerated; and that the internal consciousness of their high-minded discharge of duty produces on their own reflections a more adequate recompense in the form of that peace which the world cannot give or take away. ·

a far more impressive personality. Milton was not so oppressed by piety and the desire to portray a saint. For him Samson is the type of man who has sinned through the same weakness as brought about the fall of Adam, but has bitterly repented. He has no prevision of what is in store for him; but when his father tells him of the approaching feast in which the Philistines are to celebrate their triumph and do dishonour to God, Samson's reply is that the strife is now between God and Dagon:

> Dagon hathe presum'd,
> Me overthrown to enter lists with God,
> His deity comparing and preferring
> Before the God of Abraham. He, be sure,
> Will not connive or linger, thus provok'd,
> But will arise and his great name assert:
> Dagon must stoop, and shall ere long receive
> Such a discomfit, as shall quite despoil him
> Of all those boasted trophies won on me,
> And with confusion blank his worshippers.

But Samson is speaking in faith, not in virtue of any dream; and it is in a like mood that he foretells his own death:

> All otherwise to me my thoughts portend,
> That these dark orbs no more shall treat with light,
> Nor th'other light of life continue long,
> But yield to double darkness nigh at hand:
> So much I feel my genial spirits droop,
> My hopes all flat, nature within me seems
> In all her functions weary of herself;
> My race of glory run, and race of shame,
> And I shall shortly be with them that rest.

To the scenes which follow it has been objected, by Dr. Johnson and subsequent critics, that they form no succession of dramatic events leading up to the catastrophe, that "the poem has a beginning and an end which Aristotle himself could not have disapproved, but it must be allowed to want a middle, since nothing passes between the first act and the last, that either hastens or delays the death of Samson". But in this it does not differ very much from some Greek tragedies such as the *Oedipus Coloneus* of Sophocles which was probably in Milton's mind as he composed his picture of the last day in the life of a national hero. Moreover the critics have overlooked the fact that the action is of a kind which was not to be led up to as a deliberate choice of the hero. Milton accepts Saint Augustine's statement that Samson's action is the effect of a divine prompting, but he shows the working of that prompting in a more natural and gradual way than Vondel had done. In the first choral chant that follows the entrance of the chorus and their dialogue with Samson, Milton elaborates the thought, that God may inspire men to actions which are not to be judged by ordinary moral precepts. He does so in reference to Samson's marriages with Philistine women. "Just are the ways of God," the chorus declares, "unless there be who think not God at all", but such are few and fools. But there are more who "doubt his ways not just,

> As to his own edicts found contradicting,
> Then give the reins to wand'ring thought,
> Regardless of his glory's diminution",

for they forget that God is not bound by His own laws:

> As if they would confine th'interminable,
> And tie him to his own prescript,
> Who made our Laws to bind us, not himself,
> And hath full right to exempt
> Whom so it pleases him by choice
> From national obstriction, without taint
> Of sin or legal debt;
> For with his own Laws he can best dispense.
> He would not else who never wanted means,
> Nor in respect of the enemy just cause

To set his people free,
Have prompted this Heroic Nazarite,
Against his vow of strictest purity,
To seek in marriage that fallacious bride
Unclean, unchaste.
Down Reason then, at least vain reasonings down.

What justified Samson in wedding Philistines will justify
him in the last action of his life, even though it involve his
death by his own hand. The scenes of the play, therefore,
though they do not develop an action like that in, say,
Racine's *Bérénice*, do lead on to the catastrophe, for they show
us Samson gradually awakening from the depression in which
he is plunged at the outset, the quickening of the spirit that
has begun to revive with the growth of his hair. When at
last the challenge comes, and he is ordered to play before the
Philistines, he at first rejects the proposal with scorn, and
then suddenly it is borne in upon him that God has something
for him to do, a last service to render to God and his people:

Be of good courage, I begin to feel
Some rousing motions in me which dispose
To something extraordinary my thoughts.
I with this messenger will go along,
Nothing to do, be sure, that may dishonour
Our Law or stain my vow of Nazarite.
If there be ought of presage in my mind,
This day will be remarkable in my life,
By some great act, or of my days the last.

Samson appears to be still unaware of what that great act
shall be, but he feels that he is led by the Spirit. When,
after the display of his strength, he is conducted to the pillars
to rest:

he stood as one who pray'd,
Or some great matter in his mind revolved,

and then he saw what he was to do. The chorus at once

emphasizes the thought which has guided Milton, the thought formulated by Augustine. The death of Samson was not a case of *mors voluntaria* such as Christianity forbids:

> O dearly bought revenge, yet glorious!
> Living or dying thou hast fulfill'd
> The work for which thou wast foretold
> To Israel, and now liest victorious
> Among thy slain *self-kill'd*
> *Not willingly*, but tangl'd in the fold
> Of dire necessity, whose law in death conjoin'd
> Thee with thy slaughter'd foes in number more
> Than all thy life had slain before.

I have touched on this aspect of Milton's tragedy because I do not think it has been sufficiently emphasized, and because it explains to some extent the peculiar character of the plot, which has been the subject of much criticism. But it has possibly a second interest. Every critic, English and continental, has recognized that in composing *Samson Agonistes* (1660) in the closing years of his life Milton had his own life and fate in mind, was finding relief for his pent-up feelings in a dream, a wish-fulfilment. He too was blind and "fallen on evil days", living among the triumphant enemies of the cause to which he had devoted the best years of his life; he too had wedded a wife from among the Philistines and she had betrayed his fondest hopes; he too had driven from the field of battle a boasting Harapha in the person of the great French scholar Salmasius. Of himself as a poet he had always thought as of one inspired by the Spirit of God. Is it possible that, as he sat in solitude amid the triumph of his foes and looked back on the events through which he had lived, and of which he had been a part, some of the deeds of the party he had served seemed to him of a kind that could not be justified by the normal laws of right and wrong, that in a revolution men's actions were not to be judged by such canons, that they must be judged by the event, the degree to which history proves that they had the sanction of God? He had identified himself in the closest way with the republican, the regicide party. He had defended the execution of Charles before the bar of Europe and adhered to Cromwell till his death. But it would appear from his writings after the death of Cromwell that he had not approved of the dismissal of the Long Parliament; and he had disapproved of Cromwell's meditated assumption of the crown and his allowing the clergy to hold the tithes. After the Restoration all approval of the execution of the King or of Cromwell was silenced. Milton must have known, even from a friend and sympathizer like Marvell, what was the general feeling as to that great crime; and I imagine that if he held his tongue his thought was expressed in *Samson*—"these acts are not of man but of God and God will vindicate his cause". He did not live to see the end of the Stuarts.

V

CARLYLE AND HITLER

The Adamson Lecture
in the University of Manchester—1930

Who ere thou beest that read'st this sullen Writ
Which just as much courts thee, as thou dost it,
Let me arrest thy thoughts; wonder with mee,
Why ploughing, building, ruling and the rest,
Or most of those arts whence our lives are blest,
By cursed Cain's race invented be,
And blest Seth vext us with Astronomie [i.e. *Astrology*].
There's nothing simply good, nor ill alone,
Of every quality Comparison
The only measure is, and judge Opinion.

JOHN DONNE
The Progresse of the Soule

I WAS much struck, writes Carlyle to Emerson in 1853, some two years after the publication of *Latter Day Pamphlets* had shocked many of his most sincere admirers:

> I was much struck with Plato and his ideas about Democracy, mere *Latter Day Pamphlets* saxa et faces (read *faeces*, if you like) refined into empyrean radiance and lightning of the Gods!— I for my part perceive the use of all this too, the inevitability of all this; but perceive it at the present height it has attained to be disastrous withal, to be horrible and even damnable. That Judas Iscariot should come and slap Jesus Christ on the shoulder in a familiar manner; that all heavenly nobleness should be flung out into the muddy streets there to jostle elbows with all the thickest-skinned denizens of Chaos, and get itself at every turn trampled into the gutters and anni-

65

F

hilated: alas, the reverse of all this was, and is, and ever will be the strenuous effort and solemn heart purpose of every good citizen in every country of the world, and will reappear conspicuously as such (in New England and in Old first of all) when once this malodorous melancholy Uncle-Tommey is got all put by! which will take some time yet I think.

So, in words as forcible as if they had been spoken by the author of *Also Sprach Zarathustra*, does Carlyle express his sincere conviction regarding the advent of Democracy as he sees it pouring in through the sluices successively opened by Whig, Radical, Tory, and Liberal alike. But if Carlyle's contempt is as sincere and as vehemently expressed as that of Nietzsche, he arrived at that conviction from a different angle of approach. It is with no naturally aristocratic contempt for the lower orders, or Junker's hardness of temper, that he speaks; quite otherwise. Carlyle did not share, he had not much respect for, Shakespeare's and Scott's ambition to win for themselves a place among those privileged beings who bear coats of arms, whom birth and fortune allow to cultivate the graces and splendours of life, a life that, whatever its faults, has a certain aesthetic appeal, the appeal of distinction if it be only of manner and tradition. Of the Scottish nobility he writes, after reading *Tales of a Grandfather*:

> Lastly, it is noteworthy that the nobles of this country have maintained a quite despicable behaviour from the time of Wallace downwards. A selfish, famishing, unprincipled set of hyaenas, though toothless now, still mischievous and greedy beyond limit.

Later indeed, he said more than once in conversation that it was among the English nobility he had met on the whole the best specimens of humanity this country had to show.

But it was with no aristocratic prejudice that Carlyle became the critic and foe of democracy; quite the opposite. The humour or temper of the young peasant who tramped to

Edinburgh University and, turning away from the Presbyterian Ministry, spent bitter years in teaching, translating,
hack-work of every kind, and spiritual wrestling, was more
akin, he confesses, to that of a Sansculottist. You remember
his description of Professor Teufelsdroeckh:

> lifting his large tumbler of Gug-guk, and for a moment lower-
> ing his tobacco-pipe, he stood up in full coffee-house . . . and
> there with low soul-stirring tone and the look truly of an angel,
> though whether of a white or of a black one might be dubious,
> proposed this toast: *die Sache der Armen in Gottes und Teufels
> Namen*—the cause of the poor in Heaven's name and the —'s.

Die Sache der Armen, the cause of the poor, was Carlyle's
abiding preoccupation, the inspiring motive of almost everything he wrote, but it did *not* make him a democrat or a
philanthropist of the kind he saw around him, interested in
the negroes of Borrioboolah Gha, or Jamaica, or the criminals
in model prisons at home. Negroes were happiest, he
thought, when made to work; and model prisons and poor-
houses were the sores, the scabs, which betrayed a deeper
seated disease. It was not by doctoring the scabs at the
expense of the struggling tax-payer that the disease was to
be cured. It was his diagnosis of the disease that led him
away from his friends, the whole Manchester school of *laissez-
faire* and the Radicals—"Hide-bound Radicalism; to me a
well-nigh insupportable thing—a breath as of the Sahara and
the Infinite Sterile". It was this that brought him to a
position not very remote from that of Nietzsche, if the spirit
which animates it be different, if he demands the rule of the
best not for *their* sake but for the sake of the poor, the victims
of *laissez-faire.* But to understand Carlyle's political position
and his doctrine of the Hero, of the relation of Might to
Right, requires some consideration of the history of his
thought.

For the best of a man's thinking is the work of his early

years and this is pre-eminently true of the Prophet. When Christ entered on his three years' mission it was no longer as a learner but as a teacher: One who spake "with authority and not as the Scribes and Pharisees". Mohammed "was forty before he talked of any mission from Heaven". But thereafter he knew what his mission was. "I had a good talk", says Emerson, "with Carlyle last night. He says over and over for months, for years, the same thing." But that is the note of the Prophet. "There is one God and Mahomet is his Prophet" is the burden of the Koran. The Kingdom of Heaven in the sermons of Christ is likened unto many things.

Well, Carlyle came to Edinburgh in 1808 and was a student there till 1814. He taught for two years with Edward Irving at Kirkcaldy. From 1818 to 1822 he was tutoring, hack-writing and wrestling with dyspepsia and the devil in the beautiful but draughty city of Edinburgh. In 1822 he became tutor to the Bullers, while continuing his literary work. In 1826 he married, and two years later retreated to Craigenputtock, where he composed *Sartor Resartus*, with which one may say his *Lehrjahre* end, though there were still years of suffering and financial uncertainty to follow. By that time he had come through deep waters to the message he had to deliver, religious and social. For the two foci around which his thought moved elliptically during these years were just these—religion, what to think of the Universe in which we find ourselves, and the social problem, the "condition of the people" question, as he calls it, presented in the acute forms of those years which have been so well described recently by the Hammonds.[1]

He had parted from his early Christian moorings as com-

---

[1] *The Village Labourer*, 1760–1882 (London, 1920), and *The Town Labourer*, 1760–1882 (London, 1925), by J. L. Hammond and Barbara Hammond.

pletely as Schopenhauer or Nietzsche. Through regard for his old mother, he continued to use in a sense of his own the language to which she and he were accustomed, with an effect that has sometimes bewildered his readers, sometimes perhaps himself. But of that later. No reader of his life and conversation can doubt that he thought of Christianity as something that had had its day. "Jesuitism", the title of one of his *Latter Day Pamphlets*, means in the broad sense in which he uses it, just what he thought Coleridge and Maurice and others were busy doing, trying to discover esoteric reasons for believing what had ceased to be believable.

> For the old eternal Powers do live forever; nor do their laws know any change, however we in our poor wigs and Church-tippets may attempt to read their laws. To *steal* into Heaven by the modern method of sticking ostrich-like your head into fallacies on Earth . . . is forever forbidden. High treason is the name of that attempt; and it continues to be punished as such.

> Strange enough [he says of Coleridge]: here once more was a kind of Heaven-scaling Ixion; and to him as to the old one the just Gods were very stern! The ever-revolving, never-advancing wheel (of a kind) was his through life; and from his Cloud-Juno did not he too procreate strange Centaurs, spectral Puseyisms, monstrous illusory Hybrids, and ecclesiastical Chimeras—which now haunt the earth in a very lamentable manner!

The effect of this definite severance of old ties is the theme of the three most famous chapters of *Sartor Resartus*, and one must ask what was the faith to which in this crisis Carlyle attained. In the chapter called "The Everlasting No" he gets down to his own consciousness of good and evil, his own rejection of evil:

> Thus had the Everlasting No (*das ewige Nein*) pealed authoritatively through all the recesses of my being, of my Me: and then it was that my whole Me stood up in native God-

69

> created majesty and with emphasis recorded its Protest. . . .
> The Everlasting No had said: "Behold thou art fatherless,
> outcast, and the universe is mine (the Devil's)": to which my
> whole Me now made answer: "*I* am not thine, but Free, and
> forever hate thee!"

The experience is not unlike that which Professor Elton
describes as the feeling with which we contemplate the close
of a great moral tragedy like *King Lear*. Here is evil apparently triumphant, no solution of the mystery of things divin-
able, but yet we feel that we would rather be with Lear and
Cordelia than with wickedness even triumphant. Whatever
the moral character of the universe, the human soul remains
the impregnable citadel of its own values. The next step is
more difficult to follow. It is a step which Nietzsche and
Schopenhauer felt unable to take, for it is a judgment about
the moral character, the fundamental justice of the universe
however mysterious its operations. There is a *saltus*, in faith.
It is a little difficult to follow the exact implication of the
"Everlasting Yea" chapter, but one may divine its trend
towards an idealistic conception of God and the World for
which Carlyle found support in the philosophy of the Germans, though he has none of Coleridge's interest in the
systems of Kant or Schelling or Fichte.[1]

> Often also could I see the black Tempest marching in anger
> through the Distance: round some Schreckhorn, as yet grim-
> blue, would the eddying vapour gather, and there tumultuous
> eddy and flow down like a mad witch's hair; till, after a space,
> it vanished, and in the clear sunbeam your Schreckhorn stood
> smiling grim-white, for the vapour had held snow. How thou
> fermentest and elaboratest, in thy great fermenting vat and
> laboratory of an Atmosphere, of a World, O Nature!—Or
> what is Nature? Ha! why do I not name thee God? Art not

[1] For Carlyle's interest in and partial understanding of Kant and
Fichte, see Storrs, *The Relation of Carlyle to Kant and Fichte*, Brynmawr, Pa.
1929.

thou the "Living Garment of God"? O Heavens, is it in very deed, He, then, that ever speaks through thee; that lives and loves in thee, that lives and loves in me?

And so from his own soul Carlyle makes the *saltus* to God. The working of the Infinite in the Finite—is not that the explanation of the interminable controversy of the origin of evil?

Man's Unhappiness comes of his Greatness: it is because there is an Infinite in him which with all his cunning he cannot quite bury under the Finite. Will the whole Finance Ministers and Upholsterers and Confectioners of modern Europe undertake in joint stock company to make one shoeblack HAPPY? They cannot accomplish it above an hour or two; for the shoeblack also has a Soul quite other than his stomach . . . ,

and so :

Es leuchtet mir ein, I see a glimpse of it, there is in man a Higher than Love of Happiness; he can do without Happiness and instead thereof find Blessedness. . . . On the roaring billows of Time thou art not engulfed, but borne aloft into the azure of Eternity. Love not Pleasure, Love God. This is the Everlasting Yea, wherein all contradiction is solved: wherein whoso walks and works it is well with him.

So Carlyle recovered for himself, or believed he had, a religious outlook on life, a faith that, inscrutable as is the nature of God, there is a meaning in the word God—there is justice at the heart of things.

Of the bearing of this on the doctrine of the Hero I shall speak, but first must consider briefly how he approached the other great problem—the social problem, the condition of the People under the rule of industrial *laissez-faire*, the Creed of Manchester. *Die Sache der Armen in Gottes und Teufels Namen.* Carlyle came of poor people, had known the problem of poverty at almost as close quarters as Burns, and his life in Edinburgh had made him familiar with the darker

71

fate of the industrial poor of the city. In the strange chapter in *Sartor* called the "Dandiacal Body"—for *Sartor* was in part a satire on the dandiacal novel of Lytton and Disraeli—he describes in two picturesque figures the ever-widening gulf in society between the two sects of the Dandies and the Drudges,[1] and what it seemed to him likely to lead to; and the problem of industry and the poor was the theme of his most passionately felt work, *Past and Present*, *Chartism*, and *Latter Day Pamphlets*. The last of these with its "Nigger Question", "Model Prisons", "Hudson's Statue", "Jesuitism", etc., has been a sad choke-pear to liberal philanthropists and many of Carlyle's admirers, but, with all its extravagances, it is a central work. It is in the light of what he says there that one must read his earlier works, for in this he turned on the head-lights with illuminating if also with somewhat dazzling effect. From it, as from *Past and Present*, it becomes clear what was to Carlyle the central evil in the condition of the poor. It was the effects of the great Manchester Gospel of *laissez-faire*, what the Americans call "rugged individualism". In an interesting letter of 1820, Sir Walter Scott describes

[1] " I could liken Dandyism and Drudgism to two bottomless boiling whirlpools that had broken out on opposite quarters of the firm land: as yet they appear only disquieted, foolishly bubbling wells, which man's art might yet cover-in; yet mark them, their diameter is daily widening; they are hollow cones that boil-up from the Infinite Deep, over which your firm land is but a thin crust or rind! Thus daily is the intermediate land crumbling-in, daily the empire of the two Buchan-Bullers extending; till now there is but a foot-plank, a mere film of land between them; this too is washed away: and then—we have the true Hell of waters." In the second comparison they are "two boundless, and indeed unexampled Electric Machines. . . . Hitherto you see only partial transient sparkles and sputters: but wait a little till the entire Nation is in an electric state; till your whole vital Electricity . . . is cut into two isolated portions of Positive and Negative (of money and of hunger); and stands there bottled-up in two World-Batteries! The stirring of a child's finger brings the two together; and then—What then? The Earth is but shivered into impalpable smoke by that Doom's-thunderpeal; the Sun misses one of his planets in Space, and thenceforth there are no eclipses in the Moon." *Sartor Resartus*, iii. 10.

what had come about. While industry was dependent on water power, the manufacturer set up his mill in some country place, and around it grew an industrial village. He knew his workers. Their health and welfare were his interest. His relation to them was to some extent paternal.[1] With the advent of steam and the growth of great cities, all that had disappeared. The employer's relation to his hands had become only that of a weekly wage-payer, the only tie between them what Carlyle calls a "cash nexus".

All this dire misery . . . of our Chartisms, Trades-strikes, Toryisms, Corn-laws and the general down-break of *Laissez-faire* . . . may we not regard it as a voice from the dumb bosom of Nature saying to us: "Behold! Supply-and-demand is *not* the one law of Nature; Cash-payment is *not* the sole nexus of man with man—how far from it!" . . . Ah me, into what waste latitudes, in this Time-Voyage have we wandered; like adventurous Sinbads:—where the men go about as if by galvanism, with meaningless glaring eyes and have no soul, but only a beaver-faculty and stomach! The haggard despair of Cotton-factory hands, Coal-mine operatives . . . in these days is painful to behold; but not so painful, hideous to the inner-sense as that brutish, God-forgetting Profit-and-Loss Philosophy and Life-theory which we hear jangled on all hands . . . as the Ultimate Gospel and candid Plain English of Man's Life from the throats and pens and thoughts of all but all men![2] . . . *Laissez-*

[1] "When the machinery was driven by water the Manufacturer had to seek out some sequestered spot where he could obtain a suitable fall of water, and there his workmen form'd the inhabitants of a village around him, and he necessarily bestow'd some attention, more or less, on their morals and on their necessities, had knowledge of their persons and characters, and exercised over them a salutary influence as over men depending on and intimately connected with him and his prospects. This is now quite changed. The manufacturers are transferred to great towns where a man may assemble 500 workmen one week and dismiss the next, without having any further connection with them than to receive a week's work for a week's wage, nor any further solicitude about their future fate than if they were so many shuttles." To John B. S. Morritt, 19th May, 1820.

[2] "It is not by the intermeddling of Mr. Southey's idol, the omniscient and omnipotent State, but by the prudence and energy of the people,

faire on the part of the governing Classes, we repeat again and again, will, with whatever difficulty, have to cease; pacific mutual division of the spoil and a world well let alone will no longer suffice. A Do-nothing Guidance; and it is a Do-something World.

But it is not my purpose to discuss Carlyle's social teaching in detail, though it has acquired a new interest and significance from the social and political condition of England and Europe to-day. What I wish to indicate is that Carlyle's cult of the Hero had its roots in both his religious and his social conclusions and convictions.

Jesus Christ was not God, in the sense which he had been taught to believe—but the divine spirit was revealed in him and in other great men.

> But now, if all things that we look upon are emblems to us of the Highest God, I add that more so than any of them is man such an emblem. You have heard of St. Chrysostom saying in reference to the Shekinah or Ark of Testimony, visible revelation of God among the Hebrews: "the true Shekinah is Man!" Yes, it is even so: this is no vain phrase; it is veritably so. The essence of our being, the mystery in that which calls itself I . . . is a breath of Heaven; the Highest Being reveals himself in man . . . "there is but one Temple in the Universe", says the devout Novalis, "and that is the Body of Man . . . we touch Heaven when we lay our hand on a human body". . . . *We* are the miracle of miracles—the great inscrutable mystery of God. . . . And now if worship even

that England has hitherto been carried forward in civilization; and it is to the same energy that we now look with comfort and good hope. Our rulers will best promote the improvement of the nation by strictly confining themselves to their legitimate duties, by leaving capital to find its most lucrative course, commodities their fair price, industry and intelligence their natural reward, idleness and folly their natural punishment, by maintaining peace, by defending property, by diminishing the price of law, and by observing strict economy in every department of the state. Let the Government do this: the people will assuredly do the rest." Macaulay, "Southey's Colloquies on Society", *Edinburgh Review*, Jan. 1830.

of a star had some meaning in it, how much more that of a Hero! Worship of a Hero is transcendent admiration of a Great Man. I say great men are still admirable; I say there is at bottom nothing else admirable. . . . It is at this hour and at all hours the vivifying influence in man's life. Religion, I find, stands upon it; not Paganism only, but far higher and truer religions—all religion hitherto known. Hero-worship, heart-felt, prostrate admiration, submission burning, boundless, for a noblest, god-like Form of Man—is not that the germ of Christianity itself? The greatest of all Heroes is One whom we do not name here. Let sacred silence meditate that sacred matter; you will find it the ultimate perfection of a principle extant throughout man's whole history on earth.

That will suffice as a statement of the religious aspect of Carlyle's Hero-worship. Nietzsche scoffs at the religious cast given by Carlyle to the admiration of the Hero, but Gundolf, a disciple of Nietzsche to some extent, but more of Stefan George, puts the case for the Hero on much the same basis. The opponent's case is, he says, threefold: (1) that all greatness is relative; (2) that past greatness has no longer significance for us; (3) that no man has any significance, beside the Ideas or God. The case for the Hero is (1) that all claims, traditions, conceptions are in the end beams and emanations from great men; (2) that there is no absolutely past but only differently effective degrees of eternity . . . (3) that there are for men no superhuman, free Ideas, that only in Man are ideas incorporate, made actual, including the Idea of God.[1]

[1] The transcendental, abstract German style is always a little difficult for a sober Briton to reduce to concrete terms but I take this to mean that (1) everything of excellence to which the human race has attained, whether a useful machine, a good ballad, a higher moral or spiritual standard, is ultimately due to some gifted individual; (2) that nothing is really dead, man or language or idea, which is still a moving and quickening force; (3) that only when and as they become *incarnate* are concepts capable of moving us to love or worship: "Lessing has said that in the religion of reason there is neither religion nor reason, and rightly; for religion, without fear, hope, faith and love for the Supreme Being, is

But of Nietzsche and Gundolf later. I wish now to consider the relation of Carlyle's social ideas to the cult of the Hero. Looking out on the chaotic world of industrial and governmental *laissez-faire,* employers and employed connected only by a cash nexus, Government convinced that its sole clear duty was to do as little as possible beyond keeping an open field for the mutual play or warfare of competitive forces, he found one doctrine of a cure for the accumulating evils being industriously preached—Democracy. Intensify still further this mutual warfare by giving every man a vote, and mechanically the warring elements will begin to take form, to crystallize, and through the mystic machinery of the hustings and the ballot-box we shall secure the Benthamist ideal of the greatest good of the greatest number. This doctrine Carlyle regarded with contempt:

> The notion that a man's liberty consists in giving his vote at election-hustings and saying: "Behold I too have my twenty-thousandth part of a Talker in our National Palaver; will not all the gods be good to me?"—is one of the pleasantest; Nature nevertheless is kind at present; and puts it into the heads of many, almost of all. The liberty especially which has to purchase itself by social isolation, and each man standing separate from the other, having no "business with him" but a cash account: this is such a liberty as the Earth seldom saw; as the Earth will not long put up with, recommend it how you may.

impossible. A concept can arouse neither fear, hope, belief nor love. . . . In order to love beauty or the Divinity, we must feel their impress within ourselves and somehow represent them to our imagination." Vossler, *Mediaeval Culture.* The progress of religious thought and experience that led to Christianity might be described as circular—from particular, individual but imperfect, at best National, gods to a purified concept of God such as along different lines Hebrew prophet and Greek philosopher had made their way to, and thence, in the Incarnation, to an embodiment of that higher concept in a person who could be loved and worshipped. The identification of Christ with the Deity has been compared to similar deifications of heroes and emperors. It was something quite different because He became the Incarnation of an infinitely higher conception of the Godhead.

This liberty turns out, before it have long continued in action, with all men flinging up their caps round it, to be for the Working Millions a liberty to die by want of food; for the Idle Thousands and Units, alas, a still more fatal liberty to live in want of work; to have no earnest duty to do in this God's World any more

—The War and consequent unemployment have greatly added to their number to-day.

But as to universal suffrage again,—can it be proved that, since the beginning of the world, there was ever given a universal vote in favour of the worthiest man or thing? . . . John Milton, inquiring of universal England what the worth of *Paradise Lost* was, received for answer, Five Pounds Sterling. George Hudson, inquiring in like manner what his services on the railways might be worth, received for answer (prompt temporary answer) Fifteen Hundred Thousand ditto. Alas, Jesus Christ asking the Jews what *he* deserved, was not the answer, Death on the Gallows!

We may depend on it, Heaven in the most constitutional countries knows well who is slave and who is not. And with regard to voting I lay it down as a rule: No real *slave's* vote is other than a nuisance, whensoever or wheresoever or in what manner soever it be given. No *slave's* vote; . . . the fact is, slaves are in a tremendous majority everywhere; and the voting of them (not to be got rid of just yet) is a nuisance in proportion, a nuisance of proportionately tremendous magnitude, properly indeed the great fountainhead of all other nuisances whatsoever.

Nietzsche could not have used a more naked word to describe what the majority of men are and must be, or denounced the potential evil of Democracy more forcibly.

On two things Carlyle seems to me to rest his doctrine of the social need of heroes, the rule of the best:

England will either learn to reverence its heroes and discriminate them from sham-heroes and valets and gas-lighted histrions, and to prize them as God's voices . . . or else England

77

will continue to worship new and ever new forms of Quackland, and so, with whatever resiliences and rebounds, it matters little, go down to the Father of Quacks.

The first of these is the natural desire in the heart of the great majority of men to be governed, to be guided, to obey (witness Russia and Italy and Germany to-day). Nietzsche dwells always on the envy felt by the slave, the weakling, the lower classes, for the great, the strong, the wise; and there is an element of truth in this, had I time to analyse it; but a much more obvious fact is the almost pathetic readiness of the mass of men to accept leadership in things political, intellectual, and spiritual. We in educational circles are always declaring that the end of education is to teach people to think for themselves. But can the majority ever do so? My experience is that eighty per cent of a class do not want to think for themselves, or are incapable of doing so. The man who can does so from the beginning. The majority want to be taught what to think, and the practice of Communist Russia and Fascist Italy points to the same conclusion. Men can and must be taught what to think. So the Catholic Church has always taught, and so the Communist and Fascist insist to-day. Freedom of thought and of the Press have had a short and precarious history. Men desire to believe: hero-worship is not only an instinct, it is a need of the human spirit.

The other fact on which Carlyle leans is that, this being the case, and society being a complex organism, the laws of whose being are not open to every man, are only slowly being discovered even by the few; but whose laws, like all the laws of Nature, are relentless and irreversible (make no allowance for ignorance, giving no place to repentance); it is folly to suppose that mechanically, through the free play of contending egoisms, or the mechanism of the ballot-box, society can be safely and wisely governed. It can only be done by giving the government to the wise, to those who have what he calls "the seeing-eye", which in political as in other practical matters anticipates the findings of science, may guide where, as Pascal taught, science will never be able to lay down fixed principles because of her abstract character. Life, social and individual, is a conflict in which Justice in the long run will prevail: in the long run, Right and Might will be found to be identical; but this brings us to the difficult question—what did Carlyle mean by the Justice which in the end always prevails, which he had, in the "Everlasting Yea", persuaded himself lies at the heart of the Universe? "Effected it will be", he says, speaking of the just regulation of labour, "unless it were a Demon that made the Universe; which I for my part do at no moment . . . in the least believe"; and again: "All fighting, as we noticed long ago, is the dusty conflict of strengths, each thinking itself the strongest, or, in other words, the justest;—of Mights which do in the long run, and forever will in this just Universe in the long run, mean Rights". Note the emphasis by repetition put on the "long run". Nietzsche considers these vehement assertions to be a confession by Carlyle that he does not really believe.

> Carlyle stupefies himself by means of the *fortissimo* of his reverence for men of strong faith, and his rage over those who are less foolish; he is in sore need of noise. . . . At bottom he is an English Atheist who makes it a point of honour not to be so.

And others besides Schopenhauer and Nietzsche have doubted if justice were traceable in the workings of the universe:

> Great is the Truth, and will prevail
> When none cares whether it prevail or not.

For in a great deal that he says about Law and the inevitable working of things, Carlyle has in view rather a scientific conception of Law than a moral one. He means the fact, as it is, rather than a law, of cause and effect. Things are what

79

they are and their consequences will be what they will be. Whether one should call such an arrangement of things just or not is a question, is a judgment of Faith rather than Experience. In his talk of Law and Justice, two different strains in Carlyle's education come together, his study of science—he was an able and interested mathematician—and his earlier puritanical Old Testament upbringing. He would link the scientific law, or rather fact of cause and effect, with that other conception of Law as imposed by God, so that national prosperity is the reward, national disaster the penalty of disobedience:

> And it shall come to pass, if thou shalt hearken diligently unto the voice of the Lord thy God, to observe to do all his commandments which I command thee this day, that the Lord thy God will set thee on high above all nations of the earth. . . . Blessed shalt thou be in the city, and blessed shalt thou be in the field. Blessed shall be the fruit of thy body, and the fruit of thy ground, and the fruit of thy cattle, the increase of thy kine and the young of thy flock, etc.

But there is in Carlyle's mind a link between the two conceptions, and that is this: Among these laws of the Universe, irreversible and relentless, is the social nature of man and the desire ineradicable from his heart for justice in his social relations. That too is a cause which has to be reckoned with. Man is bound to his fellows by more than a cash nexus. Carlyle in *Past and Present* returns again and again to the instance of the Irish widow who, refused charity on every hand, proved her common humanity by infecting the lane with typhus fever, whereof seventeen people died. In treating men as isolated atoms, connected only by the mutual attraction and repulsion of money-making, society is ignoring the real nature of man and sinning against the law of justice. Here the two conceptions become one. Justice is the demand of every human heart:

It is not what a man outwardly has or wants that constitutes the happiness or misery of him. Nakedness, Hunger, Distress of all kinds, Death itself, he has cheerfully suffered when the heart was right. It is the feeling of injustice that is insupportable to all men. The brutalest black African cannot bear that he should be treated unjustly. No man can bear it or ought to bear it.

The French Revolution was to Carlyle an event that justified the ways of God to men, because it was a long delayed but finally achieved vindication of the poor and the unjustly treated, as it had seemed to the young Wordsworth. But the doctrine of justice has another implication for Carlyle that is not so commonly found; here Carlyle draws nearer to Nietzsche. The desire for justice is the vindication not only of the poor man when he rises at last in rebellion. It also, Carlyle seems to think, is the vindication of the strong man, the Hero, even of the conqueror, for

no man at bottom means injustice. It is always for some obscure distorted image of a right that he contends . . . could a man own to himself that the thing he fought for was wrong, contrary to fairness and the law of reason, he would also own that it thereby stood condemned and hopeless: he could fight for it no longer.

Your great conquerors are not inspired purely by greed of possession and lust of power.[1] They were not merely destructive forces like Attila. However they may have erred, what moved them was an instinct of right, a belief that they could order things better, make a better use of what they conquered, and they are to be judged by the result. So Carlyle seems to think, though, as we shall see, he is a little

[1] That is the difference between the true conqueror and the buccaneer: "Victory is the aim of each. But deep in the heart of the noble man it lies forever legible that as an Invisible Just God made him, so will and must God's Justice and this only, were it never so invisible, ultimately prosper in all controversies and enterprises whatsoever." *Past and Present*, iii. 10; and see iii. 13.

81   G

uneasy about some of his heroes. Dr. Johnson said that he *loved* the University of Salamanca because, when asked by the Pope if it were just to conquer America, that University alone replied, NO. Carlyle would not have agreed, and it is clearly a very difficult question to answer in the abstract whether it had been juster to leave America to contending tribes of Red Indians, or the South Sea Islands to such amiable cannibals as Melville describes in *Omoo*, or to clear them out and to establish such a civilization as that of America to-day with all its complexities of good and evil.

But it is just this complex nature of human society, the difficulty of deciding what is just and then getting it done, that makes the need of a Hero so insistent; and what I wish to consider is Carlyle's conception of the Hero, especially in the field of action, on whom it is that his choice falls, and the significance of that choice. When we turn to *On Heroes, Hero-Worship and the Heroic in History*, we find, of course, that there are different types of the Hero, Heroes in different spheres of human activity. All the leaders of men have not been Kings or Captains. Some have been Prophets and Poets. The various classes that Carlyle distinguished for the purpose of his lectures will be found, I think, to fall into the two main classes of King and Prophet. Carlyle has little interest in poets who are not also prophets. He cannot away with a Keats, who seems to him to be the artist alone, and therefore a Hedonist.[1] A German writer on *Helden und*

---

[1] "Milnes has written", he comments in 1848, "this year a book on Keats. This remark to make on it: 'An attempt to make us eat dead dog by exquisite currying and cooking. Won't eat it. A truly unwise little book. The kind of man that Keats was gets ever more horrible to me. Force of hunger for pleasure of every kind, and want of all other force— that is a combination! Such a structure of soul, it would once have been very evident, was a chosen 'Vessel of Hell', and truly for ever there is justice in that feeling. At present we try to love and pity, and even worship, such a soul, there being enough of similarity. Away with

Dichter has made, I think, a clearer distinction of three main classes—the men of action, the Kings as Carlyle would say, Alexander, Caesar, Napoleon: the heroes of the spiritual life, prophets who have created a tradition of Being, Suffering and Teaching, Buddha, Christ, and Mahomet; and lastly the Heroes who live in their work, their creation, their word— as Dante, Shakespeare, Goethe, and one might add surely heroes such as Rembrandt, Beethoven. But the hero that Carlyle as a social reformer was chiefly concerned with was the Hero as King, and it is he that presents the chief difficulties in the study of the Hero. To the others I must make only a passing reference.

Now Carlyle's choice of a Hero in this field is very illuminating. He touches on Mirabeau and Napoleon, and he was to write the Life of Frederick, but there is only one Hero whom he accepts with his whole heart, and that is Oliver Cromwell.

But before speaking of Cromwell, let me just say a word on one of Carlyle's heroes, because he illustrates what one might call the lowest common denominator of the hero, and that is Dr. Johnson, a rather strange figure in this setting, if Burns is a stranger. Carlyle places Johnson among the Men of Letters, but it is *not* as a great writer, or as the "Great Moralist" of the *Rambler* whom Boswell revered, that he gives him his place, but "in virtue of his sincerity, his speaking still in

it! There is perhaps no clearer evidence of our universal immorality and cowardly untruth than even in such sympathies." A sweeping and a cruel judgment, and quaint, if one thinks, coming from the unlimited admirer of Burns whose love of pleasure was as keen as Keats's and his recklessness in its pursuit far greater. "We have said", writes Scott, who had known more of Burns's life than Carlyle, "that Robert Burns was the child of impulse and feeling. Of the steady principle which cleaves to that which is good, he was unfortunately divested by the violence of those passions which finally wrecked him. It is most affecting to add, that while swimming, struggling, and finally yielding to the torrent, he never lost sight of the beacon which ought to have guided him, yet never profited by its light." Whether either the one or the other be right there can be no doubt that Scott's is the more charitable judgment. Charity, Carlyle had come to think, was a weakness.

some sort from the heart of Nature, . . . that Johnson was a prophet". But sincerity hardly describes exactly what Carlyle means. Pepys was, I think, sincere. What he means by Johnson speaking from the heart of Nature is that Johnson spoke and thought from the depths of his own nature, was absolutely indifferent to what others around him thought or said. With all his prejudices, Johnson is a Hero in that his own soul was his guide through life. For the fashions of the day in thought or history he cared not a whit. Others might be sceptics, or Whigs, because that was the right thing for an "enlightened" man to be: Johnson was a believer and a Tory. "Clear your mind of cant", was his watchword, and so in his small way he was a centre of force, a fountainhead; and this is the first, the basal note of the Hero. He is neither impelled nor inhibited by others. His thoughts, his deeds, his words are his own. The great Disciple, as we might describe another class of men, may achieve much—sometimes even effect what the master failed in—St. Paul, Abu Bekr, Augustus. But each has caught his inspiration from a master, looks back to him, acknowledges him as master even after his death.

Oliver Cromwell is the one historical man of action for whom Carlyle has no apology to make in the *Lectures*; and to clearing of Cromwell's character, and establishing his fame, he devoted years of research; producing, Professor Trevelyan declares, in *Oliver Cromwell's Letters and Speeches* his most original and solid contribution to history.[1] It is a strange work. Cromwell is never censured, never made responsible for the ultimate failure of the Commonwealth. Carlyle accompanies his speeches with a running comment of approving interjection in a manner that used to be customary in

[1] But see the edition of this work by S. C. Lomas, 1904, with Introduction by Sir Charles Firth, and *Carlyle, His Rise and Fall*, by Norwood Young, 1927.

Methodist churches. The failure of Cromwell to make good
in the end, the "blessed Restoration" which brought back
"Charles Second and merry Nell Gwynnes", is for Carlyle
the great tragedy in English history.

> Oliver is gone; and with him English Puritanism, laboriously
> built together by this man, and made a thing far-shining to
> its own Century and memorable to all Centuries, soon goes.
> Puritanism without its King is *kingless*, anarchic. . . . King,
> Defender of the Puritan Faith, there can now none be found;
> —and nothing is left but to recall the old disowned Defender
> with the remnants of his Four Surplices and Two Centuries
> of *Hypocrisis* (or Play-acting *not* so called), and put up with
> all that, the best we may. The Genius of England no longer
> soars Sunward, world-defiant, like an Eagle through the storms,
> "mewing her mighty youth", as John Milton saw her do: the
> Genius of England much liker a greedy Ostrich intent on
> provender and a whole skin mainly, stands with its *other*
> extremity Sunward; with its Ostrich-head stuck into the
> readiest bush, of old Church-tippets, King-cloaks, or whatever
> other sheltering Fallacy there may be, and *so* awaits the issue.
> The issue has been slow; but it now seems to have been in-
> evitable. No Ostrich, intent on gross terrene provender and
> sticking its head into Fallacies, but will be awakened one day
> —in a terrible *a posteriori* manner if not otherwise! Awake
> before it comes to that; gods and men bid us awake! The
> Voices of our Fathers, with thousandfold stern monition to
> one and all, bid us awake.

Carlyle's choice of Cromwell as Hero is luminous, because
in him the two strains of thought in his conception of Justice,
Law, combine. Cromwell had "the seeing eye" that gained
the victory for the Puritan Rebellion, because he saw what
things are and what their consequences will be, while others
were lost in the tangles of constitutional or ecclesiastical
theory: "I beseech you in the bowels of Christ, think it
possible you may be mistaken", as Cromwell said to the
Scottish Presbyterians of Scotland, in their eyes alone ortho-

dox, alone righteous. He drove through where others discussed abstract rights. But he was also the first of Heroes, because he was the soldier of God, had, as no other of the great soldiers of history, a moral and religious end:

> To see God's own law, then universally acknowledged for complete as it stood in the Holy Written Book, made good in this World; to see this, or the true unwearied aim and struggle towards this: it was a thing worth living for and dying for! Eternal Justice: that God's will be done on Earth as it is in Heaven: corollaries enough will flow from that, if that be there; if that be not there, no corollary good for much will flow. It was the general spirit of England in the Seventeenth Century.

But alas! it is difficult not to feel that Carlyle is deceiving himself about this union of qualities in Cromwell. The man who believes as Cromwell did that he finds the whole law of God written in a book; that in all he does, the dispersion of the Parliament which had given him his power, the execution of the King, he is following the leading of God; and finds God's sanction for all his doings, for the victories he has gained from Marston Moor, Naseby, Drogheda, Tredah, Dunbar, to the "crowning mercy" of Worcester, has lost the "seeing eye", and is walking in a vain illusion which will bring its consequences. One may or may not defend all these actions on prudential grounds or grounds of necessity, but to claim divine inspiration for every deed of violence is a dangerous thing. When he has finished describing how all the Friars were knocked on the head at Tredah, Cromwell goes on: "And now give me leave to say how it comes to pass that this work was wrought. It was set upon some of our hearts that a great thing should be done, not by power or might, but by the spirit of God. And is it not so clearly?" Comment which gives Carlyle much solemn satisfaction:

CARLYLE AND HITLER

An armed soldier solemnly conscious to himself that he is a Soldier of God the Just—a consciousness which it well beseems all soldiers and all men to have;—armed soldier terrible as death, relentless as doom; doing God's judgments on the enemies of God . . . art thou worthy to love such a thing; worthy to do other than hate it or shriek over it?

One is tempted to ask Carlyle: "Are you yourself really justifying the action, or are you taking refuge from a decision in a cloud of words that would have one meaning for your mother and another for yourself?" Does Carlyle really believe with the Jews that God's will is written down in black and white to the last tittle, known to us definitely, that obedience to this known law is the guarantee of prosperity, all misfortune a punishment for the neglect of this known law? The result of that for the Jews was that when One came who believed he had a deeper insight into the Will of God, they felt bound by the Law of God to account him a blasphemer and crucify One who claimed to be the Son of God. Even in Cromwell's age there were those who did not think that God's Will was thus known and written down, but believed that God had given us reason wherewith to explore it—that was the tenor of Hooker's *Ecclesiastical Polity*. It is, I fear, what Carlyle most admired in Cromwell that most distinctly marks his limitation as a Hero, his fanaticism—or if his personal fanaticism was less than his language suggests, his too great dependence on the fanatical element in his following, so that he could not free himself and the country from the tyranny of Saints and Major-Generals. The sword of the spirit and of steel had placed him where he was and could alone uphold him:

> And for the last effect
> Still keep the sword erect:
> Besides the force it has to fright
> The spirits of the shady night,

The same arts that did gain
A pow'r must it maintain.

Yet it is a prejudiced, short-sighted person who would deny heroic stature to Cromwell. He is in a sense the one Hero in our history, this man who when already middle-aged, untrained in arms or diplomacy, rose by the innate force of character and genius to be the ruler of the English people, the conqueror of Ireland and Scotland, and who made the name of England feared and respected throughout Europe. In some ways he did more than Napoleon, for no revolution had reduced England to the condition from which Napoleon rescued France, and he made himself master of a people with an ingrained constitutionalism of mind, a passion for at least the appearance of inherited right, so that even Cromwell's Parliaments would not get to business, but must waste time and weary out his patience debating *their* right and *his* right. His power had to rely on the sword, and when he died the order of things he had established melted away, and, even by the Whigs, Cromwell was remembered as the "great, bad man" Clarendon had called him, though a bad man who communicated his own power to the people he ruled.

> These disturbers [says Burke] were not so much like men usurping power as asserting their natural place in society. Their rising was to illuminate and beautify the world. Their conquest over their competitors was by outshining them. The hand that like a destroying angel smote the country communicated to it the force and energy under which it suffered. I do not say (God forbid), I do not say that the virtues of such men are to be taken as a balance to their crimes; but they were some corrective to their effects . . . such was, as I said, our Cromwell.

It was left for Carlyle to do for Cromwell what Mommsen has done for Caesar.[1]

[1] Mommsen's conclusions are not accepted by all historians. See Prof. Conway's article in the *Quarterly Review*, July, 1933.

But Carlyle's choice of Cromwell is an interesting and instructive one in several ways. If, as I think, this cult of the Hero, especially on its religious side, was in part a result of Carlyle's early enthusiasm for Novalis and the German Romantics, yet his insistence on the moral requirement is characteristic not only of Carlyle but of the British people, especially the English, generally. They have at no time been altogether willing to accept the strong man as the arbiter of their destinies—even Cromwell found the English a stiff-necked generation—and they have always required their leaders to present their moral testimonials. Even in the sphere of the Prophet, a Knox and a Calvin were more whole-heartedly accepted as Prophets in Switzerland, France, and Scotland than in England. The Anglican Church through Hooker appealed to reason and tradition; the Independent or Quaker vindicated in different ways and measures the claim of the individual's experience, the "inner light". The acceptance of Napoleon in France was at first practical, the need of peace and order, but the practical demand was soon intensified by the French love of "La Gloire", which in the twelfth and thirteenth centuries had given Europe the cult of chivalry. But Germany is the home of the mystical worship of the Hero. It is hard to believe that a German could endorse Bernard Shaw's recent dictum on Napoleon that it would be better if he had never lived. It would seem to him almost blasphemous. A man like Napoleon, he would say, is not to be measured by a moral yard-stick; and if the blood he shed condemns him, might not the Hero as Prophet be in danger of condemnation—Mahomet, even Christ: "I came not to send peace on earth; I came not to send peace but a sword". These are not the least true words that Christ uttered. To Nietzsche, Napoleon represents the passion of new spiritual possibilities, and he cites Taine on Napoleon as the reincarnation of the great man of the Renaissance:

Suddenly the master faculty reveals itself; the artist which was latent in the politician comes forth from his scabbard; he creates *dans l'idéal et l'impossible*. He is once more recognized as that which he is: the posthumous brother of Dante and of Michael Angelo; and verily in view of the definite contours of his vision, the intensity, the coherence and inner consistency of his dream, the depth of his meditations, the super-human greatness of his conception, he is their equal . . . *il est un des trois esprits souverains de la renaissance.*

To Carlyle Napoleon is but half a hero; to Lord Morley he was only a Corsican brigand of transcendent ability and transcendent good fortune.

But instead of Napoleon, I will for the moment take another Hero concerning whom also one can study the contradictions in the estimation of the Hero, and that is Julius Caesar. The most vivid exponent of German Hero-worship to-day, the late Professor Gundolf, has written a history of the fame of Caesar from his own day to the end of the nineteenth century, and it is very instructive. The greatness of Caesar as soldier and statesman and man was felt and acknowledged from his own day even by his enemies, and not only his greatness, but the charm of his personality—his magnanimity, what one might call his *style* in life and writings. Napoleon, at close quarters, exercised no such fascination over men like Talleyrand, Fouché, and others as Caesar did over Cicero and Brutus. Caesar was a *gentleman*, which Napoleon with all his greatness was not. And Caesar's star has never set. In all ages have been men willing to echo Antony's words in Shakespeare's play:

> Thou art the ruins of the noblest man
> That ever lived in the tide of time.

In the Middle Ages, Caesar became more of a formula than a personality, the founder of the Empire; but with the Renaissance his personality revived. The greatness of Caesar, says

90

Gundolf, was rediscovered by Petrarch; his charm by Montaigne. "When I reflect", says the latter, "upon his incomparable greatness of soul, I can excuse victory for not having been able to shake off his fetters even in that very unjust and iniquitous cause." [1]

But Montaigne's closing words bring us face to face with the other side of Caesar's reputation throughout the centuries, leaving the Middle Ages out of the count. As Cromwell by Clarendon, Caesar, by the moralists of his own and succeeding ages, moralists and constitutionalists, was accounted a *great but a bad man*. This two-fold judgment goes back to Cicero.

> Cicero's picture of Caesar [says Gundolf] varies like the colours of an opal from that of a god to that of a knave. In eulogistic speeches he treats him as the glory of his age, speeches in which he celebrates his exploits in war, his magnanimity, his power of intellect, in a more sincerely elevated strain than any writer has done since; and that not only to Caesar's face, when he is speaking as the flattering pleader for his clients and himself . . . or under the influence of a concealed anxiety before this enigmatically mild man whose power he knew, but even after his death, in an outbreak of feeling, oppressed by hatred, sated with revenge, moved even against his will with admiration. In the *Second Philippic*, it is true, Caesar's mighty shadow is evoked to put to shame Antony strutting in the mantle of the giant; yet the conjuration is no mere rhetorical trick, but expresses Cicero's conviction. Thus has he seen Caesar through all the oscillations of party feeling and personal relations—a miracle of power, of intellect, of refinement, of completeness—and withal the reckless destroyer of the state and corrupter of the people.

That is the judgment which passed down the centuries till

---

[1] "On parle beaucoup de la fortune de César; mais cet homme extraordinaire avait tant de grandes qualités sans pas un défaut, quoiqu'il eut bien des vices, qu'il eût été bien difficile que, quelque armée qu'il eût commandée, il n'eût été vainqueur et que en quelque république qu'il fût né il ne l'eût gouvernée."—Montaigne.

the nineteenth; and over against the Great Man appeared the
Moral Man, the virtuous hero, Cato or Brutus:

> *Victrix causa deis placuit, sed victa Catoni;*
> Where is now the soul
> Of God-like Cato?   He that durst be good
> When Caesar durst be evil; and had power
> As not to live his slave, to die his master?
> Or where the constant Brutus, that being proof
> Against all charm of benefits did strike
> So brave a blow into the monster's heart
> That sought unkindly to captive his Country?
> O they are fled the light! . . .
> . . . nothing good,
> Gallant or great: 'tis true that Cordus says
> "Brave Cassius was the last of all that race".

So speaks the old Roman republican in Ben Jonson's *Sejanus*,
and you have there the idealization of the virtuous hero, the
Harry Vanes and Lafayettes with whom Carlyle can at times
grow impatient, even if it is with some uneasiness that he
accepts as hero one who is not also good, and prefers Cromwell to Caesar or Napoleon because of his more religious and
moral aim.   It is a rather puzzling dilemma this, presented
by the great man who does great things and the good
man often apparently quite inefficient but nevertheless
"good".

The Gordian knot, if it is one, is cut of course by Nietzsche,
who denies validity to the "good" as thus conceived.   If
Ruskin led to Oscar Wilde, as a recent French critic declares,
Carlyle led direct to Nietzsche.   His superman is a further
development of the Hero.   Might is right, says Carlyle,
because in the long run, if it is not also right, the might will
prove delusive.   He blends, as I have said, a scientific with a
religious pronouncement.   If the power you rely on is not a
power in nature you must fail; if you have made a mistake
your air-ship will fall; or, to speak religiously, if you are

violating the fundamental instinct of justice, if you are not acting in accordance with God's Will, you must be defeated. Nietzsche, accepting from his first teacher Schopenhauer the doctrine that there is *no* providential order in the world, no law revealed and sanctioned by a power external to man, obedience to which is rewarded, disobedience punished, as set forth clearly in the Book of Deuteronomy; but that we are our own guides and create our own values, Nietzsche makes the *saltus* and declares Might is Right. Ultimately it is the only Right, imposed on the mass, *das Gesindel*, by the superior class and accepted by them. If morality becomes something different, then it is a kind of miasma rising *from* the mass and paralysing the strong, the authentically good, a device by which the Will to Power that is in us all, directed by the priest, the strong in craft though wanting in nobility and courage, succeeds in restraining the strong and noble, dragging all down to the anarchic level of equality, or, under the disguise of doing so, subjecting the generous and noble warrior to the crafty and revengeful priest, so that the Emperor comes to Canossa. Christianity especially has been one long conspiracy of the weak against the strong, exalting the so-called virtues of humility, meekness, pity, over the natural and essential virtues of strength, pride, and courage. Nietzsche indeed pushes the superiority of the great man to all morality so far that one feels tempted to find his supermen to-day in gentlemen like Mr. Hatry and others (who, having risen beyond good and evil, are now serving their time), or at least in the oil or rubber or newspaper magnates of modern trade. Nor indeed would he quite deny the affinity of the hero to the criminal.

> Dostoievsky [he writes], this profound man . . . found the Siberian convicts among whom he lived for many years . . . those thoroughly hopeless criminals for whom no road back to society stood open—very different from what even he had

expected—that is to say, carved from the best, hardest, and most valuable material that grows on Russian soil.

The criminal type [he says again] is the type of the strong man amid unfavourable conditions, a strong man made sick. . . . Almost every genius knows the Catilinarian Life as one of the stages in his development, a feeling of hate, revenge, revolt against everything that exists, that has ceased to evolve —Catiline—the early stage of every Caesar.

But Nietzsche would not, I think, have admitted to the rank of Hero merely the great capitalist, the profiteer, for he sees one of the perils to society in their lack of distinction, of any claim to superiority beyond their great wealth. They cannot evoke the sentiment of hero-worship.

But it is not my intention to follow Nietzsche in the quest of the superman, compared with whom all the heroes of history gradually lost interest, so that he could not disguise his contempt for Carlyle's devout attitude: "Never yet has there been a superman. Naked I considered the greatest and least of men—all too like were they the one to the other; truly even the greatest I found—*all too human.*"

I think that the difference, if there is one, between the English and the Continental attitude towards the Hero is explicable without going quite so far. It is partly a symptom of the Continental inclination to allow a more absolute value to what appeals to the imagination than *we* are altogether willing to do. In judging of both men and works of art, we are more unwilling to allow an absolute value to anything that does not justify itself on practical or on moral grounds. By the German, the French, and the Italian critic, the greatness, the sheer abstract greatness, of a man like Caesar or Napoleon, his force of intellect and will, is accorded an admiration, that we are more disposed to modify by a demand that he shall approve himself also by his moral worth, just as in art they are more ready to admire and accept a great work

94

without submitting it to the test of moral value, at least as measurable by fixed and recognized standards. Things and men that appeal to the imagination have thereby worth. To deny the greatness of Caesar or Napoleon is as blasphemous or foolish as to deny the greatness of the sea or the tempest:

> What! alive and so bold, O Earth?
>   Art thou not overbold?
> What! leapest thou forth as of old
> In the light of thy morning mirth,
> The last of the flock of the starry fold?
> Ha! leapest thou forth as of old?
> Are not the limbs still when the ghost is fled,
> And canst thou move Napoleon being dead?

Shelley catches there, as a poet might, whatever his final judgment on Napoleon, the sense of his greatness not to be ignored. To Mr. Shaw and Mr. Wells as much as to Carlyle such a feeling is repellent. The moral judgment is insistent. Carlyle can with difficulty overlook the youthful immoralities of his hero Frederick: they would not have weighed with Goethe for a minute. Even Sir Walter Scott, whose imagination so much dominated his view of history, is yet well aware that the final estimate must be moral and practical. His Claverhouse makes but a poor defence of his conduct to Morton. Scott refused to write the Life of Mary Queen of Scots, so well aware was he that his judgment and imagination were not on the same side. He is far more of a Jacobite in his letters to Miss Clephane than in the novels that close with *Redgauntlet*, in such a clear perception of the fatal flaw of character which was the doom of a House, the best of whom had, as Laud admitted, neither greatness nor the capacity to be made great.

But this is not all. There is another explanation of this difficulty of reconciling greatness and goodness in the Hero. The antinomy of Great but Bad man may be due to a too

95

abstract conception of both "greatness" and "goodness", the Hero and the Moral Man. The moral man, Cato and Brutus and Harry Vane and Lafayette, is, as Carlyle too feels, a rather empty ideal. Cato is approved, Caesar condemned, by the application of a very abstract standard of Platonic and Stoic Virtue. I do not know why it is that the word "virtue", "virtuous", so much in favour in the eighteenth century, has so much lost colour, if it be not due to this distrust of abstract virtues and moral commandments, whether engraved on stone or painted in our chancels, with the appropriate penalties expressed or implied. "Thou shalt not kill" —"Penalty, a drop not exceeding twelve feet"! Or the sanction may be more purely prudential:

> Do not adultery commit;
> Advantage rarely comes of it.

And it has been the mission of the Hero as Prophet to wage war against such legalism and substitute for it the less definite but more searching rule: "Thou shalt love the Lord thy God with all thy heart, etc., and thy neighbour as thyself". But the Hero also has often been considered too much in the abstract of an aesthetic admiration of his gifts and exploits. Plutarch was mainly taken up with such descriptions of his qualities, interlarded with all the indications of his favour in the eyes of the Gods, the oracles and other signs and wonders that accompanied his career or his death. It was only gradually that the question became not what were his personal qualities, intellectual or moral, but what did he achieve of permanent worth for his nation or for civilization generally. Gundolf traces the rise of this demand to the constitutional wars of England, but the English approach to the question was, he thinks, too strictly practical and legal. It was Montesquieu who first, taking the ruler in close relation to his people, brought this aspect of the Hero to the front; and one result of it, in the survey of the heroes of antiquity, was, Gundolf points out, that for a time Alexander was given a place superior to Caesar, because he had rendered real service to humanity as the bulwark of the West against the East and the disseminator of Hellenic civilization, whereas Caesar was still held to be the destroyer of the liberty of Gaul and of his own country. It remained for Mommsen and the historians of the nineteenth century to vindicate Caesar both as the conqueror of Gaul and as the founder of the Empire, to show that it was Caesar and not the virtuous constitutionalists who had the "seeing eye" which Carlyle exalts as the special gift of the Hero. It was but natural that Froude, the disciple of Carlyle, followed Mommsen in the glorification of Caesar, and looking round for another hero, was tempted to try his hand on Henry VIII.

Now this estimate of the Hero had established itself before Carlyle wrote, and underlies all he has to say on the subject, as it does, say, Mr. Wells' reconsideration of various heroes. If we now mean anything by a Hero, it is, I suppose, someone who has quite definitely, we believe, carried mankind a step forward, hard as it may be to decide what are the real steps in advance that humanity has taken. But what I wish to suggest now is that, from this point of view, one may perceive the reason of the difference between the British and the Continental conception of the Hero, and understand why Carlyle and the English writers generally have laid greater stress on the moral aspects of his character and work than, for example, Machiavelli in *The Prince*, or the Continent generally in their estimate of Napoleon. The Hero as King, as ruler and soldier, is to some extent the creation of an emergency, the saviour. The emergency will not always produce him, witness the Italy of Dante and Machiavelli, but the emergency is the great man's opportunity. In peril of its existence a nation is more willing to place its fate in his hands, as the Dutch in 1672, the French after the Revolution, and, say, Germany when Bismarck came to the top, or at the present juncture. Dante had looked for a saviour from beyond the Alps; Machiavelli had hoped to find him in Cesare Borgia. We have been hitherto less often in such a predicament, perhaps, as our Continental critics say, because of our insular position; and we have been able to "muddle through" our constitutional crises without his aid; for in the ordinary course of political business, a cabinet of Heroes is as little to be looked for as a cabinet of Archangels, and might prove as ineffectual as a Cabinet of all the Talents. And this may explain also the almost mystical reverence of Continental writers for Napoleon, whom, with a few striking exceptions, English critics have never quite accepted as a Hero, a Benefactor. The Continental admiration is not purely imaginative and artistic. To western Europe Napoleon, if in the end he became the enemy and so the quickener of national feeling, was at the outset both a deliverer and a promise—a deliverer from what Shelley calls the old Anarch Custom and the promise of a United Europe, one who might do for Europe what Machiavelli had hoped Borgia would do for Italy. Byron, who understood the European point of view as few Englishmen at the time did, has put that thought into four lines:

> A single step into the right had made
> This man the Washington of worlds betrayed;
> A single step into the wrong has given
> His name a doubt to all the winds of heaven.

That is the feeling which inspires Nietzsche's admiration of Napoleon, "that synthesis of Monster and Superman".

What I am concerned with—for I see it preparing itself slowly and hesitatingly—is the United Europe. It was the only real work, the one impulse in the soul of all the broad-

minded and deep-thinking men of this century—the prepara-
tion of a new synthesis, the tentative effort to anticipate the
future of the European. Only in their weaker moments,
when they grew old, did they fall back again into the national
narrowness of the Fatherlander—then they were once more
patriots—I am thinking of men like Napoleon, Heine, Goethe,
Stendhal, Schopenhauer. . . . Enough; here as in other matters
the coming century will be found following in the footsteps of
Napoleon—the first man and the man of greatest initiative and
advanced views of modern times.

If the Hero be in part the child of the emergency, to ask
that he should always also be a good man is to say that in a
political emergency we can always act in accordance with
principles that are sufficient for normal conditions. It is
more; it is to assume that we know more completely what is
right, what is good, than perhaps is the truth. Even the
Hero as Prophet has presented himself as a challenge to the
standards of his day; has not been at once accepted as a
Saint, but as a blasphemer and a friend of Publicans and
Sinners. And he too is the response, to some extent, to the
emergency—Mahomet, Christ. One aspect of the social and
moral conditions of man when Christ appeared is supplied by
St. Paul in the *Epistle to the Romans*, supported by the evidence
of the satirists. "The pictures so constructed are mosaics of
singular vices, and they have led to the not unnatural impression that those centuries constituted an era of exceptional
wickedness." But the late Edwin Hatch in the Hibbert
Lectures for 1888 showed that there was another aspect of
the emergency: "that the age in which Christianity grew was
in reality an age of moral reformation. There was the
growth of a higher religious morality, which believed that
God was pleased by moral action rather than by sacrifice.
There was the growth of a belief that life requires amend-
ment." It was the age of Epictetus. And if the great men
who were captains and kings are to be judged solely by the

blood they shed, what of the Prophets? In their name rivers of blood have been poured out.

The late Lord Acton thought that most great men in the field of politics and warfare had been more or less bad men; Swift maintained that they had been *lunatics*:

> For, if we take a survey of the greatest actions that have been performed in the world, under the influence of single men; which are the establishment of new empires by conquest; the advance and progress of new schemes in philosophy; and the contriving as well as the propagating of new religions—we shall find the authors of them all to have been persons whose natural reason had admitted great revolutions from their diet, their education, the prevalency of some certain temper, together with the particular influence of air and climate. . . . For the brain in its natural position and state of serenity disposeth its owner to pass his life in the *common* forms, without any thought of subduing multitudes to his power, his reasons or his visions; and the more he shapes his understanding by the pattern of human learning the less he is inclined to form parties after his particular notions, because that instructs him in his private infirmities as well as in the stubborn ignorance of the people.

Carlyle but a few years ago was reckoned a mightily discredited prophet. The editor of the Centenary Edition of his works, the late H. D. Traill, could affirm in the opening introduction with confidence that: "Carlyle is neither prophet nor ethical doctor, but simply a great master of literature who lives for posterity by the art which he despised". When a few years later he came to introduce *Past and Present*, he could boast complacently that "this pronouncement . . . has on the whole been received with a greater amount of assent, express or tacit, than one would have ventured to count on when the sentence was penned", and for final confirmation he appeals to the very work in hand, *Past and Present*.[1] Such was

[1] "It is with some unwillingness that we pass from this picturesque and romantic episode to the two concluding books, and find ourselves at

our complacent mood before the last War. Will anyone say to-day, when we are standing amid the wreck of that industrial order which Carlyle arraigned, and of that democracy at which he scoffed, that he was no prophet? "Let inventive men cease to spend their existence incessantly contriving how cotton can be made cheaper; and try to invent, a little, how cotton at its present cheapness could be more justly divided among us." Is not that the problem with which we are faced to-day, grown infinitely more pressing? And what of democracy in the Europe of Lenin and Stalin and Mussolini and Hitler and smaller varieties of the Hero type? Or the United States and Roosevelt? The feelings with which Russian and Italian and German turn appealingly to the Hero show the same blend of religious mysticism and economic demand as Carlyle felt and proclaimed. Men will worship the great man, but they will demand of him (as of their God) that he feed them. He must find them loaves and fishes. And in our own country from different angles Sir Oswald Mosley and Sir Stafford Cripps point the same road. So far as democracy and constitutional government and liberty are concerned there is not a pin to choose between them.

What Carlyle would have thought of the happenings in Russia, Italy, and Germany to-day is hard to say, for he was

hand-grips with professors of the dismal science, commercial capitalists, *laissez-faire* theorists, Plugson of Undershot, Sir Jabesh Windbag, and the rest of Carlyle's favourite bogles. They are all fallen silent—all gone dead to-day, etc." It is strange to see how many of them have come alive again—professors of the dismal science were never so much in evidence, if a little less confident than of old; commercial capitalists leading us the same glorious round from fortunes made to fortunes lost in the twinkling of an eye; and all the problems not solved and done with, as Mr Traill believed, but very much alive. A Government of Business Men—there is not much cry for that to-day! They had been so shortsighted in their own sphere, made such a melancholy mess of their own and other people's money, that in America they were in the recent Presidential election discredited, and for once in history Plato's philosophers, or at least University professors, are being allowed an innings—how long it will last remains to be seen.

never quite unaffected by his humours and prejudices. He would certainly not have joined in the varied and inconsistent outcries of horror, for since the last War we have been divided, in the most odd manner, into those who approve of certain things done in Russia and regard them with horror when they are transferred to Italy or Germany, and *vice versa* those who accept them with complacency when directed against Socialists in Italy or Germany but shrink with horror from the same cruelties in wicked Russia. One can hardly doubt that Carlyle would have seen in the War and all that has followed it the fruits of *laissez-faire* and Democracy. Competition for trade, the cash nexus as the sole link, had failed between nations as between individuals in the state. And Democracy? A Society to promote what was called Democratic Control was instituted as the War drew on and people were growing weary. I remember putting myself sadly through a catechism. Why could neither France nor Italy afford (perhaps Britain *might* have done so) to make a reasonable peace with concessions on all sides, say in 1917? Democratic Control. No government could have gone to the people and said "the War has brought us no gain, only the *status quo ante*". Why was the Peace of Versailles so much worse than the Peace of Paris of 1814–15? Democratic Control. Recall the election and the promises extracted from candidates to exact reparations and hang the Kaiser. Why did America fail to implement President Wilson's signature and insist on leaving Europe to stew in its own juice? Democratic Control. It is part of the cant of the moment, when we have all grown wise after the event, that Lord Grey declared war without consulting the people. If it had been possible to do so they would have voted for war. The fear was not that we should be brought in but that we should leave France in the lurch, especially among the generous young whose successors are now so critical of their elders.

CARLYLE AND HITLER

What Carlyle would have thought of the particular Heroes themselves is even more difficult to say. He was not quick to discover heroic traits in a contemporary. And the Hero, to-day as ever, presents the same dual aspect, good and evil· If in measuring that good and evil we may be misled, as I have suggested, by too abstract standards alike of goodness and greatness, the problem yet remains. But the solution is after all perhaps not so difficult. The good and evil in what your hero does—Caesar, Augustus, William of Orange, Cromwell, Napoleon, Frederick—remain and each bears its fruit. Good may outweigh the evil. It cannot annul it. No hero in the world of action but has left behind a legacy of evil as well as good. There is only one class of Heroes who can plead that if they have achieved no great exploits, they have done no harm; they have come to us only in the attractive power of love and beauty, and that is the Hero as Poet— Dante, Shakespeare, Goethe. There is no debit side to their credit balance as there is to so many, not only Caesar and Napoleon, but, may one say it, St. Paul and Mahomet. Even of the Prophet the most enduring of the victories he achieves may prove to be not those which were won for him by arms or inquisitions, but by the penetrating and pervasive influence of his character and words, the poet in the prophet. But the Hero as Poet made small appeal to Carlyle unless he could also class him as Prophet. It is strange indeed that Carlyle did not rather concentrate on the Hero as Prophet; but that he did not, but was more intent on the Hero as King, bespeaks his own sense of the emergency of his time; like Plato he would fain have ruled men, at least guided them, for that seemed to him the want of his age; and ours is confirming his forecast. We are paying dear to-day for *laissez-faire*, for refusing, while we had the wealth, the natural demand, as he affirms it in *Past and Present*, of every working man for two things, a living wage and security of employment. Even our

103

Insurance for Unemployment came too late, and had not accumulated the funds needed for the emergency which has overtaken us. It is Carlyle who has led me, rather contrary to my own expectation, away from the Hero as Poet, which would have been my more natural theme; but he who sets out to write a lecture knows little of where and how it will end.

VI

ROBERT HENRYSON

*An Address to the Scottish P.E.N. Club,
at a Henryson Dinner—1933*

OF Robert Henryson's personal life we know really nothing. But this absence of knowledge has certain advantages. There is no need for any apologia; no stories to discuss such as those concerning Burns' loves and conviviality, or Scott's extravagance and tragic later days. We are concerned with the poet alone, his work and its significance and interest for us to-day. Indeed, if we abstract our minds from the poetry, we might feel as if we were attempting to-night to evoke from "the dark backward and abysm of time" one of whom we know nothing but a late report that he was "sometimes cheife schoolemaster in Dunfermling much about the time that Chaucer was first printed and dedicated to king Henry the 8th by Mr. Thinne, which was neere the end of his raigne".

But this obscurity attaches not to Henryson alone, but even to the much more noisy and self-assertive Dunbar, about whose life also we know little or nothing for certain. Indeed, and this is why I have touched upon it, this ignorance or indifference of a great mass of the Scottish people extends to the whole history of their country in the Middle Ages. Apart from the long conflict for independence with England, and the exploits of Wallace and Bruce, we trouble ourselves little about this older Scotland. Scottish history, as it appears in most of our text-books, is a rather dreary chronicle of struggles

105

between various noble families—Douglases, Hamiltons, Crichtons, Livingstones, Boyds—to gain control of the King, and of fitful efforts by the King to establish his authority—that, and recurring wars with England. "Lastly", says Carlyle, after reading *Tales of a Grandfather*, "it is noteworthy that the nobles of this country have maintained a quite despicable behaviour from the time of Wallace downwards—a selfish, famished, unprincipled set of hyenas." These be very bitter words, but not altogether undeserved. How many of the Nobles in Mary's reign were in the pay of Elizabeth? The brightest luminaries in this dark history are to be found in one or two of the Kings and in one or two of the great ecclesiastics, Bishop Kennedy of St. Andrews, Bishop Elphinstone of Aberdeen.

It is partly the facts themselves that give so wretched an appearance to much of our early history, but there is another thing to be remembered, and that is the completeness with which the great mass of the Scottish people have permitted their history to be divided into two chapters by the Reformation, have rung down the curtain on the ecclesiastical and cultural history of our country before 1560. Thereafter it became the duty of pious Scots to regard all earlier periods as a kind of Dark Ages, and to consider even such great and good men as Kennedy and Elphinstone as emissaries of Antichrist, to displace all our Saints to make room for the burly but coarse figure of John Knox, and the rather sour countenance of Andrew Melville.

The Scottish youth of to-day are determined to reclaim the whole of their inheritance, to surrender nothing of our Scottish tradition, Catholic and Protestant. They are quite prepared to honour Knox and Melville and the Covenanters according to their measure, but are equally interested to revive the memory of our great ecclesiastics and poets of these so-called "Dark Ages". Sir Walter Scott did much to recover for us the romance of Scottish history, but he left much undone. He did not, after all, understand the finer spirit of the Catholic ages. In his day, the frost of complacent Protestantism was only beginning to melt. He left, moreover, many of the most interesting figures in Scottish history untouched. It was the work of an English poet of Italian blood to give poetic enshrinement to our king and poet and his tragic and brutal end.

Robert Henryson is a more modest person, one who was not even, like Dunbar, a Court poet, but, as tradition says, and his poetry is in harmony with that tradition, a simple schoolmaster in Dunfermline, a school where, as a later master in the same school declares, "his predecessors have continued maisters and teachers of the youth in letters and doctrine to their great commodity past memory of man". It was, I suppose, in the Abbey which is now a ruin that Henryson walked and meditated in the manner one of his poems describes:

> Allone as I went up and doun
> In ane abbay was fair to se,
> Thinkand quhat consolatioun
> Was best in to adversitie,
> On caiss I kest on syd myne E,
> And saw this writtin upoun a wall:
> "Off quhat estait, man, that thow be,
> Obey and thank thy god of all".

But if we reflect upon Henryson, his pupils dismissed, wandering in the Abbey and the Abbey grounds, we may be allowed for a moment to compare, so far as we can, the Scotland on which he looked out with the Scotland of to-day. The Abbey was not then the ruin that it and almost every great ecclesiastical building is to-day. In ruined churches and abbeys Dr. Johnson saw the chief evidences of the Scottish Reformation.

It is not only in Raasay that the chapel is unroofed and useless; through the few islands which we visited we neither saw nor heard of any house of prayer, except in Skye, that was not in ruin. The malignant influence of Calvinism has blasted ceremony and decency together; and if the remembrance of papal superstition is obliterated, the monuments of papal piety are likewise effaced.

But the ruins of to-day look out perhaps upon a fairer country than met the eye of Henryson. When as a boy I came from the Shetland Islands, Scotland always struck me as a country of trees. The leaves with which the playground was strewn when I returned from the summer vacation in autumn were evidence of a very different season from that which I had witnessed,

> Where the Atlantic ocean, in vast whirls,
> Boils round the naked melancholy isles
> Of farthest Thule.

Now, the Scotland of Henryson's day was not very different from the Shetland of mine. It was perhaps while Henryson was alive that Aeneas Sylvius, later Pius II, visited Scotland in 1435, and you may remember his description:

It is an island joined to England, lying to the North, about two hundred miles in length, and fifty across: a cold land bearing few crops and to a great extent devoid of trees. . . . The cities have no walls; the houses are for the most part built without mortar; the country houses are roofed with turf, and the door of the cottages closed with the hides of bulls. The common people are poor and uncivilized; they eat their fill of meat and fish, regarding bread as a delicacy. The men are small in stature and brave; the women white-skinned, beautiful and amorously disposed. To kiss a woman there means less than to touch her hand in Italy . . . there is nothing the Scots like better than to hear the English abused.

It is not a very different Scotland after all from that which Johnson visited three centuries later.

From the banks of the Tweed to St. Andrews I had never seen a single tree which I did not believe to have grown up far within the present century . . . the variety of sun and shade is here utterly unknown. There is no tree for either shelter or timber. The oak and the thorn is equally a stranger . . . a tree might be a show in Scotland, as a horse in Venice.

You will remember with what joy Goldsmith exchanged the barren hills of Scotland for the tulip-fields of Holland.

But poverty in Scotland has ever gone hand in hand with respect for learning.

I know not [says Johnson] whether it be not peculiar to the Scots to have attained the liberal without the manual arts, to have excelled in ornamental knowledge, and to have wanted not only the elegancies but the conveniences of common life. . . . The Latin poetry of *Deliciae Poetarum Scotorum* would have done honour to any nation. . . . Yet men thus ingenious and inquisitive were content to live in total ignorance of the trades by which human wants are supplied, and to supply them by the grossest means. . . . Their tables were coarse as the feasts of Eskimos, and their houses filthy as the cottages of Hottentots.

This last *may* be an exaggeration, yet it is characteristic of Scotland that one of her best poets in these early times should have been a schoolmaster, and the work by which he is best known should have grown out of his work as a teacher.

For it was doubtless in reading with his pupils the Fables of Æsop, as they were called, in Latin, that the happy idea occurred, or was suggested to him, of translating them into his native vernacular, and of adding to each, as became an instructor of youth, an edifying moral. In the introduction to the *Tale of the Lion and the Mous*, he tells us that one beautiful June morning he was visited by no less a person than Æsop himself:

> His gowne wes off ane claith als quhyte as milk;
> His Chemeis wes off Chambelate Purpour Broun;

His hude off Scarlet, bordourit weill with silk,
On hekillit wyis, untill his girdill doun;
His Bonat round, and off the auld fassoun;
His beird wes quhyte; his Ene wes grit and gray,
With lokker hair, quhilk over his schulderis lay.

But if the schoolmaster in Henryson prompted him to translate the Fables and to add an appropriate moral, it in no
way interfered with his dramatic and humorous rendering
of them. There is nothing of the rather dreary didactic flat-
ness of a Gower or a Lydgate. Chaucer was his master,
"worthy Chaucer glorious", but the Scottish poets generally,
and Henryson in particular, were no slavish imitators. In
their technique, indeed, their love of alliteration and elaborate rhyming, both Dunbar and Henryson are more akin to
the Northern and Western poets of the fourteenth century
than to Gower and Chaucer, to the poet or poets who composed the *Pearl* and *Gawayne and the Grene Knight*. If Henryson
assimilated what was best in Chaucer's dramatic and humorous method, he gave it a turn of his own. The Scottish
poets' handling of their themes, whether narrative or alle-
gorical or lyrical, has a certain Scottish downrightness, which
gives the poems of Dunbar and Henryson a flavour of the
Scottish character. Their work does not show the courtly
over-sophistication of sentiment which one sometimes finds
in Chaucer, as in his French models, and their lyrics are
more strongly wrought than the filigree work of Chaucer's
love lyrics.

Henryson, specially, is not a courtly poet. He has not to
waste his time in flattering kings and lords, nor to consider
too carefully the refined sentiments of courtly queens and
ladies. If the *Moralitas* which he attaches to each Fable is
sometimes tedious and far-fetched, nevertheless the moral
spirit in which he writes lends solidity to his treatment, without weakening either its dramatic truth or his delightful Scot-

tish humour. A moral Fable could not be better told than his *Taill of the Uponlandis Mous and the Burges Mous*, or the two characters be better distinguished and sustained. The sage remark of the Country Mouse when she has enjoyed the superior dainties of her Burgess sister,

"Ye, dame" (Quod scho) "how lang will this lest?"

reminds one of Napoleon's mother "Si ça dure", and I have heard almost the same words from a golf caddy when my partner had commented on my good play for a hole or two: "Ah, it winna lest". Recall again the fox who confesses to the wolf, and being ordered to eat no meat throughout Lent but only fish, and finding the catching of fish beyond his capacity, seizes a lamb and plunging it in the river cries

"Ga doun, schir Kid, cum up, schir Salmond agane!"

a rather startling case of transubstantiation. But vengeance is awaiting him, for while he lies basking his well-filled stomach in the sun he says to himself unwisely:

Straikand his wame aganis the sonis heit,
"Upon this wame set wer ane bolt full meit".

Almost immediately, a goat-herd passing shoots an arrow through his stomach, and the poor fox complains while dying:

"Me think na man may speik ane word in play,
Bot now on dayis in ernist it is tane."

It is in the Fables, I think, that one finds Henryson's gifts —easy narrative, playful humour, poetry and gravity—in happiest balance. But his most original poem is the *Testament of Cresseid*. There is a little over-elaboration in the aureate style, especially in the description of the gods.[1] But

[1] A somewhat superior review (*Scrutiny*, December 1933) of Mr. Wood's edition of Henryson selects as a proof of Henryson's independ-

it is to my mind perhaps the most original poem that Scotland has produced. It was no light thing to come after Boccaccio and Chaucer, and to succeed in making a real addition to a great dramatic story, something that without needless challenging of comparison does, in its impressive way, complete that tragic tale.

Chaucer had, in his courtly and detached manner, avoided any moral judgment upon Cresseid. He tells the story and leaves it to speak for itself:

> Ne me ne list this sely womman chyde,
> Forther than the story wol devyse.
> Hire name alas is punysshed so wide
> That for hire gilt it oughte ynough suffise.
> And if I myghte excuse hire any wise,
> For she so sorry was for hire untrouthe,
> I wis I wolde excuse hire yit for routhe.

The only moral which Chaucer will enforce at the end of the whole tale is the religious one—that all earthly things are vanity. He speaks as a Christian, but so might a Buddhist. Boccaccio warns young men to beware of women such as Cresseid. Chaucer will not do that. I fancy he thinks at

ence of Chaucer "the evocation of the Ancient Gods", which the reviewer describes as something "in a manner which is scarcely Chaucerian". Yet surely Henryson had in mind Chaucer's evocation of the Ancient Gods in the Knightes Tale (III, 1580–1620), and much as I admire Henryson I cannot think anything said by the Gods is equal to the words of Chaucer's Saturn:

> My cours, that hath so wyde for to turne
> Hath more power than wot any man.
> Myn is the drenchyng in the see so wan;
> Myn is the prison in the derke cote;
> Myn is the stranglyng and hangyng by the throte;
> The murmure and the cherles rebellyng;
> The groynynge and the privee empoysonyng.
>
> .   .   .   .   .   .
>
> I slow Sampson, in shakynge the piler;
> And myne be the maladyes colde,
> The derke tresons, and the castes olde;
> My lookyng is the fader of pestilence.

heart that to have loved and been loved by Cresseid was
worth while, even if in the end she did desert you:

> O blisful night of hem so long ysought,
> How blithe unto hem bothe two thou were!
> Why ne hadde I swich oon with my soule ybought,
> Ye, or the leste ioie that were there.

But all earthly joys are fleeting, bring repentance, the legitimate as well as the illegitimate. The only true joys are in
heaven. So Chaucer changes the message of Boccaccio into
a pious exhortation:

> O yonge fresshe folkes, he or she,
> In which that love upgroweth with your age,
> Repeyreth hom fro worldly vanitye,
> And of your herte up casteth the visage
> To thilke god that after his ymage
> Yow made, and thynketh al nys but a faire,
> This world that passeth soone as floures faire.
>
> And loveth hym which that right for love
> Upon a cros, our soules for to beye,
> First starf, and roos, and sit in hevene above;
> For he nil falsen no wight I dar seye
> That wol his herte al hooly on hym leye.

But Henryson is not content with what, after all, is an
evasion—he, a Scot and a Schoolemaister, with a Scot's and
a schoolmaster's belief in retribution. The result might
have been disastrous—a dry or a piously unreal didactic
poem. But it is not, and that for two reasons. In the first
place, Henryson retains Chaucer's sympathy for Cresseid:

> Yit nevertheless quhat ever man deme or say
> In scornefull language of thy brukkilnes,
> I sal excuse, als far furth as I may,
> Thy womanheid, thy wisdom and fairnes;
> The quhilk Fortoun hes put to sic distres
> As hir pleisit, and nathing throw the gilt
> Of the, throw wickit langage to be spilt.

In the second place, his morality is sound and sincere, not the preacher's conventional acceptance of standards which he has not made his own. For the retribution which overtakes Cresseid in the poem is the retribution of her own heart. It is from within herself that the stroke which slays her comes. It is not the leprosy we think of as her penalty, but the last encounter with Troilus and its reaction on her own soul. You remember how they met when she the leper begged and he gave alms, neither knowing who the other was, though something in her face makes Troilus' old wound bleed afresh:

> Than upon him scho kest up baith hir Ene,
> And with ane blenk it come into his thocht
> That he sumtime hir face befoir had sene.
> Bot scho was in sic plye he knew hir nocht,
> Yit than hir luik into his mynd it brocht
> The sweit visage and amorous blenking
> Of fair Cresseid sumtyme his awin darling.
>
> Ane spark of lufe than till his hart culd spring
> And kendlit all his bodie in ane fyre.
> With hait Fewir ane sweit and trimbling
> Him tuik, quhill he was reddie to expyre.
> To beir his Scheild, his Breist began to tyre,
> Within ane quhyle he changit mony hew,
> And nevertheless not ane ane uther knew.
>
> For Knichtlie pietie and memoriall
> Of fair Cresseid, ane Gyrdill can he tak,
> Ane Purs of gold, and mony gay Jowall,
> And in the Skirt of Cresseid doun can swak;
> Than raid away, and not ane word he spak,
> Pensive in hart, qhuill he come to the Toun,
> And for greit care oft syis almaist fell doun.

Cresseid, too, has not recognized him, but learns from her companions who it is that has given her alms:

> "Yes" (quod a Lipper man), "I knaw him weill,
> Schir Troylus it is, gentill and fre."

That is the last straw:

> Quhen Cresseid understude that it was he,
> Stiffer than steill, thair stert ane bitter stound
> Throwout hir hart, and fell doun to the ground.
>
> Quhen scho ouircome, with siching sair and sad,
> With mony cairfull cry and cald ochane:
> "Now is my breist with stormie stoundis stad,
> Wrappit in wo, ane wretch full will of wane".
> Than swounit scho oft or scho culd refrane,
> And ever in hir swouning cryit scho thus:
> "O fals Cresseid and trew knicht Troylus.
>
> "Thy lufe, thy lawtie, and thy gentilnes,
> I countit small in my prosperitie,
> Sa elevait I was in wantones,
> And clam upon the fickill quheill sa hie:
> All Faith and Lufe I promissit to the,
> Was in the self fickill and frivolous:
> O fals Cresseid, and trew Knicht Troylus. . . ."

That, it seems to me, is a perfect end to the story, a real *catharsis* leaving us at peace with Cresseid as Chaucer's poem hardly does. Socrates contends in the *Gorgias*, first, that it is better to suffer than to do what is unjust. Troilus, at the end of Chaucer's poem, is happier than Criseyde. Secondly, that if you have done wrong the best thing which can happen to you is to suffer, not to escape, punishment:

> Now the proper office of punishment is twofold: he who is rightly punished ought either to become better and to profit by it, or he ought to be made an example to his fellows, that they may see what he suffers, and fear and become better; those who are punished by gods and men, and improved, are those whose sins are curable; still the way of improving them is by

pain and suffering; for there is no other way in which they can be delivered from their evil.

In Chaucer's poem, despite his sympathy, Criseyde is left an example to others. In Henryson's we see her healed and repentant by the way of suffering, and we are left in mind at peace with her as with Troilus. It is no small honour to a Scottish poet to have given this moving and dignified end to one of the great medieval stories.

I shall say nothing of Henryson's other poems. The best are the lyrics, especially *Robene and Makyne* and the two allegoric and devotional lyrics, *The Garmont of Gud Ladeis* and *The Bludy Serk*. One of the finest of Dunbar's lyrics is to my mind that on the Resurrection:

> Done is a battle on the dragon blak,
>   Our campioun Christ counfoundet hes his force;
> The yets of Hell ar broken with a crak,
>   The signe triumphall rasit is of the croce.

I will not say that Henryson's have all the lyrical fervour of that. As a lyrical poet of the Swinburnian kind, a master of every variety of rhyming technique, Dunbar is the greater, but in dramatic power, in gravity of temper, Henryson is the first of early Scottish poets; and his humour, if not so boisterous as Dunbar's, is finer, slyer, more Chaucerian and more Scottish.

In Henryson, then, we have a Scottish poet of the Dark Ages before Knox enlightened us, artistic, moral, religious, who well deserves to be remembered and honoured. The question is, what can we do to honour him aright? Well, we have made a beginning within this year in the both adequate and available editions of Dunbar by Dr. Mackenzie and of Henryson by Mr. Wood. That is all to the good. Yet I fear it will not carry appreciation far beyond academic and studious circles. Not many people will overcome the initial, and in great measure apparent, difficulty of the language. I have a suggestion that I am almost afraid to make. At Columbia University this year Professor Krapp brought out a complete translation in modern English of *Troilus and Criseyde*. I have not, I confess, read it, and am a little afraid to do so. But it is worth while to let a wider audience become familiar with one of the greatest of English narrative poems. Might it not be worth while trying a rendering in the Scots of to-day of some of the best of Henryson's Fables, as an experiment? I will leave it at that.

VII

LANG, LOCKHART, AND BIOGRAPHY

The Andrew Lang Lecture
in the University of St. Andrews—1933

THE duty of the Lang lecturer is, as I understand it, to
lecture on some subject from one of the many fields
explored by that extraordinarily learned and versatile mind.
It is not the lecturer's duty to accept Lang as infallible in any
one of these fields, or to make of his lecture an encomium.
Indeed I can imagine no great man who would have less
desired insincere, or even sincere, encomia being allowed to
disturb the lecturer's quest of the truth, for no one ever was
a more unprejudiced and sincere seeker of the truth. Like
Sir Walter Scott, Lang had his prejudices—a sympathy with
lost causes, an attachment to beliefs that were not the fashion
of his day; but, like Sir Walter, when his pen was in his hand
he felt it his duty to discount these prejudices, even to suspect them. It was his business to discover the truth, to find
out exactly what happened, whether, when found, these facts
were or were not what, as a Jacobite, or as one who had
felt the spell of Queen Mary, he had wished, perhaps even
hoped, to find. If Lang did fall at times into error the cause
was not his prejudices. It was due rather to the rapidity
with which his own mind worked. He caught up the points
of the evidence, and seemed to himself to see their bearing
so swiftly that sometimes, as his critics found and pointed
out, those facts were not exactly as he had believed. A quite
minor instance on which I came recently will illustrate what

I mean, because the fact is so unimportant that one cannot for a moment suspect the presence of any misleading motive. When Lockhart was in the Junior Latin Class at Glasgow University he had hoped, a certain Dr. Rainy told Gleig (who wrote a sketch of Lockhart's life for the *Quarterly Review*), to gain the second prize, awarded then by the votes of the students. He was not successful and felt it acutely. Some of his fellow-students, who shared the disappointment, subscribed to make him a present of Scott's *Lay of the Last Minstrel*, which was accordingly given out by the Professor along with the regular prizes. Lang, either glancing too quickly at the article, or trusting later to his memory, makes Rainy say that Lockhart "obtained the second prize" and being "disappointed by his second place" was presented by his backers, his supporters, with the consolation prize I have mentioned.

I make this somewhat apologetic introduction because there is no doubt that I have chosen my subject from a field regarding Lang's achievements in which there may be room for difference of opinion, as there is at the present time to a rather surprising degree concerning the biographer whose name I have coupled with that of Lang. In his *Life of Sir Stafford Northcote* (Lord Iddesleigh), a book not much read, I fancy—at least I could find no copy of it in our University Library—Lang gives his views about biography:

> On the whole subject of biography it would not be difficult and it might be pleasant to write at length. In this, as in everything, the fashion of the world changes. To Plutarch but a few pages sufficed, and in these he drew his men— imperishable portraits. The Life of Agricola in the hands of Tacitus fills but twenty folio pages, and yet Tacitus might easily have played the Boswell to his father-in-law. The ground that Izaak Walton occupied in the *Lives* was scarcely more spacious, and about our greatest name only a sheet or two of doubtful anecdotes survive. It was Boswell who began

the new method of biography, and in Lockhart he had his one worthy disciple. To their method, or at least to Lockhart's, Mr. Carlyle urged objections, asking for the picture of a man and not for the materials out of which a picture might be made. The taste of the age has preferred the accumulation and array of documents . . . this book is composed or compiled of letters, diaries, speeches, anecdotes, reminiscences, etc.

It seems a little strange that Carlyle should accuse Lockhart of failing to give us a picture of Scott, for surely by his selection and arrangement, and by descriptive digressions, such as that on Scott's life in Edinburgh or on an Autumn at Abbotsford, and other similar scenes, he composed almost as vivid a picture of Scott as Boswell had portrayed of Johnson. The charge of Lockhart's critics to-day, or of the more competent among them, is that Lockhart gave a vivid but an incomplete picture.

Be that as it may for the moment, there can be no doubt that Lang's own biographies belong to the second class of the two he mentions. He is less intent on drawing a picture than on extracting from the documents a record of what actually did happen, in the life of John Knox or Charles Edward, or the Elder Pretender, or Mary Queen of Scots. Most of his biographies, indeed, were the outcome of some challenge to his mind—a discovery that the traditional life of Knox was one-sided, had omitted or glossed over the facts which were essential to a right understanding of the man, the period, and the country—Scotland in the sixteenth century, not unlike the Serbia of some years before the War, or the Afghanistan of yesterday and to-day. If Knox was a Prophet, he was also a good deal of a Mullah or Mahdi, inciting to rebellion and civil war, and the apologist for brutal murders. Lang never, indeed, denies either the greatness or the essential sincerity of Knox, nevertheless such a biography fails to leave you with a three-dimensional picture of the man. He makes little or no attempt to get inside the subject of his biography, to estimate the spiritual factors at work. If he does not actually himself, he tends to make the reader, judge of Knox by present-day standards and circumstances, which are not those of a period when the religious conflict was one of life or death for one side or the other; when neither side dreamed of toleration except under compulsion. Toleration—like mixed marriages in a Catholic community to-day—was only to be tolerated if you had not sufficient force to suppress what were deemed heretical opinions.

In some of his biographies, indeed, Lang works almost like a detective or a Sherlock Holmes intent on solving a problem —who was the Jacobite spy signing himself "Pickle"? Was Mary or was she not art and part of the conspiracy to murder her husband? The greatest of his biographies is that on which another lecturer has dwelt—the *Maid of France*. Here, if he writes as a counsel for the defence, unravelling the evidence, exposing misrepresentations, checking illegitimate interpretations of the evidence, his heart as well as his intellect is in the work. The result of his investigation into the life and character of Queen Mary and of Charles Edward had been disillusionment, painful disillusionment, because it was the romantic and poetic side of his own nature which had made him undertake the investigation hoping for the best. But he makes no disguise of what has been the result. There was no disillusionment with regard to Joan:

> Last with a great voice she call "Jesus". Her head drooped, and the Daughter of God went home to her Father's house. Her heart, "cor cordium", was unconsumed. . . . That the world might have no relic of her of whom the world was not worthy the English threw her ashes into the Seine.

It is with the heart as well as with the head that a biographer must judge in the end, whether he approves or condemns or apologizes.

In the *Life of Lockhart* Lang was following to some extent the same line, writing in the same spirit, as in the *Maid of France*, though of course with not quite the same whole-hearted devotion. It might indeed have been a better piece of work if written in the critical and inquiring spirit of his *John Knox* and *Charles Edward*, for there are unsolved problems in the life and character of Lockhart which are not solved by Lang's *apologia*, or to be solved by the rough and ready, butcherly methods that are the fashion just now in biography.

Lang was drawn to Lockhart, first, I imagine, by a common loyalty to Scott, whom both men loved. But it is characteristic of Lang's loyalty to truth, and his high moral standards, that even Scott he will not over-estimate. Saintsbury has, he says,

> placed the book beside or above Boswell's. That is a length to which I cannot go; for Boswell's hero appears to myself to be of a character more universally human, a wiser man, a greater humorist, his biography a more valuable possession, than Sir Walter and Sir Walter's Life.

That, like his final judgment on Mary Stuart and Charles Edward, but even more so, for Lang loved Scott, is a striking evidence of his own integrity and of the pre-eminence he allots to character. "More universally human, a wiser man"—Scott, too, was human, and in his advice to others almost invariably wise; yet his wisdom failed him seriously when literature seemed to become a golden key to worldly success. He allowed his eyes to be dazzled by the promises of Lady Pecunia, not for her own sake but for the power she offered him of fulfilling his dreams of the imagination and the heart—Abbotsford, a baronetcy, the founding of a family—but also a stream of benevolence to relatives and friends and

brother authors and dependants and the poor. Yet Johnson
in his poverty, with his house full of old ladies and cats and
with Dr. Levett in the garret, is, I agree with Lang, a more
purely noble subject to contemplate.

But I must not stray so early from Lang and Lockhart to
Scott. There was another tie between Lang and Lockhart,
a fellow-feeling. Both, on the evidence alike of friends and
critics, were or could be, difficult people, prickly, rude sometimes almost to the extent of positive insolence. They were
both unsympathetic to many of the fashionable idols of their
day; detested the colossal complacency of liberals, political
and religious; had the old faith ever, in Tennyson's phrase,
"rugging at the heart". Lockhart, or so Lang was convinced, like himself, hid under this prickly and repellent
surface a depth of loyal affection for his friends and a sincere
regard for moral worth. The deeper Lockhart and the
deeper Lang come very near to one another in two poems.
Lockhart's is "a poem", Froude tells us, "sent to Carlyle. . . .
The lines were often on his lips and will not easily be forgotten by any one who reads them." So says Froude.
Lang goes on: "These lines came to him who now writes,
with Lockhart's letter to Carlyle, in an hour of sorrow and
will not be forgotten while memory endures".

> When youthful faith has fled,
>   Of loving take thy leave;
> Be constant to the dead,
>   The dead cannot deceive.
>
> Sweet modest flowers of spring,
>   How fleet your balmy day!
> And man's brief year can bring
>   No secondary May.
>
> No earthly burst again
>   Of gladness out of gloom;

Fond hope and vision vain
    Ungrateful to the tomb!

But 'tis an old belief,
    That on some solemn shore,
Beyond the sphere of grief,
    Dear friends will meet once more—

Beyond the sphere of Time,
    And Sin, and Fate's control,
Serene in changeless prime
    Of Body and of Soul.

That creed I fain would keep,
    That hope I'll not forgo;
Eternal be the Sleep,
    Unless to waken so.

These lines, it has always seemed to me, were in Lang's mind when he wrote the not often quoted poem, but to my mind one of the most moving of his poems:

Another Way

Come to me in my dreams, and then,
Saith one, I shall be well again,
For then the night will more than pay
The hopeless longing of the day.

Nay, come not *thou* in dreams, my sweet!
With shadowy robes and silent feet,
And with the voice, and with the eyes
That greet me in a soft surprise.

Last night, last night in dreams we met,
And how, to-day, shall I forget?
Or how, remembering, restrain
Mine incommunicable pain.

Nay, where thy land and people are,
Dwell thou remote, apart, afar,
Nor mingle with the shapes that sweep
The melancholy ways of sleep.

But if, perchance, the shadows break—
If dreams depart, if men awake,
If face to face at length we see,
Be thine the voice to welcome me.

The same haunting doubts, the same longing, the same deep and reserved affections.

It was thus as an *apologia* that Lang wrote the *Life of Lockhart*, a defence of one to whom injustice had been done by those who, unable to forget the stings of the "Scorpion", the sarcastic pen and haughty manner, had been fain to take their revenge upon the dead—Miss Martineau, Croker, Mrs. Gordon (though *her* Lang is prepared to forgive as the champion of her father) and others unable ever to condone attacks upon Liberal principles and the Liberal party. It is with Lang's *apologia* that I wish to deal shortly under two heads—first, his defence of Lockhart's treatment of the Ballantynes, both in the *Life of Scott* and in the pamphlet warfare which ensued; secondly, his general estimate of Lockhart's character and of his *Life of Scott*, though here I must speak somewhat tentatively, for I have not yet made up my own mind on the whole question. We should need to see more of Lockhart's own letters than have yet been made public, and know more, actually not conjecturally, of his contributions to *Fraser's Magazine* on which Mr. Sadleir has based his recent, to my mind very prejudiced, account of Lockhart.

For, as a Life professing to give a full and authentic account of Lockhart's activities in Edinburgh and London, Lang's work is not entirely satisfactory. It is written as by one who selects rapidly here and there what interests himself or will serve his defence, too rapidly, and also with scruples about the publication of private letters. One gets little assistance from Lang in fixing the exact date of events, or of letters which have subsequently come to hand, and we hear practically nothing about Lockhart's connection with *Fraser's Magazine* under Maginn. A full study of Lockhart is still a desideratum. Lang found difficulties at the very outset. He was refused access to Lockhart's letters to Croker, and therefore refused to make any use himself of Croker's letters to Lockhart, now with many others in the National Library.

But Lang does consider and discuss in considerable detail Lockhart's treatment of the difficult question of Scott's money affairs and his relations with the Ballantynes. In the light of such work as I have been engaged on during the last three years, Lang's line of defence seems to me in part just, but in part incomplete, incomplete for reasons which Lang might suspect but could not be fully aware of. Lang is just in his contention that Lockhart does not as a fact put the whole blame for Scott's disaster upon the Ballantynes, but acknowledges Scott's own ultimate responsibility for that tragedy:

> With equal clearness of insight and delicacy of statement he executed the painful task of tracing Sir Walter's misfortunes to Sir Walter's own errors of various kinds. The Ballantynes (undeniably improper instruments for Scott) aided and accelerated but did not cause the downfall. Lockhart's intention and aim was to draw a thoroughly truthful picture of Sir Walter Scott. How entirely he succeeded, how boldly and fully, yet how delicately as regards Scott, he told the truth no one can know better than the present compiler, who has followed in his steps, and handled many of the documents which he used.

So Lang; and as regards the first part of the statement, touching the Ballantynes, he is, I think, perfectly right. As regards the second half of the statement some qualification is, I think, necessary. Lockhart did not draw a complete picture; and in presenting his picture he allowed himself, quite in the modern manner, to introduce picturesque and dramatic touches which do not, I believe, falsify his picture of the main figure, but which nevertheless it is sometimes very difficult (in view of dates and other stubborn facts) to accept as descriptions of what actually happened. But of this later.

The second line of defence which Lang took is, on the face of it, sound and reasonable. In all that Lockhart says about Constable and the Ballantynes, Lang justly contends, Lockhart was relying on one who knew or ought to have known the full truth of the matter. He was guided by Robert Cadell. This is where Lang's defence halts, for he did not know, or at least fully realize, that Cadell was a prejudiced, to my mind an untrustworthy, witness. Lockhart's account of Constable and the Ballantynes was vitiated by the anger caused, explicitly, by statements about the Ballantynes which he found in Scott's letters, and by his too entire acceptance of Cadell's account of these men.

How do the facts stand, what was the gist of Scott's complaint when disaster overtook him? Too much stress has been laid on the loans raised at the last moment in the hope of saving Hurst, Robinson & Co., whose speculations and failures ruined Constable & Co., and through them John Ballantyne & Co., i.e. Sir Walter Scott. For one thing, Cadell was equally responsible with Constable for all the measures that were taken at the end, nor do these constitute the substance of Scott's serious complaint. That was, that he had been deceived throughout as to the stability of Constable's house. "Constable's business seems unintelligible. No man thought his house worth less than £120,000. Constable told me when he was making his will that he was worth £80,000. Great profits on almost all their adventures.

No bad speculations—yet neither stock nor debts to show."
Again: "I trusted too much to Constable's assurances of his
own and his correspondent's stability, but yet I believe he
was only sanguine". To Skene he spoke in the same way:
"He paid well and promptly, but devil take him, it was
all spectral together. Moonshine and no merriment. He
sowed my field with one hand and as liberally scattered the
tares with the other."

That is Scott's serious complaint, but why should the
blame be put upon Constable alone and not shared with
Constable's partner, Robert Cadell? Now that we have
access to the correspondence which passed between the
partners we know from Cadell that at least since 1811, two
years before Scott put himself into Constable's hands, the
firm had been "a labouring concern", that Constable was
taking out of the business more than the business could
afford, and that the sheet-anchor of Archibald Constable &
Co. was John Ballantyne & Co., i.e. Sir Walter Scott. "Our
most productive culture", writes Cadell, "is the author of
Waverley—let us stick to him, let us dig on and dig on at that
extraordinary quarry—and as sure as I now write to you we
will do well." Accordingly Cadell was quite as ready as
Constable to accept works which they had not yet seen, and
to pay in advance by bills discountable long before any
profit had begun actually to come in. It was Cadell who
in 1822, when Constable was recruiting his health in the
neighbourhood of London, offered Scott £1000 for *Halidon
Hill*, which he had never read, and that in bills discountable
at three and at six months, thereby providing Scott with the
means of paying at once for his son's transference to another
regiment. That was in May. In June he writes to Constable: "Hallidon Hill is *not good*, but this for *yourself* and for
no living ear".

With this awareness, at once of the shakiness of his firm

and of the value of Scott as an asset, Cadell more than Constable was averse to any step that might awaken Scott's suspicion. As I have shown in my Introduction to the Letters, when in 1823 Constable was extremely desirous of reducing the bills outstanding between his firm and that of the Ballantynes, Cadell was thoroughly alarmed at even the thought of any step being taken which might arouse Scott's suspicion. He impresses on Constable in the strongest terms that, so far from the Ballantynes' bills being a source of weakness to Constable's firm, they were absolutely essential to their stability.

> What can be the reason of your never failing remarks about Ballantynes' bills is a mystery to me but (*i.e.* except) your utter ignorance of the absolute want of your concern being as great as if not greater than those of J. B. & Co. I say *ours* are greater than theirs . . . do you suppose I have no alarms —I have many but it is not for Ballantyne, it is for A. C. & Co. . . . without them and their bills and books A. C. & Co. would not in all likelihood have existed.

If that was how things stood in 1823, two years before the failure, it seems to me clear that both Constable and Cadell did deceive Scott, and that Cadell was at least equally responsible with Constable. One may say, and not unjustly, that Scott should not have drawn on them so heavily—in bills for work not yet done and in accommodation bills, that is, loans. But to pay by bills in advance was not uncommon —at least so I gather from a letter which Scott wrote to Samuel Warren, and in any case why did Constable and Cadell agree to such terms? For fear Scott went to another publisher—but would another publisher have agreed to such speculative terms? Cadell detested the Ballantynes—the "miscreants of John Street" he calls them—just because he suspected in 1815 that they were negotiating with Blackwood and Murray. It is a thousand pities that Scott did not get into happier relations with these or other publishers. It would at least have distributed his risks.

But my subject is not Scott's finances; I wish merely to indicate that Cadell was not the unprejudiced and trustworthy witness which Lang in his defence of Lockhart seems to assume. Cadell had never really the personal regard, the affection for Scott, which Constable had. He hated the Ballantynes, but he hated Constable much more. They had quarrelled for years before the separation, and when poor Constable died Cadell wrote to a friend about his former partner and father-in-law in terms that shed a strange light on his own character:

So much for business—now for a few words to finish—Constable is now in a small space—poor man, he died very easily, he considered himself better, and had told Wallace at 3 o'clock that he would be a robust man yet, at six while eating or after he had done eating a little rice for dinner, and while his attendant was bathing his eyes which were somewhat inflamed, he sank back and expired. Thus has gone one of the vainest and most absurd men you have known. Originally ill-educated, he picked up from his intercourse with others a smattering of passable letter writing, which with some knowledge of books made a great show to ordinary persons, he had besides an ingenious mind, but I have not the slightest doubt that many of his projects were suggested by others and fathered by him—he was *not* a liberal-minded man, he was the very reverse, a liberal-minded person is liberal in all things, Mr. C. made liberal offers of money which were the offspring of sagacious calculation, but he almost always grudged his liberality so soon as it was emitted, and used to curse his folly, —his liberality was vanity—do you call it liberal to allow merit to no-one else, to be jealous of others in the same trade —and to do petty things to annoy and vex them? Mr. C. took the absurdest likings for persons—and before long equally absurd hatings—and when he did hate it was the most malignant hatred—in a word in Mr. C. there was nothing really amiable. He quarrelled first and last with every friend he

had—wife—son—and daughter—he was at one time a successful projector—and died a Bankrupt from want of knowledge
of business and calculation.

Lang allows that Lockhart might have given more consideration to the possibility that Cadell was a biased witness,
and argues that he did give some consideration; but Lang
did not know all the facts. He had before him Cadell's
correspondence with Lockhart, but not Cadell's correspondence with Constable before the failure.[1] Moreover, while
defending Lockhart, he does not approve the taste of Lockhart's pamphlet—*The Ballantyne Humbug*—though he apologizes for it (vol. ii, p. 168). Nobody will ever be able to
clear up the whole business regarding the Ballantynes. My
own belief is that John has had less than fair play—James
perhaps more. John did not die a bankrupt as Lockhart
says or implies, though it took some years to clear up his
affairs. On the other hand, in the second period of their
partnership in the printing business, after 1822, James, if I
may trust Mr. Glen's examination of the Cash Book now in
the Signet Library, drew more out of the funds than he was
legitimately entitled to. But my final conviction is that the
Ballantynes played a quite subordinate part in the whole
business, that the chief agents in the disaster were Constable,
Cadell, and Scott himself.

But now I must turn to Lockhart and his *Life of Scott*
regarded more broadly. His character is still to me somewhat of a mystery, though I have no sympathy with those
who dispute his ability. To my mind the *Life of Scott* is a
great work of art, a biography which just as a work of art is
rivalled only by Boswell's *Johnson*, and Froude's *Carlyle*, while
it has pages which in beauty of feeling and style rise to a
higher level than anything in these works. Such is the

---

[1] Except in as far as it was printed in *Archibald Constable and his Correspondents*, 1873.

account of Scott's last illness and death, to which the only parallel I can recall is Walton's narrative of John Donne's last days and death.

My concern is with Lockhart's methods, and with the *Life*, not as a work of art, but as a record of the facts; and some preliminary considerations are requisite to a fair judgment. That Scott and Lockhart loved each other is undeniable. Yet they must have been conscious of great differences in taste and character. Scott speaks of Lockhart, when announcing his engagement to Sophia, with some degree of qualification:

> He is highly accomplished, a beautiful poet and fine draughtsman, and what is better, of a most honourable and gentlemanlike disposition. He is handsome besides, and I like everything about him except that he is more grave and retired than I (who have been all my life something of an *étourdi*) like particularly; but it is better than the opposite extreme. [*To Lady Abercorn*, 15th March, 1820.]

Of Lockhart's shyness and hauteur, and his inability to push himself, he speaks more than once. The other trouble was his satiric bent of mind, and the part he had played on *Blackwood's Magazine*.

> All I have to fear on Lockhart's part is a certain rashness, which I trust has been the effect of youth and high spirits joined to lack of good advice, as he seems perfectly good humoured and very docile. [*To Morritt*, 19th May, 1820.]

> Lockhart is very much what you will like when you come to know him—much genius and a distinguished scholar. Very handsome in face and person, and only wanting something of the *usage du monde*. I mean there is a little want of ease in his manner in society. He does not laugh as thou dost, Anthony,—this is however speaking critically, for he is neither conceited nor negligent. His powers of personal satire are what I most dread on his own account—it is an odious accomplishment and most dangerous, and I trust I have

prevailed on him to turn his mind to something better. [*To ditto*, July 1820.]

On two occasions Scott expostulated strongly with Lockhart on this bent for merciless and reckless satire—after the fight over Wilson's candidature for the Chair of Moral Philosophy, and again after the unhappy duel in which poor John Scott lost his life. But never with success. Lockhart continued even after he left Edinburgh to contribute to *Blackwood*, and in London he joined the equally reckless but even more brilliant company of satirists and mockers who gathered round Maginn to run *Fraser's Magazine*. It is not surprising that he made enemies who, as Saintsbury suggests, took revenge on him after his death. To Sophia, his daughter, Scott wrote *à propos* of suspicions which had been excited in the mind of Canning at the time that Lockhart went to London: "To be one of the best and one of the kindest, as well as one of the cleverest of men I know, John's taste and talent for making enemies, and powerful enemies, is something quite extraordinary" (March 1827). This particular misunderstanding was cleared up, though Canning did not live long enough to show in any practical manner whether he had forgiven and forgotten.

This defect in Lockhart's character Lang admits throughout, and attributes to his early connection with Wilson in *Blackwood's Magazine*, and the extraordinary freedom allowed them in anonymous satire. Mrs. Gordon, in her Life of her father, Wilson, is inclined, quite naturally, to put the blame chiefly upon Lockhart, which Lang, quite justly, will not allow. In my opinion, it operated injuriously upon both men—this licence in anonymous satire and abuse. It allowed them, and Wilson took full advantage of this, to write now in one vein and now in another on the same man. Wilson will laud Wordsworth to the skies one day and almost slander him the next, and there is some sign of the same uncertainty in Lockhart's criticism, at least in his letters. The qualification in Wilson's case was his good humour. His review of Tennyson's early volume, which gave the poet so much chagrin, is a far kinder and more generous article than Lockhart's merciless satire in the *Quarterly*.[1] It is this merciless satire, unrelieved by a single generous word, that the subject of it finds difficult to forgive. Mr. Sadleir, in his *Edward and Rosina*, makes Lockhart chiefly responsible for the attacks from which Bulwer Lytton suffered at the hands of *Fraser's Magazine*, as well as of the *Quarterly*. But Mr. Sadleir takes a rather prejudiced view both of Lockhart and of *Fraser's Magazine* when he describes the brilliant group who supported Maginn as "Tory Jackals". It is a little difficult to accept this as a description of Thackeray, Carlyle, Galt, Coleridge, and others. *Fraser's* was, as a fact, a very troublesome ally of the Tory party during its first ten years, for the chief objects of its attacks were the Whig doctrine of *laissez-faire*, with the cruelties that doctrine involved for the working classes, and the cruelty of the great Whig magnates and Tory landlords in the administration of the Poor Law. Moreover, allowing for the kind of literary warfare of the day, the attacks of *Fraser's* on Bulwer's novels do not seem to me strikingly unfair. If one allows one's novels to be puffed as Bulwer's were by the publisher Colborn, and if one writes consciously (as Mr. Sadleir admits) to catch the taste of the less educated public, one can hardly expect not to be satirized. Mr. Sadleir indeed conjectures that Lockhart as one good-looking man was jealous of Bulwer as a rival. That is too much in the psychological, divining manner of modern biography to appeal to me. Lockhart was too proud a man to be merely vain. Bulwer's most

[1] But this was by Croker. Lockhart acknowledges receipt of the article (23.1.33): "You have most completely effected your purpose. It is wonderful that such folly should pass for poetry with anybody."

135

persistent and merciless critic was a Whig, Thackeray. Like Carlyle, Thackeray and Lockhart had a perfectly unfeigned contempt for the dandiacal novel of Lytton and Disraeli.

This was Lockhart, and thus Scott felt about him. What now was Lockhart's attitude towards Scott—was it entirely uncritical? The account of George IV's visit to Edinburgh, and of Scott's activities on that occasion, is in itself an almost sufficient answer. Nor, I suspect, did every aspect of the life at Abbotsford appeal to Lockhart's taste. There is a sentence in one of his articles in the *Quarterly* which gives to think:

> We are less surprised than distressed to see a child blowing up a frog, or impaling a butterfly; but, of all the world's wonders, none is to us more incomprehensible than the fact that there have been deep philosophers, solemn divines, nay, tender, thoughtful, meditative poets, who could wander from morn to dewy eve torturing fish and massacring birds.

It is difficult to imagine one who felt like this thoroughly enjoying Sir Walter's coursing parties, or young Walter's skill with the fowling-piece; though I think Sir Walter might have argued that it is no worse to torture fish and massacre birds than to torture and massacre young poets and novelists, a sport whose attraction for Lockhart was irresistible. And there were perhaps other things in the life at Abbotsford that Lockhart regarded with a detached amusement which, had it been anybody but Scott, would have found expression in his sarcastic manner. Of Maria Edgeworth's visit to Abbotsford, he speaks in the *Life* as of a period of pure enjoyment:

> The next month—August 1823—was one of the happiest in Scott's life. Never did I see a brighter day at Abbotsford than that on which Miss Edgeworth first arrived there. . . . The weather was beautiful, and the edifice and its appurtenances were all but complete; and day after day, so long as

she could remain, her host had always some new plan of gaiety. One day there was fishing on Cauldshields Loch, and a dinner on the heathy bank, another the whole party feasted by Thomas the Rhymer's waterfall in the glen—and the stone on which Maria that day sat was ever afterwards called Edgeworth's Stone. A third day we had to go further afield, he must needs show her, not Newark only, but all the upper scenery of the Yarrow, where "fair hangs the apple frae the rock"—and the baskets were unpacked about sunset beside the ruined chapel overlooking St. Mary's Loch—and he had scrambled to gather bluebells and heath flowers with which all the young ladies must twine their hair,—and they sang and he recited until it was time to go home beneath the softest of harvest moons. Thus a fortnight was passed—and the vision closed; for Miss Edgeworth never saw Abbotsford again during his life; and I am very sure she could never bear to look upon it now that the spirit is fled.

Lockhart writes to Wilson, at the time, in a less enthusiastic tone:

> Miss Edgeworth is at Abbotsford—a little, dark, bearded, sharp, withered, active, laughing, talking, impudent, fearless, outspoken, honest, Whiggish, unchristian, good-tempered, kindly, ultra-Irish body. I like her one day, and damn her to perdition the next . . . she, Sir Adam, and the Great Unknown are too much for one company.

That is a friendly letter, of course, and one must not make too much of the humour of a moment, yet I think Sir Walter's boyishness, and his tireless and lavish hospitality, must have sometimes fatigued the grave and sarcastic son-in-law. Nor did he enjoy the company of all Scott's cronies.

I have touched on these points of difference between the two men because I do not think that full consideration has been given to the difficulties which Lockhart encountered when he undertook the task of writing the Life of his father-in-law. The crash of 1826 had come on him, as on every member of Scott's family and his social friends, like a thunderclap. Then had followed the slow tragedy of the last years —Scott working himself to death under the direction of Cadell; the growth of illusion (if, indeed, Scott ever realized how things stood and the sheer impossibility of his working-off the debt with interest included); the last voyage and death—and then for the first time a full revelation of the hitherto, in the main, unknown side of Scott's life,—the crisis of 1813; the renewal thereafter of reckless anticipation and expenditure on that Delilah, Abbotsford, under the impetus of the success of the novels and the expectations raised in 1819 by the will of Scott's brother-in-law; the enormous accumulation of debt before the final disaster. And at the same time there was always the other side of Scott, alive in Lockhart's own memory, and revealed afresh in the letters that poured in from Heber and Ellis and Morritt and Lady Abercorn and Lady Louisa Stuart and the Duke of Buccleuch and Lord Montagu and dozens of others in every rank of life —the endlessly generous Scott with

> a tear for pity and a hand
> Open as day for melting charity,

unweariedly patient of claims made on his time and strength by relatives, friends, and strangers; unable to close his heart or purse to any appeal, giving money to Maturin and Bailey and Haydon and Godwin (whose politics he hated) and scores of others; finding work for Tom Purdie and Laidlaw; concerned at every hard season for his tenants at Abbotsford and the poor at Darnick; beloved by his friends and acquaintances as few men have ever been; and withal, when a clear issue presented itself, unobscured by his sanguine dreams or the passionate prejudices of the moment, an entirely honourable man; and finally, a great genius whose works, whatever they, like *all* novels, may have lost in freshness of interest for some readers to-day, give as clear evidence of a creative mind of the first order as anything of the kind produced since Shakespeare poured out his plays with the same profusion and much the same carelessness.

Lockhart quite justifiably conceived it to be his main task to present and do justice to the greater and better, the essential Scott, and not to darken the picture by too constant insistence on the reverse side of the canvas, the financial gamble, the constant drive to meet accruing bills by fresh engagements and fresh labour. He dealt with the crisis in 1813, and when disaster ensued in 1826 he did bring out this aspect of the story clearly enough to shock such different readers as Croker and Cockburn. It is possible now to see how much he left out. The mistake he made was to allow his natural impatience with many things he found in the Ballantyne correspondence—Scott's complaints about their delay in providing him from time to time with a clear presentation of the financial position—and the readiness with which he accepted the account of things he received from Cadell to cause him to make too much of the failings of the Ballantynes, and to concentrate upon Constable blame that should at least have been shared with Cadell, and to do all this in the scornful and irritating manner of which he was only too great a master. It would have been better had he acted on Miss Edgeworth's advice:

> Do pray leave out all the Accounts in Scott's Life—only make one clear general statement, and let there be an end of all that. Posterity will care nothing about Ballantyne and Constable or any one of them but Scott himself—and let me hear no more of Ballantyne-Humbug—what a vulgar word, unworthy of you.

And this brings me to a consideration of Lockhart's methods in biography, and that under two heads—his treatment of the letters, and his dramatic descriptions of persons and incidents, the method which he had used for imaginary scenes in *Peter's Letters* and in the *Noctes Ambrosianae*. The term which Lockhart applied to his manner of printing the letters is "manipulation"; and some such manipulation seems to me legitimate for one who is not editing the letters as such, but weaving them into a biography in a manner first adopted by Mason in his *Life of Gray*. But Lockhart's manipulation goes at times beyond what is legitimate, if he never, like Mason, introduced compliments to himself. His dealing with the letters may be described under one or two heads. The text is seldom quite accurate, though the changes are often trifling. He condenses letters. He corrects Scott's Scotticisms and errors in expression, sometimes in fact. (Scott not infrequently uses a wrong word, or a wrong personal name. He will call Daniel Terry Richard, and Robert Surtees is invariably called Richard.) He omits portions of letters, necessarily; but he does this in two different ways, and thus produces what may at least be described as a *suggestio falsi*. In some cases he inserts stars to indicate omissions, but as often as not he gives no such indication. But if some omissions are marked, then the absence of marks leads the reader to assume that there are no omissions. This is his method not only in the *Life* but in the *Ballantyne Humbug Handled*, in which Lockhart made use of letters access to which was refused to his opponent. Surely in this case at least it was his duty to make it clear that he was omitting portions of the letter cited. I can hardly think that in a legal case one would be allowed to submit as evidence what purported to be a continuous letter but was not so. Lockhart also "telescopes" letters, makes one letter out of what are really two or more. Even this might be done in a legitimate manner, if nothing actually misleading were introduced, though I think our modern standards of accuracy would hardly allow of such manipulation. For examples I must refer to the 1932 edition of the Letters, though we have made no attempt to indicate Lockhart's methods throughout in our notes—we have had too many other things to do. I may, however, give one example of this blending, made evident by my recent recovery in America of the letters to George Ellis. The "letter" which Lockhart wove into the text of the biography we printed in our first volume (pp. 258-9), assigning it, by reference to the immediate context, to the month of September. The originals now available show that the first part of this "letter" is taken, with omissions, from a letter the rest of which Lockhart prints subsequently without any indication of omissions, and dates "Ashestiel, 17th Oct. 1805"—there is no place or date in the original. But the final paragraph of the letter which we assigned to September, from the words "I am interrupted by the arrival of two gentil bachelors", is an extract from quite *another* letter, a long letter commenting on Ellis's *Specimen of Early English Metrical Romances*, dated by Scott himself, "Ashestiel, by Selkirk, 20th July 1805". July and October are thus combined, without a word of warning, in a letter which from its position suggests September. No essential harm is done in this case, and Lockhart did not wish to include discussions of metrical romance in his biography, but such treatment of letters makes one at least uneasy about others the originals of which are no longer accessible.

Some of these omissions in letters, and Lockhart's silence about episodes in Scott's life and experience, are readily explicable by another difficulty which the biographer had to overcome, besides his desire to do justice to the best and most attractive aspect of his hero. Lockhart was bound to consider the feelings of many persons still alive, or whose relatives were among his own friends. How much he felt this is seen from his treatment of the *Journal*, which came into his hands after Scott's death.

I had the whole diary [he tells Croker] set into type in order that I might obtain the advice throughout of his most intimate friend, Mr. Morritt, and of another person who knew very little of him but a good deal of society and all literary questions —Milman. Three copies were struck off and I now have them all, and I have no doubt that in the course of time some heir of his will sell the complete diary for a larger sum than my book brought, for the relief of his immediate representatives succeeding to an overburdened estate; nor have I the least doubt that Sir Walter foresaw this also. . . . Posterity will know that I at least endeavoured to avoid the offending of Scott's surviving contemporaries, and you will not doubt that I had to spare Tories about as often as Whigs the castigation of diarizing Malagrowther.

One wishes that Lockhart had used a little of the same self-restraint and discretion with regard to the Ballantynes and Constable; but on these he let himself go in the dramatic, satirical manner of *Peter's Letters* and the *Noctes* and *Blackwood* and *Fraser*. We owe to this, certainly, some of the most piquant pages in the *Life*—descriptions of James proposing "the Author of *Waverley*" at printing-house banquets, and of Jocund Johnnie "rattling down the Newhaven Road with two high-mettled steeds prancing tandem before him and most probably—especially if he was on his way to the races at Musselburgh—with some 'sweet singer of Israel' flaming with all her feathers beside him". Such touches as these are clever, yet not in the best of taste, for obviously if a man is known by his associates such a vivid portrayal of the Ballantynes somewhat detracts from the picture of Scott which Lockhart wished to present. But no one was more aware of the defects of Lockhart's satire than Lang:

The mass of Lockhart's *Quarterly* articles [he writes] cannot possibly be criticized here in detail. Not many of them deserve our dislike; among these are the reviews of Moore's Sheridan which displeased Sir Walter and the critique of Leigh Hunt's unhappy *Lord Byron and his Contemporaries.* The book was *une mauvaise action*; perhaps it could not be passed over. But, despite Lockhart's reputation for skill in satire, it must be said that in satire . . . he is always at his worst, and he is always at his best when he is most sympathetic.

Moreover, one's dislike of these satiric anecdotes about the Ballantynes and Constable is heightened by some distrust of their strict veracity. One suspects that he has allowed prejudice and later feelings to colour his account of past events. Lockhart, quite like the modern biographer, allowed himself to dramatize scenes, and I can see no great harm in that. Boswell did the same, though Boswell's dramatization seldom goes beyond a record of conversation. It is not often that he gives us pictures of, say, Johnson's rooms when he first visited him, or poor Goldsmith sulking at the Club after some rebuff and Johnson apologizing. Lockhart speaks a little contemptuously of the man who would record private conversations, but it is difficult to see anything like violation of confidence in Boswell's reports of conversations on general topics, though doubtless some of Johnson's satiric remarks regarding individuals must have given offence. But Boswell's account of conversations give an unmistakable impression of veracity, while for his vivid descriptions of incidents, Lockhart, it would appear, drew a good deal upon his imagination. The result is often delightful, as for example the narrative of his first visit to Abbotsford along with Wilson (chap. xlii) and others to which I have referred. But there are some of them which it is difficult to accept at their face value because they will not fit in with dates and other evidence. Of these some are of trifling importance, such as Lockhart's account of how Scott on holiday in the Highlands in 1810 first picked up and read Byron's *English Bards and Scots Reviewers.* He had, as a fact, corresponded with Southey on the subject two months earlier. The story, again, of the hand seen by the young Edinburgh advocate, which was the hand of Scott writing *Waverley*, is not quite borne out by the young lawyer himself who, on receiving a copy of the *Life*, wrote to Lockhart from the Cape, and remarked: "That in 1814 Mr. Menzies' only house was in India Street, and that the said Mr. Menzies did not reside in George Street before 1818 in the Summer of which year I imagine the incident alluded to took place". But the incident loses some of its piquancy if it did not happen when Lockhart was a young man passing through Edinburgh, but in 1818 when Lockhart was settled in Edinburgh, had met Scott and waited on him in Castle Street, and when he like many others was fully convinced that Scott was the Great Unknown.

But there are more serious difficulties. I will take two instances: one is the dramatic account of the first warning conveyed to Scott of impending disaster, and first intimation to Lockhart himself of his father-in-law's financial commitments. Lockhart's story is that he had "returned to Chief's Wood from one of my rapid journeys to London" about 22nd October (Mrs. Coutts, he tells us, arrived a few days after, and that, we know, was on the 25th), and a few days later received from his friend Wright "the eminent barrister of Lincoln's Inn" a letter informing him that it was reported in London that Constable's banker had thrown up his book. "This letter", he says, "reached me about 5 o'clock, as I was sitting down to dinner", and about an hour afterwards he rode over to Abbotsford, saw Sir Walter, was reassured by him, and "went home relieved and gratified". Next morning "behold Peter Matheson at my door, and the Sheriff rubbing his eyes as if the halt had shaken him out of a sound sleep". Scott had driven over to Polton, where he found "Constable putting on his night-cap. I stayed an hour with him, and I have now the pleasure to tell you that *all is right.* There was not a word of truth in the story—he is as fast as Ben Lomond."

It is almost incredible that so circumstantial a story should be the invention of the author. Yet the movements of both Lockhart and Constable in the autumn of 1825 are clearly traceable, both from their own and Scott's letters, and from Buckle's *Life of Benjamin Disraeli.* Scott arrived at Abbotsford from the visit to Ireland on 27th August, 1825, and Lockhart at Chiefswood on 1st September. There they both were when, on the 17th September, arrived in Edinburgh the young Benjamin, ambassador from John Murray to propose to Lockhart the editorship of his new journal, and with it of the *Quarterly Review.* He learnt that Lockhart was at Chiefswood, and dispatched a letter of introduction from the afore-mentioned Wright. If Benjamin carried out the intention which he reports to Murray in a letter from Edinburgh, he would be at Chiefswood on the 21st, whence he wrote to Murray on what seems to be the 22nd, reporting his success with Lockhart and his meeting with Sir Walter: "The Chevalier breakfasted here to-day". With the Lockharts Disraeli stayed for about three weeks: "Lockhart has introduced me to most of the neighbouring gentry, and receives with a loud laugh any mention of my return to Edinburgh". "Here has been", Scott writes on the 12th of October, "a visitor of Lockhart's, a sprig of the root of Aaron, young Disraeli; in point of talents he reminds me of his father, for what saith Mungo's Garland?

> "Crapaud pickanini,
> Crapaud himself.

Which means that a young coxcomb is like the old one who got him." To London Lockhart and Disraeli went together in the second week of October, and on the 20th of that month an agreement was signed with Murray, appointing Lockhart editor of the *Quarterly Review*, and another engaging him, not as editor (Lockhart thought such a position was socially beneath him!), but as a benevolent assistant in the work of running the newspaper, *The Representative*. Lockhart returned to Chiefswood on the 22nd or 23rd, and a few days afterwards, if we are to believe him, occurred the incident related above.

But Constable did not return to Polton from London, whither he had gone early in October,[1] till 7th November, and Scott himself went into Edinburgh on the 11th, so that the only possible nights on one of which the incident could have occurred are those of the 7th, 8th, 9th, or 10th. But on the 11th Constable wrote to Scott telling him that he had got home on the evening of Monday, 7th November, which was surely unnecessary if they had already met one another within the last few days. What Lockhart actually did when he conveyed to Scott the first warning of trouble is clear from Scott's letters. On the 17th of November, or a day earlier, he did receive a letter from Wright, possibly brought north by the young Disraeli, who had been sent back to Scotland to consult Sir Walter about objections made to Lockhart's appointment as editor of the *Quarterly* by Croker and others. That it was *this* letter which conveyed to Scott in Edinburgh the report about Constable's banker throwing up his book, is clear from Scott's reply of the 18th:

> I saw Cadell, and told him that I had heard from a friendly person towards them and me, and by a letter from London, that their affairs were in bad order, and that Constable had left town in consequence of his banker's having abruptly closed his account. He listened gravely, but without the least concern . . .

and Scott goes on to tell how Cadell reassured him. This was the first alarm, but an entry in Scott's Journal four days

[1] Before Lockhart, who brought him up a letter from Scott.

146

later shows that it was quickly followed by more indications of trouble:

> Here is a matter for a May morning, but much fitter for a November one. The general distress in the city has affected Hurst and Robinson, Constable's great agents. Should they *go*, it is not likely that Constable can stand, and such an event would lead to great distress and perplexity on the part of J. B. and myself. Thank God, I have enough, at least to pay forty shillings in the pound. . . .

To Cadell, he had just written:

> I hope to be at home all to-morrow, being Teind Wednesday. After looking into my own affairs, I am much comforted. By merely fulfilling engagements, I can bring £10,000 betwixt now and mid-summer. . . .

In all this, it will be seen, no reference is made by any single one of the correspondents to any previous warning of so startling a character as to involve a night's journey from Melrose to Polton, no trifling affair in days before motors. What is one to make of the story? Lang passes it over in a couple of paragraphs which leave one in serious doubt as to how he himself understood the incident. It is to be noted that this part of Lockhart's *Life* was written after Sophia Lockhart's death. She could hardly have let it pass. Yet I cannot but think there must have been some incident of the kind from which Lockhart's story is woven. Did he possibly, after his return in October, walk over to Abbotsford one evening and talk to Scott, not about Wright's letter, which had not yet arrived, but of the rumours which he had found flying about London with regard to Hurst and Robinson, and their speculations? Did Scott drive over next morning, as he was in the habit of doing from time to time, and report receipt of a letter from Constable? Supposing that such a call had evoked for the first time a suspicion in Lockhart's mind of Scott's financial relations with

Constable being more serious than he had supposed, then he may, recalling it afterwards, have, either by confusion of memory, or by surrender to the temptation of the artist for a vivid scene, have linked this call with the fact that he was actually, by sending Scott Wright's letter, the first to awaken alarm in Sir Walter's too sanguine mind: "I had a lesson in 1814 which should have done good upon me, but success and abundance erased it from my mind".

The other story of the same kind is that of Lockhart's interviews with Constable in January 1826, when the publisher was making his last desperate effort to avert bankruptcy. In vivid language Lockhart describes the fury of Constable confined by an attack of gout on his arrival in London to his hotel in the Adelphi:

> A more impatient spirit never boiled in a feverish frame. It was then I for the first time saw full swing given to the tyrannical temper of *the Czar*. . . . I will not repeat his haughty ravings of scorn and wrath. I listened to these with wonder and commiseration. . . . To be brief, he requested me to accompany him, as soon as he could get into his carriage, to the Bank of England, and support him . . . in his application for a loan of from £100,000 to £200,000 on the security of the copyrights in his possession. It is needless to say that, without distinct instructions from Sir Walter, I could not take upon me to interfere in such a business as this. Constable, when I refused, became livid with rage. After a long silence he stamped on the ground, and swore that he could and would go alone. I left him in stern indignation.

Lockhart then adds:

> There was another scene of the same kind *a day or two later* when his object was to get me to back his application to Sir Walter to borrow £20,000 in Edinburgh and transmit it to him in London. . . .

He continues:

> It is no business of mine to detail Constable's *subsequent* proceedings on this his last visit to London. Everywhere he

found distrust. . . . Constable *lingered on* fluctuating between wild hope and savage despair until, I seriously believe, he at last hovered on the brink of insanity. When he returned to Edinburgh it was to confront creditors whom he knew he could not pay.[1]

All this, it seems to me, implies that Constable made a stay of some length in London—"he lingered on". But letters written at the time by Constable to his partner Cadell, to Sir Walter Scott, and to Lockhart himself tell a different story. Constable left Edinburgh on 13th January and reached London on the 16th. "I was so shocked", he writes to Cadell on the 17th, "on getting to Waterloo Place yesterday morning that it had nearly unfitted me for business. I found Mr. Thomas Hurst and Mr. Robinson preparing to go into the city and I accompanied them." He describes the calls he made at various banks. On the 17th and 18th he *may* have been confined to the hotel with gout. He says nothing of this in his letter to Cadell, but tells him: "I have been engaged the whole of the day in matters connected with H. R. & Co.", and adds, "this day I saw Lockhart". On the 18th he writes again, at length, to Cadell and also to Sir Walter, to whom he says: "I had a long interview with Mr. Lockhart yesterday who feels as you would expect in the present crisis". On the same day Lockhart wrote to him in a letter which bears no mark of the "stern indignation" in which he had left Constable, according to his own narrative, the night before:

> My dear Sir, I have not stirred out in the anxious expectation of hearing something from you, nor shall I altho' I confess my desire is great to see and talk with Mr. Richardson. Probably, however, as you can have letters from Edinburgh to-morrow written after the news reached Mr. Cadell you will wish to pause until then. Yours mo' truly, J. G. Lockhart. 25 Pall Mall, Wednesday.

[1] The italics are mine.

On the 19th Constable left London for Edinburgh, arriving there on the 21st, and on the 25th wrote to Lockhart:

> You would, I trust, excuse my not having called on you before leaving London the cause of which I hope my son's note would explain. I reached this yesterday after a pretty smart going and have just returned from Edinburgh.

What is one to make of Lockhart's successive meetings with Constable, and what of Constable lingering in London till he was on the verge of insanity? It is possible that looking back over ten years Lockhart may have given to a period of intense feeling a longer duration than it actually occupied, but how Cadell could have let pass such an account of these critical days is explicable only by his animus against Constable, and it is this animus, communicated to Lockhart, which gives to his account a colour that is not found in the letters written at the time.

What one is to think of these various problems is difficult to decide, and I should prefer at present to keep them *sub judice*—and that is indeed where I must leave Lockhart himself. Some of the incidents do no violence to the general character of the picture he is presenting, but others seem to me to be coloured by prejudices conceived at a later time. It is also possible that for each of them there may have been some actual happening which either Lockhart's memory distorted or which he allowed himself to dress up dramatically. There must be some revaluation of his greatest work, but it is not to be done in the rough-and-ready method of our brilliant young men. Their method, applied to such recent biographies as for example those of the late D. H. Lawrence by the author of *The Savage Pilgrimage* on the one hand, and by Mr. Middleton Murry on the other, would reveal different accounts of the same incident which it would be hard to reconcile, yet each of which was probably quite honestly set down. Patience and sympathy are necessary to any just biography of Lockhart, as of other men, and we should need to have access to more of his letters than have ever been printed. Allowance too, as I have said, must be made for the difficulties with which he had found himself faced when all the undercurrents of Scott's life were revealed to him. He could not but wish to show him in the most favourable, which is also ultimately the most just, light. Lockhart acknowledged Scott's faults, but could not resist the temptation to divert attention to some extent from these by what one might call a covering attack upon the Ballantynes and Constable. The true causes of the disaster were not these, but Sir Walter Scott, Archibald Constable, and Robert Cadell. Scott was big enough to have the whole truth told about him. Like Rubens he loved the good things of the world,—and, like him, in a generous way; but Scott was swept along by the current of a new commercial age which made it possible to realize, by the use of credit, wealth which had not actually materialized. He paid the penalty, and he did his utmost to make good such injury as he had done to others. Lockhart, too, was a complex character. Lang's biography is not an *apologia* for his faults, which are fully admitted. He paid the penalty of his gift of penetrating and merciless, or apparently merciless, satire. If he had been a little greater, a genius of the first order, and had written a *Tale of a Tub* or a *Gulliver's Travels*, he would have been more easily forgiven, for Swift was far more savage and merciless in his satire and vituperation; was more regardless of truth in his political pamphlets; was more eager than either Scott or Lockhart to be admitted to the world of the great; and he too paid the penalty, the penalty of being befooled and bamboozled by Oxford and Bolingbroke, who never really trusted him with their secrets.

Of Mr. Lang's own work as a biographer, what a close study reveals is—his unwavering regard for the truth, his deep sense of justice, his high standards of conduct. His brilliant and rapidly working mind led him into errors, but his prejudices and sympathies never obscured his loyalty to truth. His *Life of Lockhart* was inspired by something of the same spirit of chivalry and loyalty as informed the greater *Maid of France*. He thought the man had been harshly treated —his faults allowed to obscure his real virtues of loyalty, affection, and self-sacrifice. Moreover, life and its sorrows of which he had more than his full share mellowed Lockhart in his later years. In a letter to Croker of 1838 he writes: "After my long labours in Scott's energetic and tumultuous existence—all excitement of one sort or another—I could not but feel very strongly the beautiful composing and sustaining effect of religion in Wilberforce, wishing from my heart that Sir Walter had had more of that element merged in him. Surely the decision and vivacity of your friend's nature would have been gloriously embellished by that capacity of looking on worldly things from a serene point of view which no mere philosophy ever can give. You will understand what I am driving at."

VIII

TWO DUTCH POETS

*The Taylorian Lecture
in the University of Oxford—1936*

IT is a somewhat adventurous undertaking for me to
address an Oxford audience on the subject of Dutch
poetry, for Dutch literature has been only an occasional
parergon to my regular work, to which I was drawn partly
by accident, partly by a curiosity aroused in my very early
days; and of Dutch poetry my study has been partial and
eclectic.   But if by chance one comes on something that gives
one pleasure, and does not seem to be widely known, it is a
temptation to communicate the pleasure.   It was in this spirit,
rather than as a learned student of my subject, that I yielded
to that temptation when it took the form of an invitation
to lecture at the Taylorian.   It is in the same spirit I have
chosen my subject, attempting no elaborate history of Dutch
literature in any one period, but seeking rather to illustrate
the spirit and art of Dutch poetry from the work of two poets
belonging to two very definite periods in the history of
western European poetry, in dealing with whom I can aid
myself by a pretty constant reference to literature such as
our own and that of France, which are probably more
familiar to the greater part of my audience.   The first of
my two poets belongs to the seventeenth century, when
Dutch poetry had come under the same Italian and French
influences as our own.   The second is perhaps the finest
product of a movement which took a very definite and even

violent form in Holland, but which had come a little earlier in this country and had its reactions in French poetry also.

My time will not permit me to do more than recall the political importance of the Low Countries in the seventeenth century or their as great, and perhaps more enduring, achievement in the fields of scholarship and science and painting. If, of the three main divisions of the Germanic peoples, the palm in poetry must go to the people who produced Shakespeare, in music to that which produced Mozart and Beethoven, in painting none may claim superiority to the people which can boast of Rembrandt and Vermeer, and these are but two of many names familiar to you all. In this field the achievement of this small people in one century rivals that of Athens in the art of sculpture. But in one important respect the history of Holland differs from that of Athens. She has produced no poets and dramatists whose names are familiar to the world—no Sophocles or Shakespeare or Dante or Camoens, no Goethe, or Hans Andersen I might even add. The reasons are probably more than one. Who can explain the sudden emergence of groups of great men at different epochs? But one cause may be found in the genius of the people. The practical, matter-of-fact Dutchman is not easily moved by ideals which are not in close and evident contact with experience and conduct. Liberty, religion, commercial rights and privileges —these things he understands, and has been willing to fight for. But the courtly ideals of the Middle Ages had never appealed to more than a very small class. Jacob van Maerlant in the thirteenth century was as scornful of courtly love as Jean de Meun. Of the two characteristics of Dutch painting that strike every student, the first is the extraordinary technical skill and veracity the painters have displayed in every branch of pictorial representation of the world of the eye—portraits, interiors, landscapes, seascapes, battle-pieces, pageants, popular revels, still-life, genre-pictures. The other is the comparative absence, with some great exceptions, of the transfiguring, idealizing work of the imagination. Now the literature of the seventeenth century was the product of the same wealthy burgher class as was then building fine houses and decorating them with rich furniture and noble pictures. The language of the Court was Spanish or French. Dutch poetry never came under the courtly influence which in England and France produced much that was conventional and artificial, but also did much to refine and heighten the spirit of poetry and free it from too great subservience to a didactic and prudential morality. At the same time, the merchant burgher class formed an aristocracy—wealthy, privileged, and highly cultured—who looked down on the common people (*de gemeente, het grauw*). They read Spanish, French, and Italian. Many of them wrote Latin, French, and Italian poems as easily as Dutch. Thus they were led to eschew the homely realism for which the Dutch genius is well adapted, and to cultivate conventions that for them were seldom more than mere conventions. They loaded their poems as their pictures with classical gods and goddesses; they played at being shepherds and shepherdesses; they wrote love poems in the style of Petrarch and Ronsard; they imitated the tragedies of Seneca and the comedies of Plautus —and all this without being able to catch the grace and dignity and ease necessary to carry off such elaborate and conventional attire. At heart they remain homely Dutch burghers with a strong bent towards piety and edification and a decided taste for realism and coarse humour:

> Just here [writes Professor Huizinga of Leyden] comes the difference between Netherlander and Englishman. The Netherlander is a seafarer, a merchant, an inventor, an industrial organizer; he is a magistrate, a theologian, a scholar, a painter. The Englishman is all these too (except a painter)

but he is over and above these a courtier, a soldier and a poet
—the three frequently united in one person. The English
temper has all the fundamental traits in common with the
Netherlander, but is more passionate, more coloured, more
sparkling, more adventurous. We have a Linschoten, a
William Barentsz, but not a Walter Ralegh; a van der Does
but no Sidney. The aristocratic is wanting in us. The Dutch
spirit, *even when the landed nobility are its representatives,* is bourgeois
or rustic. Here was no courtly Renaissance-milieu such as
was the Court of Elizabeth. In every trait of the history of
the two countries that deeply penetrating distinction shows
itself. The history of the Netherlands is not only drier but
also more orderly and regulated in comparison with that of
England, which is full of the most violent, passionate and
romantic incidents, and stands in the same relation to their
drama as our social life to Jacob Cats.[1] The drama, aristocratic in heart and nerve, was possible in England because it
vividly reflected the actual life of the upper classes. This
highest and last bloom of the Renaissance was denied to us.[2]

But the courtly poetry of the Renaissance, Italian and
French, did penetrate to the Low Countries, and one poet
of the seventeenth century, if his work exhibits some of the
fundamental traits of the Dutch character, yet did for
Holland something of what Wyatt and Surrey attempted
and Sidney and Spenser achieved for English poetry—grafting
and naturalizing the elegant, dignified, and musical poetry
of the Renaissance, which, raised and ripened in Italy, had
been already transplanted across the Alps by Ronsard and
his fellows. In each country where this poetry took root
it acquired fresh properties from the genius of the soil, in
none more charming and fruitful than in England. In
Holland too it assimilated something of the native soil, as
we shall see by a very brief survey of the life and work of

[1] Jacob Cats (1577–1660) corresponds to some extent to Francis
Quarles but more closely to Martin Tupper, to whom our Royal Society
of Literature once gave its medal.
[2] Huizinga, *Tien Studien*, 1926. The italics are mine.

this my first poet, P. C. Hooft (1581–1647). The son of
a wealthy and influential burgher of Amsterdam, the younger
Hooft became the most typical representative of the scholar
and poet of the Renaissance which his country produced.
Vondel is an outcome rather of the Counter-Reformation,
a great Catholic, lyrical, baroque poet. Hooft is the bourgeois aristocrat, cultured and a little pedantic, sceptical and
epicurean, nourished on Plutarch and Seneca, Tacitus and
Virgil, Petrarch and Ronsard. When only sixteen years
old he was admitted a member of the Eglantine or Old
Chamber, *i.e.* Chamber of Rhetoric, for these, in the
fifteenth century, had been the great centres of literary
activity, and were still active, especially in dramatic pro-
duction. To this Chamber belonged two older writers,
Roemer Visscher and Hendrick Spieghel, who had been
leaders in the purification of the language and the refinement
of style and verse. Hooft spent three years in Germany,
France, and Italy (as our Sir Henry Wotton had done and
many other young Englishmen), and there, like Wyatt and
Surrey earlier and Milton and Drummond later, imbibed
the taste for Italian and French love-poetry, romance and
lyric. From Florence in 1600 he addressed a long verse-
epistle to his friends of the Eglantine, a poem characteristic
of the feeling of all cultured men of the day, in every country,
for Italy, and an index to Hooft's own character and the
work he was to do. He describes how, wandering at dawn
along the banks of the Arno, he meets Italia, dark-eyed but
golden-haired. She congratulates him on having come so
far, drawn by her fame; and she proceeds to point out, one
after another, her glorious towns, naming the poets who
have made them famous:

"There lies Ferrara whose fame shall know no limit as the
birthplace of the immortal poet whose pages tell of the Spanish,
French, and Moorish chieftains; he who won such favour of

knights and ladies that they render him due praise who san
their arms, and loves, and deeds of courtesy. The virtues c
old times he sang, and their vices too—Charles's long-sufferin
patience, the madness of Agramant, brave Roland's deeds c
prowess, of Holland's faith in her Olympia shown—in a wor
it is Ariosto."

When Italia has departed, Hooft is turning to quit the spo
when he is arrested by another figure enveloped in a dar
vapour (*gansch van een bruine wolck*). It is Holland, who cries

"Hooft, forget not me, let not what you have seen act a
powerfully on you as the lotos on the Ithacensian fleet wh
forgot in dreams the return to their native land. In Hollan
the path of duty is the way to glory, though I cannot boast o
Italy's splendours of art and song":

In Holland climtmen mee tot lof langs des Deuchts trappe
Al can Ick niet van my gelick Italia clappen.

The two lodestars of Hooft's life, art and his native land, ar
here made clear. To the service of his country and t
literature he devoted all his energies and unwearied patienc
throughout a life harassed by many domestic bereavements
but also full of refined, cultured, and dignified pleasures.

But of his life I shall not speak in detail. His educatio
as a lawyer and scholar completed, he was appointed Dros
or Sheriff of Muiden, near Amsterdam, and, living in th
city in winter, at the Muider Slot on the Zuider Zee i
summer, he drew around him a cultivated circle, and wa
the husband of two charming wives, the first Christina va
Erp, and the second Eleonora Hellemans. Among the poet
of the circle were two of those women-poets who have bee
throughout a feature of Dutch literary history. These wer
Anna and Tesselschade Visscher, whose poems were mor
admired in their lifetime than later; but in the group of poet
of whom I am to speak later we shall find women-poets again
To many Hollanders to-day the greatest living poet i

158

Madame Roland van der Holst Schalk. Of Hooft's plays, his pastoral *Granida*, his two Senecan and historical tragedies, *Geeraerdt van Velsen* and *Baeto*, his Plautine comedy *Warenar*, I have not time to speak; still less of his Tacitean history of the epic struggle with Spain, for which he prepared himself by a Life of Henry IV and by a translation of Tacitus. His declared purpose in the History was to "put on record the piety of his countrymen, of his fellow citizens, and of his kinsfolk". I wish merely to illustrate shortly his lyrical and reflective poetry, Renaissance poetry of the lighter and the graver kind.

The general character of Renaissance love-poetry, songs, and sonnets is familiar to you all. Mr. Lewis has traced, as completely as it can be done, the sources and history of Courtly Love, or sublimated adultery, which gave its colour to the romances of Lancelot and Guinevere, of Tristan and Isolt, and to the lyrical poetry of Provence and France, and was still further sublimated by Dante and his school; and Mr. Lewis has shown how Spenser undertook a task, perhaps more difficult than Dante's, to make marriage and not adultery the consummation of chivalrous love. The charm and the weakness alike of this poetry lie in the fixity of its conventions. These poets will make no attempt, at least till John Donne appears, to analyse love or illustrate its varying moods, except some of its more obvious contradictions. One knows beforehand what will be its themes—the beauty of the lady, her coldness and cruelty, the fleetingness of time and beauty: "Gather ye rose-buds while ye may". Everything depends on the art with which the poet can handle the themes. The worst of the poems, especially the sonnets, are purely literary exercises. The best are warmed and inspired by the love of love and the love of song. But both these passions the epicurean Hooft, for whom the society of beautiful and cultured women was an indispensable condition of life, possessed in ample measure. His songs and sonnets (in Alexandrines) may not compare in intensity of feeling and exquisite art with Petrarch's *canzoniere*; in passion and thought and vision with the best sonnets of Shakespeare; he never catches the tone of epicurean melancholy and chivalrous courtliness of Ronsard, or the fine insolence of Sidney. Hooft is always a Dutchman, with abundance of common sense and much homely humour. But his poems are elegant and musical, varied in form and rhythm, touched at times with passion, warmed always by a sensuous love of woman and song. He is indeed a more careful and conscientious artist than many of the lyrists who contributed to *England's Helicon*, not so gay and careless but more "orderly and regulated". He can use the trisyllabic foot which Gilbert Murray tells us the Elizabethans could not, and his interchange of longer and shorter lines is effectively managed, which the same critic says is not always achieved even in Shakespeare's songs, though I do not quite accept Dr. Murray's condemnation of:

> Come unto these yellow sands
> And then take hands.

Unfortunately nothing is more difficult than to illustrate this side of Hooft's art, for who can translate such light strains with success, verses like:

> Vluchtige Nymph, waarheen so snel?
> Galathea, wacht u wel
> Dat u vlechten
> Niet en hechten
> Met haer opgesnoerde goudt
> Onder de tacken van dit hout;

or:

> Schoon Nymphelijn
> Ach mindje mijn,
> Wat soud' ick al versieren

TWO DUTCH POETS

Om na mijn wensch
Dees Ledetjens
Soo wel gemaeckt te cieren.
Met blinckend gout
Of perlen, sout
Ghi voelen ras belasten
U halsgen soet;
Soo crael als bloet
Daerom niet beter pasten.

Or in quite a different movement:

Sal nimmer meer gebeuren
Mij dan na dese stondt
De vriendschap van u ooghen,
De wellust van u mondt?
De vriendschap, etc.

and again for well-woven-together lines of different length:

Ghi suchten heet
Uit bange borst gedrongen,
Diet alles weet
Wat mij de dertel jongen,
Dertel maar wreet,
Maar wreet en onbedwongen,
Cupido deed.

or:

Amaryll de deken sacht
Van de nacht,
Met sijn blaeuwe wolken buijen
Maeckt de wereldt sluimerblint,
En de wint
Soeckt de maan in slaep te suijen.

I will attempt to translate one in which he uses a trisyllabic
foot:

Amaryl, had ick hair uit u tuitjen,
'K wed ick vleughelde' het goodtjen, het guitjen,
Dat met sijn brandt, met sijn boog, met sijn flitsen,
Landt tegen landt over einde kan hitsen,

161

M

En beroofde den listighen stoocker
Van sijn toorts, sijn geschut en sijn koocker. . . .

My translation is free but endeavours to keep the rhythm:

The Net

Amaryllis, with a net of your tresses
I would snare the knave-god in the meshes,
Whose torch and whose far-shooting bow
Turned the joy of Troy's kingdom to woe;
Make the crafty one stand and deliver
His torch and his bow and his quiver.

Could I capture the sparkles that broke
Even now from your eyes as you spoke,
They should shine, as a star shines by night,
In Love's cheek, and the blind one have sight,
That if yet he must vex us and kill
He may know where his arrows to spill.

But you wager that, grant me but one
Of my wishes, and soon there is none
I shall beg as I beg now in vain.
The door opened who closes again?
So no tress will you give lest I snare
Yourself in the toils of your hair.

When Hooft's mood is graver or more passionate his lines
become iambic and have a full and stately music. In such
moods the thin veil of courtly convention is thrown aside to
give utterance to passion as full-blooded as in the poems of
Donne or Carew, and that at times in language as natural
as that of some of the lyrics of Burns or Goethe. Of the
sonnets, "Mijn lief, mijn lief, mijn lief" is a rival to the
"Bridal-Sleep" of Rossetti. But I shall take for translation
another, to illustrate the blend in Hooft's poetry of realism,
simplicity, convention, and musical cadence: the heading

in Hooft's poems is the name of an air to which the poem
may be sung.   I have called it:

Remembered Kisses

'Tgemoedt herwenscht verlooren vrolijckheden,
Eh wentelt in den schijn des tijts voorleden,
Wanneer 't de stappen ziet die 't heeft getreden, . . .

O'er vanished joys the awakening heart makes moan,
Dwells in the glow of days for ever flown,
If I retrace the path I once have known.

To hear her name, to pass her in the street,
Brings to my brain the blood's resurgent heat.
And you, my love, does your heart quicker beat?

Whither are flown the memories of delight
That melted once your body's tender might,
Do you remember, love, that summer night?

Do you remember how the golden day
With kisses laden winged its joyous way?
Ah, set me back on that old wagon gay!

We thanked our friends but waived their offer kind:
Keep your front seats, they are not to our mind,
With like good reason you would sit behind.

And would, indeed, that you were sweethearts paired,
Then not so often had you backward stared,
And us poor lovers from our kisses scared!

Ah, shame, to think that of the reluctant night
Sleep gave some hours to time's relentless flight,
When the Gods spread their banquet of delight!

With bread of heaven we drank of heavenly wine.
Ah, give once more your golden face to shine
As then on us Venus and Boy divine!

These tuneful epicurean love-songs are only one section of Hooft's poetry. The same serious spirit as animated his sententious and patriotic tragedies and his great Tacitean history appears in many of his sonnets and epigrams and didactic poems. Dutch poetry, like Dutch painting, reflected vividly the civic life of the Low Countries, a result partly of the smallness of the community and the intensity of its public life, an inheritance also from the Chambers of Rhetoric whose poetry had all of it been of an occasional character. But over these poems also I must pass, quoting only as illustrations one sonnet and some reflective lines of a rather remarkable content. The sonnet is on the birth of a child to his brother then living in London:

> O fair young fruit, that from the quiet night
>   Of slumber in the womb awaked must go—
>   Time that lets nothing rest hath willed it so—
> Forth to the whirl of sense and realms of light,
> Now has birth given thee o'er to Fortune's might.
>   Her school is change. She mingles joy with woe,
>   Sorrow with joy; exalts and hurls below,
> Till dazed with hope and fear we darkling fight.
> May He who giveth all things grant thee a heart
> Undaunted to withstand the fiercest dart
>   Fate in her anger at thy life may speed;
> Her gifts, too, when in milder mood she pours
> Riches and joys and honours in full stores,
>   Be it thine to use grateful, but with good heed!

A very interesting sidelight on Hooft's character is thrown by lines in one of the Epithalamia which, like Donne and Jonson and Spenser and other poets, he composed on special occasions. When he is half-way through the usual compliments he comes to speak of the bride's culture, the wisdom she has imbibed from the masters of those who know, Seneca, Plutarch, and one wiser than either of these, Montaigne. Like Pascal, Hooft recognizes in the French sceptic and epicurean the most unerring judge of the human heart, its aspirations, and its shortcomings, and he puts into a few lines the gist of the famous colloquy in which Pascal compares Montaigne and Epictetus:

> Den Godlijken Gascoen! zoo magh men billijh heeten
> Die zoo wel wat wij zijn, en hij was, heeft geweten. . . .

> The Godlike Gascon! So we justly may him call
> Who knew so well what he, and what mankind are all.
> Cunningly the ancient sage would mould us to his plan,
> *He* cries: in vain your toil, the stuff is but a man.
> So diversely we're formed that for true happiness,
> There is no rule which holds alike for great and less.
> One in adversity stands firm, another breaks,
> As God of sound or less sound clay his creature makes.
> All is as Fate's inexorable laws ordain,
> Nothing so small but forms a shackle in her chain
> Made fast at either end. Learning supplies safe rule
> For hearts made fit to learn; the fool remains a fool.
> What beauty is in things the ancient sage saw well,
> Montaigne sees where they halt, pierces the outer shell,
> Sifts Nature's changing shows, dissects her to a hair—
> Teacher more wise than all his teachers, or I err.
> If in his hand he takes what has won men's esteem,
> He will not trust his eyes, or deem as others deem,
> But tries; and lest it prove a vain and hollow sound
> He knocks, he weighs, he blows, he turns it round and
>   round.
> Upright and innocent, to him life's sweet turns crude
> Wanting the joy of friends, the joy of doing good.
> Fame for fame's use he woos, but labours not that she
> Follow him to the grave, he knows her vanity.

And now, leaving Vondel and Brederoo and Huyghens and other contemporaries of Hooft, and making no attempt to follow the history of Dutch poetry, I will make a long leap to another period of that poetry, a period in which a movement that was shared by other countries took in Holland a specially agitated form. A wave, that was traversing England and France, in Holland broke into surf and spray.

The movement of the critics and poets in Holland of the 'eighties of last century was one of furious revolt against the bourgeois, didactic, sentimental poetry which had been in vogue throughout the century. A number of young men took the field against the older generation in a review named *De Nieuwe Gids*, a counterblast to the established *De Gids*. The leaders were: the critic and poet and founder of the review, Willem Kloos; the critic, prosaist, and realistic novelist (taking Zola as his model), L. van Deyssel (his true name was Alberdingk Thijm and he was the son of a well-known critic and literary historian of the older generation); Albert Verwey, poet; Frederik van Eeden, a poet also, but best known by his imaginative and symbolic story *De Kleine Johannes*; Herman Gorter, the most Shelleyan of the group, and others whom I need not name, as it is not my intention to dwell on these, the first of the *tachtigers* as they are called. A newer and finer poetry had made its appearance earlier in the sonnets of Jacques Perk and the poems of Hélène Lapidoth-Swarth; but it was in the new review that their work received its first full recognition.

The attitude of the young men was one of declared rebellion and contempt for their predecessors.

I have swept [cries van Deyssel] the whole of Old Holland out of my mind. Call it injudicious, call it one-sided, call it what you will, that is in a word what I have done. When I think of sitting down to write as an artist, the first thing I do is to blow the literature of the last generation from my table. For we are not the continuers of, we are the reaction against, the work of our literary fathers. Vondel, Hooft and some others of *that* period may be able to give us some technical aid in the choice of words and their combination, but there is not one of those who came between them and us to whom a writer could go for artistic literature. Multatuli, Busken Huet, Potgieter, Vosmaer are the chief of these. The rest are a troop of rhetoricians or society littérateurs whose works, for men that know much or little of world-literature, are unreadable. Beets, Ten Kate and so forth are preachers who have nothing to do with literature as such.

Elsewhere the same writer declares that the characteristic of the period in question was "that none of the literary men of the day had the courage to be a man, or the gifts to be an artist". So politely do young pioneers speak of their predecessors.

But though the movement in Holland was of this violent, almost Bolshevist, character, it was not an isolated phenomenon. "Art for Art" was the device, the "Excelsior", under which they rallied and fought; and they found the first symptoms of what they sought in French poetry of the 'forties and later. In this country it is the movement which was represented in the poetry of Rossetti and Morris and Swinburne; in the criticism of art by Ruskin, strangely as the artistic passion was in Ruskin blended with the temper of the moralist and the prophet; and in the pictures of the Pre-Raphaelites. It was in each and every country a revolt against the ugliness of the world of industrialism, and even more against the conventional, respectable, timid morality, distrustful alike of truth and of beauty, of the middle classes whom the age of industrialism had made wealthy and dominant. It took, accordingly, in every country the same double character, the new realism and naturalism of the novel as represented, say, by Zola, and the pursuit of the beauty revealed by the imagination and in well-chosen words and rhythms, for their own sake. But "art for art" as a cry in literature (whatever it may be in music and painting) is always a symptom of something deeper. It is never *only* a revolt against moralizing, didactic poetry.[1] It is also a revolt against the morality itself of which the older poets have made themselves too complacently the mouthpiece, whether Beets and others in Holland or Tennyson in England. Swinburne, who, in his *Life of Blake*, is the most intransigent champion of the freedom and independence of art, is also a critic of the morality and complacent philosophy which the chief Victorian poets preached:

> Thus runs our wisemen's song:
> Being dark it must be light,
> And most things are so wrong
> That all things must be right,
> God must *mean* well, he works so ill by human laws.
>
> This, when our hearts are failing
> Falls on us like a benison,
> This satisfies our Browning,
> And this delights our Tennyson,
> And sooth'd Britannia simpers in serene applause.

In fact, in England and in Holland some poets whose creed was art for art, at least to begin with, became in the long run ardent reformers of society, champions, like Swinburne, of Italian and Greek Liberty; Socialists like Morris and Gorter and Madame Roland Holst and Frederick van Eeden; and some of them have passed from Socialism into the bosom of the Catholic Church.

Still, the impelling motive of the movement, here and in Holland, was artistic, an assertion of beauty as an end in itself, and a determination to give to poetry beauty of vision and diction and music. The young men were in quest of

[1] For a very intelligent and full study see *L'Idée de l'art pour l'art dans la littérature anglaise pendant la période victorienne*, par Louise Rosenblatt, Instructor in English, Barnard College, Columbia University, New York (Paris, 1931).

a purer poetry, neither didactic nor rhetorical nor sentimental, but passionate and lyrical. And, like their pre-
cursors in England and some of their contemporaries in
France, they found what they sought in poetry in the work
of two English poets of an earlier generation. The influence
of Scott and Byron had passed, leaving its wreckage of
historical novels and gloomy rhetoric; and now came the
discovery of Shelley and Keats, so long in getting their due
even in their own country. In Keats, the first poet to assert
the doctrine of art for art, and that in its most profound form,
untouched by decadence, they found that rich sensuousness
and felicity of diction which they would fain substitute for
the dulled and outworn phrasing of sentimental verse, and
Tennyson came in for some of the interest aroused by Keats,
in virtue of the precision and delicacy of his descriptive
poems and the fine use he makes of sensuous detail to suggest
a dominant mood. But Shelley was the more quickening
force. In Germany Shelley appealed primarily through the
sympathy of young liberals with his ideals of a new social
order. Not so in Holland, or in France. There, and more
strongly in Holland than in France, Shelley was recognized
as the quintessentially lyrical poet, both in virtue of the
winged music of his verse and of the imaginative passion
with which he enters into the life of what he describes, lends
to it his own passionate sense of liberty and love.[1] From
Keats they might learn to describe the luxurious beauty of
the nightingale's song, and the scents and sounds of the wood
where the nightingale sings:

> But in embalmed darkness guess each sweet
> Wherewith the seasonable month endows
> The grass, the thicket, and the fruit-tree wild;

[1] See *Die Invloed van Keats en Shelley in Nederland gedurende die Negentiende
Eeuw*, Deur Dr. G. Dekker, 1926, and *Shelley et la France, lyrisme anglais et
lyrisme français au XIX siècle*, Henri Peyre, 1935. The first work is written,
not in continental Dutch, but in Afrikaans.

> White hawthorn, and the pastoral eglantine;
> Fast-fading violets covered up in leaves;
> And mid-May's eldest child,
> The coming musk-rose full of dewy wine,
> The murmurous haunt of flies on summer eves.

But it was Shelley who seemed to them to enter the very soul of the cloud, and the skylark, and the west wind, and

> The Naiad-like lily of the vale
> Whom youth makes so fair and passion so pale

or:

> The rose like a nymph to the bath unveiled.

And Shelley thus enters the life of natural things without any savour or suggestion of what Swinburne disliked in Wordsworth, his tendency to "use nature as a vegetable fit to shred into the pot and pare down like the outer leaves of a lettuce for didactic and culinary purposes".   There is no limit to the enthusiasm with which the young Dutch poets spoke of Shelley, and in the earlier work of several of them one finds not only affinity but imitation.   You will recognize, even without a translation, the movement of Shelley's *The Cloud* in Perk's *Iris*:

> Ik ben geboren uit zonne-gloren
> En een zucht van de ziedende zee,
> Die omhoog is gestegen, op wieken van regen,
> Gezwollen van waanhoop en wee: . . .

Shelley's *Defence of Poetry*, too, became a kind of gospel for the young men of the 'eighties.   "The wisdom of Shelley", writes van Eeden in 1891–2, "has for years been the foundation stone and the cement of the edifice of Dutch poetry, and what I and Verwey have written on poetry has been in great measure an elaboration, a working out in detail, or a further building on the ideas thrown out by Shelley."   There were, of course, other influences besides those of Keats and Shelley

—French poets, such as Hugo, de Musset, Baudelaire, Verlaine; later English poets, such as Tennyson, Mrs. Browning, Rossetti; of German poets, perhaps especially Novalis.

The new poetry was then essentially lyrical in character, but lyrical in a far fuller sense of the word than when we speak of the lyrical poets of the seventeenth century, more subjective, more passionate, more varied in theme. The charm of the older lyrists was the skill with which they played variations on a limited number of themes (and I venture to think that this is true even of Donne and the Shakespeare of the sonnets, for we are apt to read back into them more of our subjectivity than is perhaps just); but in the nineteenth century the lyric had become in England, France, Germany the chief medium for the expression of every shade and mood of personal feeling. In the seventeenth century it was only religious feeling that had found expression so passionate and personal. The Dutch had made their full contribution to this religious verse, and indeed, on other themes, they were to my mind somewhat ahead of other countries in the natural expression of personal feeling. But in the nineteenth century they had lagged behind. Between Luyken at the end of the seventeenth century and Kloos, the first of the *tachtigers*, a recent anthology places only seven poets, and of these the most interesting was a Fleming, Guido Gezelle. But now the revival was come, the revival of passion and the love of song, and with it a new feeling for beauty of form, an enrichment of the diction of poetry, sensuous and imaginative, a new delight in the music of verse. The sonnet became a favourite form, and there were some experiments in longer poems, narrative and reflective, such as Gorter's *Mei*, which shows the influence of *Endymion* and *Hyperion*, or van Eeden's *Het Lied van Schijn en Wezen*; but the best of the poetry is lyrical, song not so easy to set to music, because richer in the music that is proper to poetry as such. But I must not attempt to give any general or detailed account of the poetry of the *tachtigers*, for I am not fully qualified to do so. I wish to speak, in closing, of (and to illustrate by some examples) the work of one who belongs to the second generation, whose work, taking up into itself the qualities of the earlier poetry, has added to these the effects of a more developed and educated artistic temperament, and a deeper intellectual and philosophical outlook, too intellectual and subtle to make him ever a quite popular poet.

P. C. Boutens' first volume, *Verzen*, was published in 1897 with an introduction by the leader of the movement, L. van Deyssel, and most of his work belongs to the present century: *Praeludien*, 1902; *Stemmen*, 1907; *Sonnetten*, 1907; *Beatrijs*, 1908; *Vergeten Liedjes*, 1909; *Carmina*, 1912; *Liederen van Isoude*, 1919; *Zomerwolken*, 1922—to mention only the more important collections. Boutens is a learned Greek scholar who has translated from Aeschylus and Sophocles and Sappho, and is at work on a translation into hexameters of the *Odyssey*. But his knowledge of modern and medieval poetry is as extensive, Italian, French, English, and German. He has made translations of poems by Rossetti, by Wilde, Alfred Douglas, Goethe, Novalis. He is essentially a lyrical poet, has written no long poem, indeed shares Poe's distrust of the long poem. He has some of Keats' fine sensuousness of description, but draws closer to Shelley in his symbolic use of nature. His nature poems are rather, as Swinburne says, in comparing the "Euganean Hills" with Keats' Odes, "a rhapsody of thought and feeling coloured by contact with nature, but not born of the contact. . . . His aim is rather to render the effect of a thing than a thing itself", an emotional rather than a purely sensuous effect. He is like Shelley, too, in his passion for coining compounds to express the subtle reactions of his imagination to what he describes;

in his *synaesthesia*, the transference of the impressions of one sense to those of another, as in Shelley's various comparisons of the skylark's song, or the lines in the *Sensitive Plant*:

> And the hyacinth purple and white and blue
> Which flung from its bells a sweet peal anew
> Of music so delicate, soft and intense,
> It was felt like an odour within the sense.

The music of his verse is not so light and winged as Shelley's, but has a very distinctive beauty, a clear, soaring rhythm in the individual line, with a satisfying transition between lines of different length. I will cite one verse from his *Droom-Huis*: [1]

Weet ook gij dat stille diepe huis?
Achter breede blinde poort
Kruisen eindelooze gangen en portalen
Waar men tijdelooze tijden kan verdwallen
Tusschen echo's die men klaar vermoedt en nimmer hoort.
Weet ook gij dat stille diepe huis
Door welks schaduwigen vreê
Voet zoo licht en onvermoeibaar stijgt en daalt langs treê na treê?
En zijn plotselinge helle kaamren op de maanbeglansde zee? . . .

Ah! do you too know that house of silence
Where behind the broad, blank door
Endless paths at portals meet and sunder,
That for ageless ages there one seems to wander
Following echoes that the sense seemed to hear yet hears no more?
Ah! do you too know that house of silence
Through whose shadow-haunted peace
Light and indistinguished footsteps on the stairway never cease,
And clear chambers open suddenly over moonlight-flooded
                    seas? . . .

[1] I have had to make my own translations, for few exist in English. See for earlier poetry Bowring's *Batavian Anthology*, 1829, and Gosse's *Northern Studies*, 1879.

Here again is one of his simpler but passionate transcripts of nature:

Liefdes Uur

Hoe laat is't aan den tijdt?
  Het is de blanke dageraad:
  De diepe weî waar nog geen maaier gaat,
  Staat van bedauwde bloemen wit en geel;
  De zilvren stroom leidt als een zuivre straat
  Weg in het nevelicht azuur;
  En morgens zingend hart, de leeuwrik, slaat
  Uit zijn verdwaasde keel
  Wijsheid die geen betracht en elk verstaat,
  Vreugd zonder maat,
  Vreugd zonder duur. . . .
Hoe laat is't aan den tijdt?
  't Is liefdes uur. . . .

Love's Hour

"What hour o' the day may it be?"
  The pale dawn opens like a rose;
  The breast-deep meadow, where no mower yet mows,
  Stands yellow and white with hanging flowers dew-weighted;
  The silver stream, a clean-swept highway, flows
  Far to the horizon's milky blue;
  And morning's singing heart, the skylark, throws,
  From throat intoxicated,
  Wise words wherewith the heart unwitting glows,
  Joy that no measure knows,
  Joy that seems ever new . . .
"What hour o' the day may it be?"
  Love's hour for thee and me!

"What hour o' the day may it be?"
  The sun draws nigh the summit of his stair;
  And in an ocean of light-saturate air
  The cornfield smoulders under glowing gold;
  The sickle glitters in the dry, ripe grain;
  The shadow shrinks into the wood's dark hold;

174

O'er water-course or in the sky
No cloud goes by;
Only the moon's transparency
Moves ghost-like in the blue unpastured wold . . .
"What hour o' the day may it be?"
Love's hour for thee and me.

"What hour o' the day may it be?"
'Tis Evening; in her russet gold
Grows fair and old
The world's day-lit gaudy face;
A shower of light falls from the heavens apace;
The voices of the winds awake again;
The last wain staggers to the old barn door;
Grey headstones glimmer on the darkling moor;
Above the shining wall
Of the western clouds, in the green of heaven's plain,
Suddenly the Evening-star lets fall
Her rays tender and pure . . .
"What hour o' the day may it be?"
Love's hour for thee and me.

My translation of:

> Vreugh zonder maat,
> Vreugd zonder duur

by:

> Joy that no measure knows
> Joy that is ever new . . .

is perhaps misleading, for, by the antithesis of joy that no
limit knows and joy that has no duration, I suspect Boutens
has in view his own mystical doctrine of joy as an experience
of moments only and yet of perennial significance, that in
moments of joy, of ecstasy, we come nearest to the understanding of the mystery of life, which is the doctrine of the
mystics; though I doubt if the religious mystic would admit
that the path he has travelled is the poet's, who has also
known his dark night of the soul. Boutens is, as I have
said, a classical scholar and a great student of Plato, whose

Symposium and *Phaedrus* are among the works he has translated. With the help of Plato, while adhering to the doctrine of art for art's sake, of the independence of art, which he has stated in the most definite terms in an introduction to a translation of Wilde's *De Profundis*, he has, without turning aside like Gorter to Socialism or van Eeden to Catholicism, developed his own mystical, passionate faith in God and Immortality. His early poems are full of the *Wehmut* in which German poetry has always excelled, but which had been given a new delicacy and subtlety of expression by Verlaine; and even in his maturer poetry there are poems of a more profound and sombre cast, *Wanhoop* and *Lethe*. But it is not in sorrow, he contends, that the meaning of life is best descried. In a fine poem in the volume *Stemmen*, a poem that owes its conception and its form to Shelley's *Invocation to Misery*, Boutens' *Van Vreugd en Verdriet*, *Of Joy and Sorrow*, the Dutch poet has stated his divergence from Shelley. You probably recall the poem I mean:

> Come, be happy! sit near me,
> Shadow-vested Misery:
> Coy, unwilling, silent bride,
> Mourning in thy robe of pride,
> Desolation deified!

and you will recognize the movement of Shelley's verse in:

> Luister, donkerblond Verdriet,
> Sluit die onrust-oogen niet
> Aan de peluw van mijn borst,
> Of gij mij niet zeggen dorst
> Iedren twijfel, elke waarheid,
> 'Raadsel dat de jonge klaarheid
> Nevelt van uw oogenschijn
> Tot een ouden troeblen wijn.

But Shelley's poem ends on the despairing note on which it opened:

All the world, beside us,
Show like multitudinous
Puppets passing from a scene;
What but mockery can they mean,
Where I am—where thou hast been?

Boutens works round to a different close.　He too tells how
Sorrow has been his bedfellow, how with her he has kept
watch till she slept, how to her he has dedicated life and
song.　But at last he has betrayed her.　One early May
morning he left her sleeping, and in the meadows was found
by Joy, whom so often they had seen glide past their window
like a glint of sun.　Her voice began to sing and in it suddenly, and to his surprise, he heard the same notes as in the
song of Sorrow.　Sorrow's name came into the song like
a sombre, low-toned *motif* which gradually, with the movement of the music, rose to a clearer harmony till purer,
raying like a star, it faded away in the heavens.　And his
conclusion is:

> Nay, not sorrow and not joy
> But the wealth of fullest life
> Which to sorrow gives itself,
> Lets my song of sorrow speak,
> Yet must joy again become
> For the man who, trusting Life,
> Feeds and cherishes his sorrow
> From his heart's rich overflow—
> Joy, joy shall life's meaning be.

The same theme is that of one of his most ecstatic lyrics:

Morgen-Nachtigal

Het dunne zand van sluimering
　　Waarmee de koele nanacht overblies
　　Mijn stilgewoelde wanhoop-van-verlies
Midden in de eindelooze rekening,
　　　　Verstuift—

Mijn oogen oopnen over 't gladde dek
Door het vreemd-herkende slaapvertrek
Naar venster en halfneer gordijn
Waardoor de melken morgenschijn
     Naar binne luift.

Een vogel tjilpt de stilte stiller nog,
     Drinkt dauw en dagbegin
      Met zachte halen in.
Ik roer niet uit bloeds blij bedrog
Dat leven nieuw en ongerept te herbeginnen slaat
     Met elken dageraad. . . .

The Morning Nightingale

The shallow sand of slumbering,
Wherewith the last cool hours of night had strewn
My brain for ever turning to the tune
Of hopelessness, her losses numbering,
Is blown away—
And my eyes opening over the smooth bed,
In strange familiar room, are led
To the window and the blind half-drawn,
Through which on milky waves of dawn
Flows in the day.

A lone bird pipes the stillness stiller yet,
Drinking the dewy light of dawn
With breath softly indrawn;
And I surrender to the blood's conceit
That life begins anew, unmarred of pain or sin or scorn,
With every reddening morn.

Listen!   Like sudden rain from a blue sky
Downpour of melody,
Heaven's overflow of cleansing harmony,
Hail-shower of pearls of song and ecstasy,
Spring-tide of happiness
Bursting each sluice;
With miracle of flowing sound
Life's plains and heights are drowned.

TWO DUTCH POETS

I know a nightingale nests near,
Deep in the wood beyond the stream,
And from my distant study often hear
The crackle of the cool up-leaping flame
Of song; as when in some outlandish tongue
A beautiful woman sings or says
Some tale of Love when Life was young,
So blithe that their own loveliness
Makes every word seem clear,
Though all is strange to the ear.

It is the voice of no bird's soul:
From heaven's precipice I hear
Cascade
Of super-aerial joy invade
And flood to one level all the sky's wide mere,
Wave-tossed but moveless till the whole
In this deep dale
O'erflows in steep-ascending scale.

The still white light swells open with the swelling strain,
The heavens shed across transparent pane
Sweet tears of melody and dew
And colour-broken light;
And all that I in darkest night
Of sorrow divined was true,
Breaks with the clearness of morning on my soul:
Joy is life's meaning and goal,
Not sorrow or pain;
And may that joy not be
For me,
Joy, only joy shall be my song's refrain.

With sorrow I have wept, have laughed with joy,
Yet never even as a boy
Has so sweet laughter, from bitter tears distilled,
My spirit filled.
There stands on earth no highest cloud-capped hill,
Lies here no darkest dale,

179

No deep-digged mine,
But underneath bubbles this spring;
Nor will I fail
To seek until
That hidden water my spirit's rod divine,
My mouth its virtue sing.

I shall no more walk stumbling in the day,
Dazzled by Youth's clear eyes that laughing say:
"Tell us the golden secret, O poet, in golden rhyme,
Of Life and Time!"
But I shall speak as one who knows the Way:

"Laugh, Golden Girl and Boy,
Heart of Life's opening rose!
For I found Pain my guest more oft than Joy,
But Pain has bounds; Joy . . . Joy no limit knows."

Give me one look of love, my hand but press,
One draught of happiness,
And straight I hear, from sunny lands of dream,
The murmurous laughter of that stream

Which, broad or narrowing,
Or deep, or swift, or lost in sand,
Glides without tarrying
Through the green and misty land.

"Laugh, Golden Girl and Boy,
Heart of Life's opening rose!
For I found Pain more oft my guest than Joy,
But Pain has bounds; Joy . . . Joy no measure knows."

Of the sorrows of Boutens' early poems some are, like those of so many poets, luxurious moods, others the fruit of personal experiences, or reflection on the tragedy that all life is. A poignant note came into the poems issued as *Zomerwolken* in 1922, which bear the mark of the reflection

in a sensitive spirit of the tragedy of the War.   Like the late
Mr. Lowes Dickinson, Boutens has a great admiration for
and sympathy with young men, and he could not but feel
intensely the horror of the mowing down day after day of
the flower of Europe.   *Ave praemortui te salutant* is the title
of the longest poem in the volume, its motto *Quia nondum
viximus*.   In it he adumbrates in imagination how the soul
of one, conscious at the moment he has passed beyond, might
lament that he has had too short a lifetime to understand
either life or death.   In other poems of the volume he turns,
like many poets, back to the themes of Christian devotion
and tradition—the Descent from the Cross, a Pietà, the
women preparing the body of Christ for the tomb in Joseph's
garden, as if these things derived a new poignancy from the
facts of life and the War.   In one, *The Christ Child*, an infant
seen at a railway station on Christmas Day in the evening
becomes a symbol of the helplessness of innocence and love
in conflict with the brutal facts of life.   It is too long to read,
nor can I dwell on other aspects of Boutens' poetry, his
sonnets, his medieval poems, his translations.   I will con-
clude by reading two poems.   The first is on the theme of
old age.

As one who has warmed both hands before the fire of life,
Boutens' latest poetry is prone to dwell on the thought of
age and death.   Can one who has drunk of the cup of life
with no Puritan distaste find in the advancing years any
pleasure?   Mr. Yeats thinks not.   Boutens will have it that
a finer, purer pleasure may come in the rearward of youth's
more heady joys:

Old Wine

Wine of joy so long in cellar,
  My feast to-day, my song to-morrow,
On my board grown daily clearer
  In the crystal cup of sorrow!

181

In the gold cup that I hammered
   For your draught when youth was mine,
To my thirsty lips I lifted
   Another, darker, purpler wine.

But the years, the silent years,
   While the fates your use withhold,
These have wrought you to this clearness,
   The quintessence of pure gold,

Which to the thirsty heart reproffered,
   Youthtime seeming born anew,
Makes the soul's fine senses drunken
   With a joy the Immortals knew.

Every drink calls for its own cup,
   Sweetest, purest this I rate,
Drinking your unfailing gladness
   From this crystal delicate.

Wine of joy so long in cellar,
   My feast to-night, my song to-morrow,
On my board grown daily clearer
   In the crystal cup of sorrow.

My last is on the great mystery of death:

Terra—*Vallis Nimis Amœna*

By what strange impulse won
   To quit the light of the sun
Is that wild swan the soul, avid of distances,
   From this her house of life,
   Where breeze and calm are rife
With echo of sweet songs or sweeter silences?

   Desire no habit inures,
   Hating all that endures,
Living only to taste the honey of fresh wonders,

Finds here an infinite
Woven tent of rare delight,
Ecstasies knit to-day only to-day to sunder:

Sees stars that dance to a tune,
The changes of the moon,
No lovely night as other lovely night the same;
And each succeeding dawn
Opening wide gaze upon
Eyes of new flowers, flowers of new eyes, in endless game.

She may not tell the tale
Of friends in this green dale,
Prisoners, like her, in the body's beautifully transparent limbs;
O Fortunate, that divines
By light of eyes the lines
Of the soul's naked beauty that beauty of body dims!

On every side confin'd,
Her love breaks through to find
Soul answering her soul, as light enkindles light.
Of life's horizon far
No corner lacks her star,
Stars which are souls that swirl around the Infinite:

O far-flung wheeling dance
In the wide blue expanse!
Kisses that break like fire from souls that part and meet,
Galaxy paving the way
By which march Night and Day,
Drawing Life's chariot in Law's compulsion sweet!

From hence how comes it then
The soul, that lovely swan,
Would part, loosening herself from her green mother's arms?
How hopes her thirst, and where,
Water more sweet and fair?
Where has she scent of food that hunger better charms?

What land beyond their sight
Of heavenly chrysolite
Breaks through to dying eyes, and wakens longing there?
That ineluctable death
Is desired, and their last breath
Goes out in joy to escape from all they cling to here?

I saw them gray and old
Abandoning child and gold,
Folding the loneliness of their forsaken hands.
I saw them young and glad
From out the chorus tread,
Only the fire of longing burned in their eyes like brands.

I saw them turn to go,
As if forsaking show
They sought the beauty of undream'd-of certainty.
The first the loveliest,
As from a marriage feast
The bride and bridegroom pace in seemliest dignity.

Asleep or waking none
To sound the depths has won,
The depths of heaven's sea where all earth's voices fail.
No thought has ever plumb'd
To where the wealth unsumm'd
Lies of the blessedness by which the stars grow pale.

No one that e'er drew breath
Of the mystery of death
Can speak, no poet sing; earth's songs are as bells tolled.
The soul asks no reply
But her one certainty,
The wonder unsearchable our bodily eyes behold.

So surely as I keep
Of those eyes clear and deep
The memory, I know nothing shall dim their joy;

That his the highest renown
Who here the most lays down,
Bliss shall clasp hands with bliss in endless ecstasy.

Nothing, I know, has won
From the sweet light of the sun
That soaring swan, the soul, in all-forgetting flight,
But that through death's thin veil
Her eyes the red dawn hail,
See with the feet of Love's sun all the distance grow white.

IX

THE UNIVERSITY AND A LIBERAL EDUCATION

*The Rectorial Address
to the University of Edinburgh—1937*

MY first duty is to thank you, as I do most sincerely, for the great and unexpected honour you have done me in electing me as your Rector in succession to so many men of the highest distinction in every line of life—politics, law, literature, the services, and not least the great and gallant soldier, my immediate predecessor.[1] While appreciating the honour you have done me personally, I may say at once that I recognize that the personal was only one of the factors in your choice, that my election represents an effort on your part to revive this ancient office as not only an opportunity of doing honour to some distinguished man, but as one channel through which you, the students, may constitutionally make your contribution to the ends for which this and every free and self-respecting University exists. Indeed, in the peculiar position in which I stand to-day, supported and surrounded by your representatives, I am compelled to feel myself, however inadequate for the post, your spokesman, and in what I have to say I will endeavour to look at the questions I raise from a student's point of view, to consider, what you who enter the University have a right to look for and a duty to seek after.

You will not, therefore, expect me to follow my distin-

[1] The late Field-Marshal Lord Allenby.

187

guished predecessors and discourse on some large topic, whether liberty or courage or any other. Least of all do I propose to follow in the footsteps of the most eminent, as a literary man, of these, Thomas Carlyle, and descant on the evils of democracy and the advantages of dictatorships. We have a closer vision, a more poignant awareness, of these things than Carlyle, who saw them mainly through the letters of Oliver Cromwell or at the distance of Paraguay in South America. I wish to speak from the history of the Scottish universities in the last one hundred years and from my own experience of nearly fifty years, on the question, what do you come to the University in quest of? What have you the right to look for, the duty to pursue?

The answer you would have received from most voices in the middle of last century would be: to complete a liberal education. What is a liberal education?

A University [said John Stuart Mill, speaking at St. Andrews the year after Carlyle spoke here] is not a place of professional education. Universities are not intended to teach the knowledge required to fit men for some special mode of gaining a livelihood. . . . Its function is not to make skilful lawyers or physicians or engineers, but capable and cultivated human beings.

Universities do well to have schools of Medicine and Law and Engineering and the Industrial Arts, but

Men are men before they are lawyers or physicians or merchants or manufacturers; and if you make them capable and sensible men they will make themselves capable and sensible lawyers or physicians. What professional men should carry away from a University is not professional knowledge, but that which should direct the use of their professional knowledge and bring the light of general culture to illuminate the technicalities of a special pursuit. Men may be competent lawyers without general education, but it depends on general education to make them philosophical lawyers—who demand and are capable of apprehending principles instead of merely cramming their memory with details.

A LIBERAL EDUCATION

That is high-sounding doctrine, and it raises important questions. The idea of a liberal education came to us ultimately from the Greeks, and in Greece, and later in Italy at the Renaissance, it was an education for leisured people whose livelihood was secured to them by slave labour or some other means of exploitation. Those who received such an education were to be citizens and soldiers, perhaps rulers, and the education was intended to make them civilized beings in mind and manners. But very few Scottish students were ever in that position, and even in the two great English universities the number of such is growing less. Sir Farquhar Buzzard told me recently that some sixty per cent or more of the students at Oxford were receiving financial help in one form or another.

It is not surprising, therefore, that two years after Mill spoke, when the students of St. Andrews chose as their rector James Anthony Froude, the friend, disciple, and biographer of Carlyle, he spoke in quite a different strain, threw his whole weight on to the side of a specialized and professional education:

> What I insist upon is that in a country like ours where each child that is born among us finds every acre of land appropriated, a universal "not yours" set upon the rich things with which he is surrounded . . . such a child, I say, since he is required to live, has a right to demand such teaching as shall enable him to live with honesty, and take such a place in society as belongs to the faculties which he has brought with him. . . . History, Poetry, Moral Philosophy, Classical Literature are excellent as ornament. If you care for such things they may be the amusement of your leisure hereafter; but they will not help you to stand on your feet and walk alone; and no one is properly a man till he can do that. You cannot learn everything; the objects of knowledge have multiplied beyond the power of the strongest mind to keep pace with them all. You *must* choose among them, and the only reasonable guide to choice in such matters is utility. If we mean to

thrive we must take one line and rigidly and sternly confine our energies to it. . . . We are ourselves made of earth; our work is on the earth; most of us are commonplace people who are obliged to make the most of our time.

That is the other view sharply stated—a University is a group of professional, technical schools for the training of doctors, lawyers, engineers, teachers, etc. And there can be no doubt that this is the direction in which we have moved, are moving more and more, if here in Edinburgh we still somewhat halt between two opinions. One of my colleagues said to me recently that the greatest credit which had accrued to our University of late is that we had supplied a number of capable recruits for the chemical industry; that and the doctors we turn out, he said, are our chief honour and glory. If the Arts Faculty counts for anything, it is, I suppose, that we supply some excellent teachers to schools and an occasional University Professor. The statement startled me, not because I do not value the work done in our costly chemical laboratories and our great Medical School, but simply that I had never heard the fact stated quite so nakedly that we are a professional, technical school; that the old idea of a liberal education has, in the opinion of some of my colleagues, "gone with the wind". And if that be so, then many of the things which the Arts Faculty, and myself as a member, have done of late years are wrong; instead of endeavouring to retain in the curriculum for the Ordinary Degree of M.A. certain elements of what was once regarded as a liberal education, such as Latin, Mathematics, etc., we should endeavour to make our curriculum more practical, endeavour to adapt it more readily to the professional needs of this or that individual student. Moreover, there can be no doubt that it is in this direction that the universities of France and Germany have moved. They are professional schools; only it has to be remembered that they claim in France and Germany to have given in the schools, up to the age of nineteen, a liberal and in the main a literary education. The highest classes in the French *lycées* are known as Rhetoric and Philosophy. In the German schools (at least before the revolution), there was no specialization—all alike "teach literary and scientific subjects, but in all the bulk of the instruction is literary". (Burnet, *The German Universities and the War.*) In the German universities to-day, I gather from a recent study, stress is laid increasingly on the practical. Of that I shall have something to say later.

Such being the general trend, it is remarkable that a passionate protest against this conception of a University, as intended to give a practical, technical, professional education, has come from the most practical country in the world, from the President of the University of Chicago, one of the greatest industrial and mercantile cities in the world. President Hutchins does not believe that the greatest credit which can accrue to his University is to supply capable young recruits for either the chemical or the pig-packing industry. No; he goes in his revulsion to the opposite extreme. There, amid the roar of traffic in Chicago, he dreams, with Plato in Athens, of a course of study which should raise us to the contemplation of the Idea of Good, source alike of being and knowing, and should from thence deduce all the first principles of natural and moral science.

> The aim of higher education is wisdom. Wisdom is knowledge of principles and causes. Therefore metaphysics is the highest wisdom. . . . Metaphysics then as the highest science ordered the thought of the Greek world, as Theology ordered that of the Middle Ages. One or the other must be called upon to order the thought of modern times. Without theology or metaphysics a unified University cannot exist.

But I do not propose to follow the President in his reconstruction of a University curriculum. What I wish to call attention to is what he considers are, or what he has found to be, the results of the practical, professional conception of a University education.

> The pursuit of knowledge for its own sake is being rapidly obscured in Universities and may soon be extinguished. Every group that is well enough organized to have an audible voice wants the University to spare it the necessity of training its own recruits. They want to get from the University a product as nearly finished as possible, which can make as large and inexpensive a contribution as possible from the moment of graduation. This is a pardonable, perhaps even a laudable, desire. But the effect of it on the Universities will be that soon in a University everybody will be there for the purpose of being trained for something.

When I was at Cornell University in 1927 I saw some men busy erecting large tents on the campus, and on inquiring was told that the hotel-keepers had established a department in the University, and that these were their students learning to erect marquees. The effect of a practical, technical stress on education is that the students are impatient of work on the fundamental sciences, say in law or medicine; they wish to be taught at once what you might call the tricks of the trade.

> A friend of mine [says the President] took an hour to explain to his law-school class the economic and social background of the fellow-servant rule. At the end of the discussion one student inquired: "What's this got to do with the law?" There is a good deal to be said for the boy's position. He had come to the University under the impression that it would prepare him for the Bar examinations and teach him the rules of the game. He felt that he was being cheated. Under these circumstances the temptation [for the teacher] is irresistible to tell your students stirring anecdotes of your own days at the Bar, to let them in on the tricks of the trade, and to avoid confusing their minds by requiring them to think about anything except what the courts will do.

192

A LIBERAL EDUCATION

We on this side of the Atlantic hear at times similar murmurs regarding the scientific basis of a medical education, demands for a more practical training.

I should like to approach the question raised by such statements from the history of our own universities during the last hundred years, some fifty of which I have spent in one way or another at universities. When I entered King's College, Aberdeen, in 1883, it was to follow a course of study for the degree of M.A. which had been mapped out by the Commission of 1858, for which the way had been prepared by the Commission of 1830 of which Sir Walter Scott was a member. It was a very wise Commission, that of 1830, and some of its *obiter dicta* are worth remembering, as that "the attempt to introduce into the Scottish universities any system of government or instruction similar to that which subsists in the English Universities would be inconsiderate and hurtful". Where the Scottish universities fell obviously short in comparison with Oxford and Cambridge was in classical scholarship. John Gibson Lockhart, who had gone to Oxford from Glasgow as a Snell Scholar, is never tired of making sarcastic comment on Edinburgh's ignorance of Greek. The Commission, more wisely, points out that this was only to be expected in universities which had no fellowships to reward such proficiency.

> There is no encouragement therefore to prosecute to any great extent those branches of literature which do not directly tend to useful objects; and without the strongest natural bias it is vain to hope that many will devote themselves to classical literature as their peculiar pursuit with the zeal exhibited in other countries, when they cannot thereby attain any immediate honour or future advantage.

In short, whereas in England an elegant performer in classical metres or the editor of a Greek text (with the help of a German predecessor) could count on a fellowship and might aspire to a bishopric, there were no such prizes in a country whose universities had no fellowships to offer, and whose Church has no Bishops nor many rich livings. The Commission of 1858 did not therefore endeavour to set up various schools or triposes such as in Oxford and Cambridge quite overshadowed the pass or poll degree. Their first concern was with the pass or ordinary degree. They found in 1830 that in Edinburgh "graduation was the exception, that students attended individual classes as they chose, and that the majority of the students were young men, not intended for any learned profession, but sent for one or two years to College in order to carry their education farther . . . before they are engaged in the pursuits of trade or commerce". There is much to be said for such a practice, and some of my late colleagues have wished that it might be revived.[1] The Commission thought that it led to too much lecturing and too little of the closer attention and discipline required by regular students. Accordingly a course of study for the degree was fixed in 1858 and, as I have said, was still in force when I became a student. We entered a class and with that class went through the whole curriculum—two years of Greek and Latin, two years of Mathematics, one of Physics, two of Philosophy. The Commission added to these a year of English Literature, taught at Edinburgh and Glasgow by Professors of the subject, at Aberdeen and St.

[1] It is, I think, regrettable that the organization of our studies with relation to this or that degree has produced an impression that no one should attend University classes unless proceeding to a degree. There seems to be even an idea abroad that the entrance examination admits to the universities. This is not strictly its function, but to admit to a course for this or that degree. Every citizen has a right to attend University classes if he pays the fees and behaves properly; and I think that now, as in 1830, young men of reasonable ability who contemplate leaving school in their seventeenth year, before entering business would profit more by attending individual classes in Philosophy, History, or Natural Science, at the University, than by spending the same years at school—but of this more later.

Andrews by the Professors of Logic, an arrangement traceable to the old connection between Rhetoric and Logic.
The Commissioners also made it permissible to require a
year of Natural Science (Chemistry, Geology, Botany, or
Zoology), but Aberdeen was the only University which
availed itself of this permission.

Such was the system and, without being a *laudator temporis
acti*, I do think it had certain great advantages. There was
first the mutual interest which the members of the class came
to take in one another. One of the most delightful sections
in the biography of the late Lord Bryce is that in which he
describes his years at Glasgow—the eager but entirely generous interest with which the members of a class followed the
successes of its gifted students in one subject or another.

> The class-work [he writes] kept us on the *qui vive* and nearly
> the whole class wanted to learn and enjoyed learning. When-
> ever we had a chance we talked about our work, discussing
> the questions that came up, an incessant sharpening of wits
> upon one another's whetstones. We spoke very little about
> theology and not much about politics, and though we cared
> about classics, the ambition of most of us would have been
> to be metaphysicians. That seemed the highest kind of mental
> exertion. . . . We were most of us young . . . some were much
> older . . . but there was little difference between young and
> old. In the competition for prizes neither age nor youth told.
> All alike were eager in the pursuit of knowledge, those who
> had come from parish schools of low degree and the sons of
> wealthy merchants who had got all that the best schools of
> Edinburgh or Glasgow could give. . . . There was no better
> way of understanding the Scottish spirit as it had been since
> the middle of the sixteenth century than to be a student of
> Glasgow College.

That was still much the spirit prevailing in the classes I
attended, though we were beginning to take a little more
interest in athletics, and in our debating society we did

discuss politics. I led for the Conservative party in 1885 and had over eighty supporters and over ninety opponents.

Moreover, by my time the Commission had made it possible, in addition to the class-work, to graduate with Honours in Classics, Philosophy, Mathematics, or Natural Science. But the Honours student was not cut off from the rest of the class. He competed with them in all the other subjects, and this gave us in our student societies a wider common range of subjects for discussion. Sir Peter Chalmers Mitchell, who graduated with Honours in Philosophy and then turned to Natural Science, was a distinguished member of the Literary Society. The same is true of Sir Leslie Mackenzie, who, after graduating with Honours in Philosophy and Classics, went on to the study of Medicine. To the Professor, too, this arrangement gave the opportunity of lecturing to students of first-rate ability who were not proceeding to Honours in his own special subject. Dr. Alexander Bain left the mark of his clear, methodical, honest teaching in both Rhetoric and Logic, especially Inductive Logic, the logic of the natural sciences, on innumerable minds, if some were repelled by certain of his spiritual limitations. Even that may be useful in sharpening the mind, in quickening one's thought. The bad teacher is not the man by whose views one is roused to contradiction, but the teacher to whose dissertations one remains entirely indifferent; and certainly our teachers in some subjects such as Moral Philosophy were farcically incompetent. What was true of Bain was true of many others, as Lushington, Kelvin, Caird, Tait, Sellar, Jebb, Butcher. It was not their Honours students alone who benefited by coming under such men.

It was, of course, a narrow curriculum—no history, no modern languages, no economics, and little science; and little or no attention was paid to our life outside the classroom, our health, manners, or morals. But if the range of subjects we studied was narrow it had some of the elements of a liberal education. To Mill it seemed to include all the subjects proper to a University curriculum. He defended even its limitations—the ignoring of modern languages and even of history. "The only languages and the only literatures to which I would allow a place in the ordinary curriculum are those of the Greeks and Romans." "The University is the place where the student should be introduced to the Philosophy of History."

To continue with the history of our universities, the work of the Commission of 1889–93 was to smash this uniform, if narrow, curriculum and to introduce the blessed principle of options. The impulse to this change came from two sources. It came from America, which is the wrong direction. George Herbert tells us that true religion has moved from East to West. I think it is the same with regard to education. The other impetus came from the great Liberal doctrine of the nineteenth century, the doctrine of *laissez-faire*, which to Lord Macaulay was the last word in political wisdom, to Carlyle was an inspiration of the Devil. It was at Harvard that President Eliot introduced the so-called free elective system, which the President of Chicago University now tells us amounts to a denial that there is a content to education, any common body of knowledge which should be the common possession of civilized humanity, any philosophy of life and ethics, any common principles of scientific truth. The practical effect of the system of free election has proved to be threefold: (1) vocationalism, the direction of all one's studies towards a money-making profession; (2) the quest for the easiest path towards something that can be called a degree; (3) purely fanciful combinations. I asked one young lady at Cornell who wished to join my special class for the study of the literature of the seventeenth century what other subjects she had included in her curriculum and she replied,

Anglo-Saxon and World Philosophies. Another young lady at California, Professor Blyth Webster tells me, asked by her Bishop what were her studies for the term, answered, swimming and Browning, meaning by the latter the English poet, not the effects of the sun on her complexion. But on the way in which options have affected our own curricula for the Ordinary or Pass Degree I do not propose to dwell, because I think that after some trying experiences we have, with the help of Directors of Study and some pressure from outside, succeeded in securing for our students at least creditable courses. But strangely enough it is for the Ordinary Degree candidate that we have insisted on the inclusion of certain subjects, such as Latin or Mathematics, which may not as a fact be of use to him in his profession, while we have exempted the Honours candidate from any reasonable requirement. I have come to think it should be the other way round, that the student who comes here to take an Ordinary Degree might be considered as having got at school all the general education he is likely to benefit by, and might now select his studies mainly with a view to his later career. It is, in my opinion, the Honours students, an ever increasing body, who, whatever their special subjects, should be compelled to include in their course an adequate broader training in subjects philosophical, historical, and scientific. It was in their regulations for the Honours candidate that I now feel sure the Commission of 1889 did the greatest harm. Before that year, you will remember, an Honours student was not exempted from the other subjects of the curriculum. His Honours work was something additional and done largely off his own reading. Some of us groaned a little, especially over the requirements in Mathematics. But good men got through it and were none the worse. It was thought by the Commissioners, with their eyes on Oxford and Cambridge, that we might attain to a higher standard if the Honours candidate were allowed to take nothing outside his Honours course but two subjects. The result has not been a happy one. We have given no poorer degree than a second or third class Honours degree with only two other subjects in the graduate's curriculum. In Aberdeen the favourite combination for a classical Honours candidate was Botany and Education, Botany because it could be completed in a single summer course, Education, well, I cannot say why. We have thrown away our birthright, that broader training which when we went, as some of us did, to Oxford or Cambridge, gave us one advantage. We might feel ourselves somewhat behind our public school rivals in the special subjects, Classics or Mathematics, but we had a broader range of knowledge and interest. This last statement must be qualified by the recognition that many of the young Englishmen came from wealthier and more cultured homes and had read more widely for themselves. But that very fact pleads for the need of a wider University education for the average Scottish student. Nor did the handicap of a wider training hinder many of those who thus did go on to more specialized study, at what my old Greek professor used to call "the arenas of the south", from obtaining high places and fellowships. One has only to recall the names of W. R. Hardie, James Adam, J. A. Stewart, Hector Macdonald, Chrystal, and many others. And that raises the question, if we have sold our birthright have we gained the full mess of pottage? Have more of our Honours graduates who have proceeded to the arenas of the south gained fellowships than did the poor lads whom we sent up burdened with a good graduate's knowledge of Mathematics, Philosophy, Physics, English Literature, and Natural Science? It would, I think, have been far better if we had retained for all Honours students the old broader course—with perhaps some modification of the subjects, I shall not discuss that—the broad course, philosophical, literary, and scientific. From those who thus graduated we could then have selected from time to time the fittest, and, now that we have Carnegie Scholarships and Fellowships, have encouraged these to go on to post-graduate work here or elsewhere, thus building up a really creditable post-graduate school, not like the present haphazard arrangements for the so-called Ph.D.[1]

But in touching on these practical and historical details you will complain that I am running ahead, am assuming

[1] I have not touched, for I cannot deal with everything, on the question of age—the rise in the age of entrance which is, of course, the factor that has tended to give to a University education an increasingly professional, practical bent. The young men to whom John Stuart Mill was speaking in 1866 entered the University in about their sixteenth year, and the general cry was that the universities were doing work proper to schools. On that I would say two things, and first I will quote again from Mill: "Every Scottish University is not a University only, but a High School to supply the deficiency of other schools, and if the English Universities do not do the same it is not because the same need does not exist, but because it is disregarded. Youths come to the Scottish Universities ignorant, and are there taught. The majority of those who come to the English Universities come still more ignorant, and ignorant they go away." That is, of course, John Stuart Mill speaking in 1867. Whether the pass degree at Oxford or the poll degree at Cambridge breeds better results now I am not in a position to state.

My second point is this. Granted that our schools are greatly improved since 1867, and are in a position to carry the education of their scholars much further, it is, I believe, and many others are coming to believe the same, a mistake to keep young men at school after the age of seventeen, bad for themselves and for the other boys. That is the conclusion to which many of the German professors, such as the great chemist Ostwald, were coming before the war: "Great men are ripe for higher study at seventeen or earlier, and it is wicked to keep them at school when they might be studying Energetik at the University". So Professor Burnet quotes in arguing on the same lines as I am: What is wanted at seventeen for intelligent boys is a change in the whole method of instruction, and it was just such a change that we enjoyed when we passed from the schoolmaster with his ferula, his daily exercises, his prescribed home lessons, and his pauses for revision, to a professor, frequently a man of high distinction, carrying you through a course which you followed, or did not follow, of your own good will and at your own peril. Does one find in boys still lingering at school after sixteen the eager buoyant spirit, the delight in knowledge for its own sake, which Lord Bryce found among the young students of his day at Glasgow College?

that there is a benefit to be got, a real want to be supplied, by an education which goes beyond the technical, professional, vocational. I have still to give my reasons for believing that John Stuart Mill and President Hutchins are, in the main, right, despite the trend in the opposite direction; and I propose to look for some light on the question in two almost opposite directions. Two recent developments seem to me to indicate that both the State and the individual recognize, however dimly, the need for something more than a purely technical, professional, practical education. The German universities have reorganized themselves, or rather been reorganized from above in a way that would have pleased Carlyle and his demand for a dictatorship. The old boasted *Lehrfreiheit* and *Lernfreiheit*, freedom for the teacher and freedom for the student, are gone. They never were so real, Professor Burnet declared, as appeared. All now is regulated from above, from Minister of Education to Rector, from Rector to Professor. And what do the new regulations point to as the goal of the dictators, what is their ideal of a right education? They, too, lay great stress on the practical.

> The National Socialists [says Mr. Hartshorne in his careful and impartial study of present conditions] are largely of lower middle-class origin, and share the popular prejudice against speculative science and the popular admiration of practical science (p. 110).

> Thus, there are three main tendencies to be observed in the Nazi influence in science. First, sciences of immediate practical importance tend to be encouraged in contrast with the others. Secondly, sciences of remotely practical importance, the subject-matters of which lend themselves readily to the moulding of public opinion, become instruments of official propaganda. Thirdly, unpractical sciences, not readily utilizable for propaganda, tend to be neglected.

Now, ladies and gentlemen, note that "secondly", and take the word science quite broadly to cover all your studies. What does it imply but just this: that the German dictators recognize the need for their purposes of studies which go beyond the professional, studies which are intended to make students not only good doctors or engineers or chemists, but good Germans holding certain views about biology, genetics, and race, about political science and economics, about history—in short, studies which will give the students a philosophy of life which it is the duty of every good German to assimilate, just as the medieval universities taught a theology which every Christian must accept; and the new rulers are as ready as the old to hand the heretic over to the secular arm, the concentration camp. Plato, some of you may remember (for Plato was a Fascist, had come to hate the democracy of Athens and admire the discipline of Sparta, though, fortunately for him and us, he was not born in Sparta or we should have had no dialogues, no freedom to follow the logos whithersoever it leads), thought it would be necessary for the philosopher in moulding his ideal state to use a continuous course of falsehood and deceit, to disseminate useful or noble lies. So do the Fascist rulers to-day, though, poor fellows, they perhaps believe them to be necessary truths. That is what Plato calls the lie in the soul, incurable because it has become a conviction for which they are prepared to die—at least, to put others to death. But if that is so, are we, who live still in a free democracy, or one endeavouring to approximate to freedom, and who believe that the sciences of biology and economics and politics and history are open studies in which we have not attained to, but are always seeking to attain to, truth, are we to neglect to give our best minds, our Honours graduates, whether in science or in arts, some introduction to the present condition of these studies? Are we not to recognize the necessity of giving them a philosophy of life in a free state, making them good citizens with a wise and tolerant outlook on life?[1]

My second evidence comes from another quarter, evidence that there is a natural demand for education which goes beyond the professional and technical. We have recently inaugurated at Newbattle a College for adult education. Now, what do the young mechanics, miners, and others come there to study? Is it to make themselves more skilful mechanics, to improve their chances of professional promotion? Not at all. It is to get some of the elements of a liberal education which they were denied through the need imposed on them from an early age of earning a living. I

[1] If I understand Professor Hogben aright, and it is always dangerous to judge from newspaper accounts, he would have our universities teach "useful lies", only they would be useful in a different direction and for a different class from those which the Fascist Dictator and his Apostles have in view. He would, that is to say, have subjects touching upon Politics, Economics, and Political Science taught with a quite definite bent. As a fact these subjects are never taught without some such bent. One may teach Mathematics and Physics without introducing one's own prejudices; never Philosophy, History, Political Science, or Economics —there are, in things that touch human life, no unprejudiced people. As Lord Passmore said in a lecture here: "If you meet what you call an unprejudiced person that means simply he has the same prejudices as yourself". The advantages of a free state are that if A teaches with one bent, B will teach with another, and C is free to follow either A or B. It is such variety of treatment and freedom to follow one or other bent that is anathema to the dictator, whether Fascist or Communist. We hear much of professors imposing their views upon young students. My own experience is that they do not succeed easily in doing so. We found it necessary in my days in certain of the Philosophy classes to say in our examination papers what the professor said in his lectures. That by no means meant that we thought the same as he did. Moreover, I still think that even in these subjects a study that is as disinterested as possible is better than one that has distinctively propagandist opinions. In the Physical Sciences the disinterested pursuit of truth has been fertile of practical consequences; and I believe that it is not radically otherwise in History, Political and Economic studies, though it may be that such fruitful inquiry results less from detached abstruse investigations than from the active competition between inquiring minds, each more or less influenced by his interests and prejudices. This, therefore, is just the field in which it is at once tempting and disastrous to stifle freedom of mutual criticism and competitive investigations.

asked Mr. Fraser, our Warden, to give me some idea of the
nature of the curricula and his reply is:

> We take as our special courses one in Philosophy and
> Psychology, another in Economics and Social History, and
> a third in English Literature. Students have mainly to con-
> centrate on one or other of these, and the teaching of these is
> done in small classes, and students have to write frequent
> essays. But all the students combined are given in the first
> term general lectures on the subjects of all these three courses.
> . . . Besides there is a course of History which consists of a
> general lecture to all on current events, history being treated
> from the point of view of present problems, their existence
> being interpreted by history treated backwards.

If knowledge of these things is sought by the more intelligent
among the artisan class, should their study be altogether
neglected by those from whom should come leaders in our
national life?

So far, then, if my argument has conducted me aright, we
may say that you come to the University to pursue, and have
the right to obtain all the help the University can give you
in pursuing, a professional education, a special line of study,
one that will help you to earn a living. But you come also
with the right to obtain and the duty to seek such help as
the University can give you in acquiring such knowledge of
Philosophy, History, Economics, and Political Philosophy as
may help you to do your duty as good citizens in a free
country. Some of you, while professional men, will yet
contribute to the right government of your city, it may be
your country, if not in Parliament yet by your pen or word
of mouth. But we are not yet done. You are to be professional workers earning your bread, and citizens exercising
the rights allowed you in a free country, but you are also
men and women, for I will close by returning to Mill's statement: "Men are men before they are lawyers or physicians
or merchants or manufacturers; and if you make them

capable and sensible men they will make themselves capable and sensible lawyers, etc.", and so he went on to defend the old fixed curriculum of the Arts Faculty. Froude's reply, you will remember, was that for most of us, as the world now stands, education must be practical and specialized. "History, Poetry, Moral Philosophy, Classical Literature are excellent as ornament. If you care for such things they may be the amusement of your leisure hereafter." But, I venture to say, despite Froude and his master Carlyle, you have the right to ornament in your lives, a right to pleasure, to what even you may call luxuries so long as you preserve a right balance in your life. "Man shall not live by bread alone." How deep is the natural instinct for what goes beyond sheer necessity is visible at times, as during the late War, when many workers came into wealth or what to them was wealth. Their first instinct was not to save and to secure their economic position, it was to have just those things that seemed to them luxuries—pianos, cars, dogs, or, if women, silk stockings and velour hats. Nothing could be more idle and stupid than to laugh at such impulses, for they have their source in the deepest instincts of human nature. A part of your education, and not the least essential part, is the games you play and the societies you frequent. These, too, the first especially, have their utilitarian aspect, for they make for health. Even Carlyle turned aside in his address to appeal to the students to give care to their health, and to deplore his own early neglect of that essential basis of all success and all enjoyment. It was more necessary in those days when no care was taken by the University of the student outside the classroom. In my own class, not a large one, we lost in the course of the four years, our best mathematical student and our two best classical scholars. We owe here in Edinburgh a very great debt to our present Principal for all that he has done in the short time he has been with us to secure for our students the possibility of the best care for their health obtainable, and his interest in the opportunities for healthy exercise. The difference between my student days and now is enormous. But the end of these things is the pleasure they give. When I look back to my schooldays the hours I remember most vividly are those spent on the football field and in the library. When I recall my days at King's College I do remember some of my classes, especially the lectures of William Minto; but perhaps even more the Friday evenings in the debating and literary societies. There are, of course, voices on the air just now which declare that the sole justification for athletics is their fitness to make us good soldiers, that the individual has no right to his own happiness, he exists only as a member of the State. Such statements are on a level with theories for producing perpetual motion or squaring the circle. It may at times, too often to-day, be necessary to lay down life and happiness that your country may live, but the ultimate justification of the State is to be found in the number of individuals for whom it is able to make possible a full and rich life. And this is indeed my final definition of a liberal education, one that enriches your capacity to enjoy what good things this our uncertain and troubled life has to offer. For you will fare best, ladies and gentlemen, if you approach your studies in the same spirit as you do your games, in the spirit of the young Glasgow students whom Lord Bryce recalled in surveying his early life. Some of your studies have for their end just this of giving us pleasure. Among the subjects which you may include in your curriculum here in Edinburgh are Literature (English, Classical, French, German, Italian, Spanish), Art, and Music. For some of you, your studies of these subjects are professional, for you wish to be teachers. But I can assure you, you will never make much of teaching these subjects unless you have come to enjoy them for their own sake. Some of you may say, can we be taught to enjoy? We either do so or we do not. That is a great mistake. In nothing does one need more careful and prolonged discipline than in learning to discriminate between the good and the inferior in every line of experience, from art and literature to, shall I say, wines and cigars. Joy is the final test and reward of achievement in every activity. Even of the highest of all spiritual activities, that of the great religious soul, though the path to it may lie through stern discipline and a dark night of the soul, the final reward is described as a joy that passes all understanding. And it is not only such subjects as I have mentioned that may give you pleasure. Every study if approached in the right spirit, a spirit of disinterested curiosity, will become a source of intellectual pleasure. However practical or professional the purpose you have had in entering on the study, the pleasure you will get from it is in proportion to the extent you can forget the purpose, forget even the examination at the end of the course. The late A. E. Housman, in an Introductory Lecture when appointed Professor of Latin at Cambridge, after dismissing various specious reasons put forward for the study of Latin, as that it improves your English, which it by no means necessarily does, or improves your taste in poetry, which a knowledge of Latin and Greek failed to do for Bentley, or refines our taste and character, which again it has certainly not done for many great scholars, comes to the conclusion that the final justification of that as of every other study is that it is one of the paths along which you may enjoy the pursuit of knowledge for its own sake:

all men possess by nature a craving for knowledge. It is, as it were, a game of hide-and-seek to which we are invited by the Power which planted in us the desire to find out what is concealed. . . . And the pleasure of discovery differs from other pleasures in this, that it is shadowed by no fear of satiety on the one hand or frustration on the other. Other desires perish in their gratification, but the desire of knowledge never: The eye is not satisfied with seeing nor the ear filled with hearing.

Summing up, I might say that, agreeing with John Stuart Mill in his conception and estimate of a liberal education, we must, recognizing the force of what Froude said, perhaps reverse the order. Mill's words were, you remember, "Men are men before they are lawyers or physicians or merchants or manufacturers", and therefore he could contemplate, as was easier to do when students entered the University at sixteen years of age, a four years' course in the liberal studies before one entered on a professional education. It was in my day still common for many of our best medical and law students to do this. It is more difficult now that the age has risen, a subject on which I touch in a note. We must recall Aristotle's words: "One must live before one can live well". We must, it may be, think first on entering the University what is to be our profession or the line of study in which we mean to specialize. But we must also, and it should be made possible for our best students even if we have to turn the wheel somewhat backward and make less of the entrance examination, we should make it possible for them to include in their course a sufficient range of study, philosophical and historical and literary, to give them the rudiments of a wider interest in their duties as citizens, and the possibility of a richer intellectual life. There is, to my mind, something melancholy in the plight of the professional man or scientific specialist who has no resources outside his profession or subject beyond golf, bridge, and perhaps the novels of P. G. Wodehouse. I stood on the Calton Hill recently with a brilliant young doctor from the Continent and said to him: "This is the monument built to Dugald Stuart. You will never have heard of him, but over there is the tomb of a man of European reputation." But he had never heard of

David Hume. To know nothing of Hume is to be ignorant
of one of the most epoch-making minds in later European
thought.

Into practical details I must, of course, not enter to-day,
so I will close with a few words to yourselves directly, you
who are students to-day. You come here with the right to
all that the University can do for you as professional earners
of your bread, as citizens of a still free country, as men and
women who have a right to enjoy the best things of life as
far as they may come within your purview. But you come
with corresponding duties to yourselves and to your University. As regards yourselves you can do much that goes
beyond what you are taught in class by your own thought
and reading and by intercourse with your fellow-students.
As regards your University, there has been much criticism
of this and universities generally since the War. That is
quite right and proper if the criticism is backed by knowledge and inspired by goodwill. But remember the old
Scottish proverb: "It's an ill bird that fyles its own nest".
The University is your own to benefit by and also to help
now and in your later life. *Spartam nactus es, hanc exorna.* All
that you do well in your later life will redound to her advantage, bring credit to your Alma Mater. May you look back
at the end of your life with the same gratitude and pleasure
to your University career as I do to Aberdeen, to Oxford
and to Edinburgh within whose walls I have spent the
happiest days of my life.

NOTE

The two recent books referred to are:
Robert Maynard Hutchins, *The Higher Learning in America*,
 1936.
Eduard Yarnall Hartshorne, *The German Universities and
 National Socialism*, 1937.

X

A Review of *Pastoral Poetry and Pastoral Drama*, by Walter W. Greg—1908

THIS is a scholarly, exhaustive, and interesting thesis which requires and repays careful study. A hasty reading is both apt to convey a mistaken impression as to the interest of the work (which is to be found in the discriminating and penetrating criticisms of the principal poems and plays passed in review) and even to mislead, for some of Mr. Greg's *obiter dicta* require the qualification and amplification which they generally receive in the course of the treatise. Moving through an elaborate argument, or complex genealogy, he sometimes raises expectation of a slightly different conclusion from that which he actually reaches.

The pastoral drama in England is Mr. Greg's theme. But to detach any one specific kind of pastoral literature of the Renaissance from the rest is impossible, because the pastoral ideal of the Renaissance refused to be confined to any single form, such as the classical eclogue, but invaded every department of literature—sonnets and lyrics, romance, and epic, as well as drama—and that so spontaneously that, although one may, and Mr. Greg does, indicate stages in the evolution of the pastoral romance or the pastoral drama, it is well to be on one's guard against any too rigid theory of origins. Quite naturally, therefore, Mr. Greg devotes the first two chapters of his book to a review of pastoral literature from Theocritus and Virgil, through Petrarch, Boccaccio, Mantuan, Sannazaro, Montemayor, and Marot, to Spenser,

Sidney, and their followers. I mention only the chief names.
In this review he discusses, in considerable detail, the regular
imitations of classical eclogue, the more spontaneous pastoral
lyric, and (though the title of his book does not suggest it)
the prose pastoral-romance. He omits only the pastoral
interludes in the romantic epics of Ariosto, Tasso, and Spenser.

Mr. Greg is too wise to attempt any precise definition of
what took so many forms. But he indicates clearly the
peculiar "note" of pastoral poetry, the artificiality of its
golden age, "the recognition of a contrast, implicit or expressed, between pastoral life and some more complex type
of civilization". Pastoral poetry is neither the spontaneous
utterance of simple and primitive feeling, nor poetry so
faithfully descriptive of rural life as Crabbe's. Pastoral
literature presents a courtly and cultured dream of country
life, from which all realistic and painful features are de-
liberately banished. With Theocritus it took its rise in
"the contrast between the recollections of a childhood spent
among the Sicilian uplands and the crowded social and
intellectual life of Alexandria". In the hands of Virgil it
began to lose some of this dream charm, becoming a more
conscious playing at shepherd life, in a word allegory. In
the most characteristic Renaissance pastorals, the *Aminta*
and the *Pastor Fido*, we get an exquisite combination of
courtly and refined sentiment with the feeling of a return
to nature. But generally the "proper pleasure" of the
pastoral shows a tendency to disappear, or change into something else, in one of two ways. The convention becomes
purely a convention, untouched by any feeling for nature,
as in the eclogues of Mantuan and the Humanists—and even
in *Lycidas* despite its compensating beauties—"ecloghe dove
di pastorale non v' ha che i nomi e le frasi: il resto è allegoria
di cose contemporanee tutt' altro che pastorali". On the
other hand, the natural feeling may become too sincere for

its conventional setting. This is the tendency of much English pastoral. Mr. Greg has laid great stress, in his second chapter, on the evidence of a dual tradition in English pastoral poetry, the older, simpler, more realistic pastoralism of the ballads and Miracle plays, and the conventional, ideal, Italian pastoralism. To the first he seems in this chapter to trace the vein of naïve realism in Spenser's eclogues, the delightful descriptions of Devonshire scenery in *Britannia's Pastorals*, and the sincere and ardent enthusiasm for nature of Wither's clear, high song; while the same vein blends and heightens the more ideal strain in the golden songs of *England's Helicon* and the *Muses' Elizium*. Later, however, Mr. Greg somewhat modifies the impression given by this chapter, and very wisely finds the link between native and Italian pastoralism rather in temperament and character than in a literary tradition. The Englishman is at bottom a countryman rather than, or always as well as, a courtier. The only exception is Donne, and he frankly detests the country. See his epistle to Sir Henry Wotton beginning "Sir, more than kisses, letters mingle Soules", or that to the Countess of Bedford beginning "Madame, you have refin'd mee", or his only pastoral eclogue (which Mr. Greg has excusably ignored) introducing his second Epithalamion. No English poet could have written the *Aminta*. But Spenser and Drayton, and Browne and Wither, are interesting forerunners of Thomson and Dyer, Gray and Collins, Cowper and Crabbe.

Indeed it is this temperamental trait which gives its only interest to the history of later pastoralism, from Pope to Crabbe, pastoral poetry which has lost entirely the courtly note and lingers merely as a literary tradition. For it was in connection with pastoral poetry that the cleavage first showed itself distinctly between the two principles of neoclassicism, "follow nature" and "imitate the classics", since "to follow nature is to follow them". Steele was too English to admit that to follow nature in describing country life was identical with the mere imitation of Theocritus and Virgil. The movement he initiated by his essays in *The Guardian* produced Gay's *Shepherd's Week* and Ramsay's *Gentle Shepherd*, and though the one is a burlesque, and the other a very genteel pastoral, still they were steps on the way to Crabbe's rejection of "the sleepy echoes of the Mantuan bard", and to Wordsworth's deeper and more philosophical idealism. Even Dr. Johnson, who began by being all for the rules and Virgil, ending by detesting pastoral poetry, in which "there is no nature for there is no truth", and which as a literary artifice is "easy, vulgar and therefore disgusting".

Mr. Greg's review of English pastoral poetry in the sixteenth and seventeenth centuries is excellent. He lays special stress on Spenser and Drayton, and has done justice to the structural as well as poetical capacity shown in the *Shepheardes Calender*. If we feel inclined to differ from him, it is when he appears to prefer the *Shepheardes Calender* to the *Muses' Elizium* on the ground of its choice of subject, after previously criticizing the incongruity of Spenser's "pastoral theology". Surely Spenser's is the greater poem simply because, despite faults of immaturity, it contains finer poetry, deeper in feeling, richer in phrase and cadence, than the fresh and charming work of Drayton ever attains to. But this finer poetry is to be sought not in the controversial eclogues but in such songs as those for June and for October. These touch a deeper and more vibrating note than Drayton's most enthusiastic strains. But possibly we have misunderstood Mr. Greg and are expressing his own feeling in a different way.

Coming to the drama Mr. Greg describes the beginnings of the pastoral plays in Italy in such mythological plays as Politian's *Orfeo*, and more directly in the *Egloge Rappre-*

sentative. The earliest English pastoral plays of Peele and Lyly were also mythological, but there seems no reason to demur to the name "pastoral" as applied to Peele's *Arraignment of Paris*, unless the name is to be confined to the Italian kind elaborated by Tasso. The actors other than the Gods are shepherds of the pastoral type. Indeed it affords an interesting illustration of the spontaneity with which the pastoral drama tended to take shape that Spenser's eclogues had hardly appeared before his shepherds were utilized for dramatic courtly entertainment. Even without the *Aminta* and *Pastor Fido* we should doubtless have had shepherd plays of more than one kind.

In discussing these so admired and so influential products of the Italian taste for artificial sentiment and for motives better adapted to music than drama, Mr. Greg has analysed and criticized, with great acumen and justice, the central motive of both pieces, the conflict between "feverish passion" and "virginal coldness"; and the lurking sense which they convey of something a little unreal in the latter and not altogether lovely in the former. And nothing is more interesting in Mr. Greg's analysis of the English masterpieces in the kind than his discussion of the treatment of this motive by Fletcher and by Milton. No critic has shown so fully and clearly the source of Fletcher's failure, despite the lyrical charm of his style and verse, and the Theocritean grace of his descriptions. Mr. Greg finds the source of that failure in the abstract manner in which Fletcher set to work to develop the fundamental contrast, and his want of sympathy with the "ideal which he sought to honour",—his failure, in a word, to appreciate the beauty either of chastity or of love. The delicate feeling of the *Aminta* is not perhaps quite sound at core, but it has a grace and charm which is wanting altogether to the cynical licentiousness of Fletcher.

To Milton's *Comus* Mr. Greg is, I think, less just, and partly

215

because he does not make allowance for the fact that it was a protest against courtly cynicism and licence. *Comus* suffers —like *Lycidas*, like *Paradise Lost*, like *Samson Agonistes*—from being too polemical. But Mr. Greg has duplicated a single charge which one may and must admit. *Comus* is not quite a masque and not quite a drama. It is not quite a masque like Jonson's *Masque of Queens*, because the change of fortune is not effected simply by a transformation scene, but is made to depend on the will of the Lady. Yet the poem is a masque rather than a drama, because both the action and persons are conceived abstractly and symbolically rather than concretely. The Lady is not Lady Alice Egerton, a girl of thirteen, but Virtue Militant. Grant this, and it seems unnecessary to accuse Milton further of bad taste in making her speak beyond her years. Some awkwardness there is doubtless in the identification, but it is not enough to mar the splendour of Milton's defence of Chastity, the magnificent poetry in which he has set forth the Puritan ideal, which Gardiner, with perhaps more strict propriety, saw incarnate in Archbishop Abbot looking on at the marriage of the Earl of Somerset and Lady Frances Howard.

To the beauty of Milton's poetry, indeed, Mr. Greg does ample justice, as to the grace of Fletcher's, the pathetic loveliness of Jonson's fragment—for the whole of which one would give a dozen *Alchemists*—and the blithe and pleasing *Amyntas* of Randolph. Indeed Mr. Homer Smith might plead that the Note at page 308 has some applicability to Mr. Greg's own criticism of *The Faithful Shepherdess* and *Comus*. In both he does a little separate the substance from the form.

These are the most direct inheritors of the Italian tradition, though Mr. Greg has shown how independently the Englishmen adapted the borrowed form to the traditions of the native stage. One departure from these traditions which

betrays the Italian origin of these plays he has not deemed
worthy of remark, their strict adherence to the rule of twenty-
four hours. Dr. R. Otto, in his preface to an edition of the
Sylvanire, has pointed out that it was the admiration felt for
the *Aminta* and the *Pastor Fido* which revived in the earlier
seventeenth century, in France, discussion of the Unities,
after Hardy had given them the go-by. And for this reason
discussion turned at first on the unity of time alone. "C'était
l'unique règle que l'on connût en ce temps-là", says Corneille
in the *Examen de Clitandre,* and it is the only one mentioned
in Mairet's preface, with which began the movement that
closed with the condemnation of the *Cid.* No such effects
followed in England. Ben Jonson had no Academy and no
Richelieu to back him. But even in lawless England, the
rule of the "astrological day" was recognized as an essential
feature of the Italian pastoral drama.

And speaking of France brings me to one small addition
which might be made to Mr. Greg's exhaustive thesis. In
his review of those hybrid pastoral plays (chap. vi.) in which
chivalrous elements, borrowed from the romances, are
mingled with the purely pastoral scenes and incidents,
Mr. Greg has ignored the possible influence of the contemporary French drama. Both pastoral plays, and tragi-
comedies combining chivalrous, pastoral, and humorous
elements, were the rule in France till the *Sophonisbe* (1635)
and the *Cid* (1636) established the vogue of tragedy. In
reading Mr. Greg's analysis of plays in the second section
of chapter vi. we noted several little points of resemblance,
and came upon one clear case of unrecognized borrowing.
Of course it is always to be remembered that in tracing an
English play to a French source we are not excluding the
possibility of going a step further and finding an Italian
original.

The mad lover who conceives himself in Elysium, drawn

217

with real dramatic touches by Randolph in the *Amyntas* (1632–5), and more artificially by Cowley in *Love's Riddle* (1638), appears in Rotrou's *L'Hypocondriaque* (1628), and the same author's *Laure persécutée* (1638). The latter play is, however, based on Lope de Vega's *Laura perseguida*. Probably the type has some original Italian source. The case of undoubted plagiarism from the French, which has hitherto escaped attention, is Rutter's *Shepherd's Holiday* (1635). Rutter translated the *Cid*, and was, therefore, presumably familiar with French plays. At any rate the purely pastoral portion of his drama—the story of Nerina and her lovers, and of the poisoned mirror—is, throughout, an adaptation, often a paraphrase, occasionally a translation, of Mairet's *Sylvanire* (1629). It cannot be said that in general Rutter has improved on the original. The scenes are shortened, with the result that the development of motives is made more abrupt. The courtly incidents which Rutter has loosely grafted on to Mairet's pastoral have a general resemblance to the same poet's more romantic and interesting *Sylvie* (1626). There a prince (as here a princess) leaves the court for love of a shepherdess, and incurs the wrath of his father. The *dénouement*, however, is different, and Rutter's solution may be his own or have a different origin. Cowley is, through Rutter, indebted for his best scene (*Love's Riddle*, iv. 1) to the *Sylvanire* (iii. 7). Mairet's own play, it may be added, is the recast of a play in blank verse written by the author of the *Astrée*, at the request of Marie de Médicis. There may be some other instances of borrowings from the French. Mr. Greg has throughout had Italy mainly in view. The first beginnings of French influence in the reign of Charles I are worthy of note.

Every student of the Elizabethan drama must be grateful to Mr. Greg for this carefully developed and discriminating study of the diverse elements which combined to produce the various forms of the English pastoral drama, and his admirable criticism of its masterpieces. If his work has a fault it seems to me to be an occasional disproportion of style to subject, and an occasional over-emphasis in the expression of his divergence from the views of others.

NOTE

With reference to what is said at page 216 regarding Milton's bad taste in making Lady Alice Egerton the defender of Chastity, it may be noted that, in the version of Milton's *Mask* prepared by Law for actual performance, the lines in which Comus depreciates Virginity and those in which the lady defends "the Sun-clad power of Chastity" are omitted. In composing the scene Milton thought only of his ideal character, when it came to the actual performance Law had to consider the circumstances.

XI

Bacon's Poem, *The World* : Its Date and Relation to Certain Other Poems—1911

IN the *Fortnightly Review* for September 1899 appeared an article by Miss Alice Law on a Caroline Commonplace-book in her possession, the most interesting part of which was devoted to a discussion of the authorship and date of the poem, generally attributed to Bacon, whose title stands at the head of this article. Of this poem Miss Law printed, from her Commonplace-book, what she describes as "a rare and curiously unique copy . . . inasmuch as the verses here given in italics now appear in print for the first time and are not found in any of the other existing MS. copies of the poem". Miss Law argued at considerable length for the thesis that the poem was written not by Bacon but by Sir Henry Wotton; and that its probable date is some time between 1610 and 1615. I think I am able to throw some light on the additional stanzas, to show that the traditional ascription of the poem to Bacon is probably correct, and to connect it with poems by Donne, Bastard, and Wotton written in or about 1598.

The poem was first printed by the classical scholar Thomas Farnaby (a contemporary of Bacon, Donne, and Wotton), in 1629, as a version by Bacon of the epigram attributed to Posidippus, beginning,

Ποίην τις βιότοιο τάμῃ τρίβον ;

"Huc elegantem V. C. et Domini Verulamii παρῳδίαν adjicere adlubuit" are Farnaby's words.

This epigram and the reply to it attributed to Metrodorus (Mackail, *Select Epigrams*, 1906, pp. 299-300) are both in the Planudean Anthology; and were translated into English by Nicolas Grimald before 1557, when his versions were printed in *Tottel's Miscellany*. Grimald's paraphrases are to some extent the source of those which followed, including Bacon's, and I propose to print them; but in doing so I should like to give the opening lines of the original epigrams, as it will be seen that in the English versions the classification of life's principal arenas underwent a gradual and characteristic alteration. "What path of life may one hold?" runs Mackail's rendering, "In the market-place are strifes and hard dealings, in the house cares; in the country labour enough, and at sea terror, etc." "Hold every path of life", is the reply. "In the market-place are honours and prudent dealings, in the house rest; in the country the charm of nature, and at sea gain, etc." Grimald's renderings are as follows:

Mans life after Possidonius *or* Crates

What path list you to tred? what trade will you assaye?
The courts of plea, by braul and bate, driue gentle peace away.
In house, for wife and childe, there is but cark and care:
With trauail, and with toyl ynough, in feelds wee vse to fare.
Vpon the seas lieth dreed: the rich in foraine land
Doo feare the losse: and there the poore like misers poorly stand.
Strife with a wife, without, your thrift full hard to see:
Yong brats a trouble: none at all, a maym it seems to bee:
Youth, fond: age hath no hert, and pincheth all to nye.
Choose then the leefer of these twoo, no life, or soon to dye.

Metrodorus *minde to the contrarie*

What race of life ronne you? what trade will you assaye?
In courts is glory gott, and witt encreased daye by daye.
At home we take our ease, and beak our selues in rest:
The feelds our nature doo refresh with pleasures of the best.

On seas is gayn to gett: the straunger, hee shall bee
Esteemed, hauing much: if not, none knoweth his lack, but hee.
A wyfe will trim thy house: no wife? then art thou free.
Brood is a louely thing: without, thy life is loose to thee.
Yong bloods be strong: old sires in double honour dwell.
Doo waye that choys, no life or soon to dye, for all is well.

In 1589 *The Arte of English Poesie* (attributed to Richard
or George Puttenham) appeared, and under the heading
"*Antipophora* or Figure of responce" the author "Englished"
these epigrams again, evidently with Grimald's version in
view, but in six-foot lines throughout.

It will be observed that Grimald takes

$$\epsilon i\nu\ \dot{\alpha}\gamma o\rho\hat{\eta}\ \mu\dot{\epsilon}\nu$$
$$\nu\epsilon\acute{\iota}\kappa\epsilon\alpha\ \kappa\alpha\grave{\iota}\ \chi\alpha\lambda\epsilon\pi\alpha\grave{\iota}\ \pi\rho\acute{\eta}\xi\iota\epsilon\varsigma\cdot$$

as referring not to the business of the market-place, but to
the law-courts, which "by braul and bate driue gentle peace
away" but where there is "glory gott and witt encreased
daye by daye". Puttenham refers also in the first epigram
to the "brawle and brabbles of the law", but in the second
he introduces a division which was a favourite Elizabethan
one—the Court, the City, and the Country. His expression
"Court gets vs great renowne" *may* refer to the courts of law,
but I think it is more likely that it refers to the Court of the
King. This at any rate, it will be seen, is the classification
fastened on by Bacon and the poets who took up the theme
later.[1]

---

[1] The view that the words

$$\epsilon i\nu\ \dot{\alpha}\gamma o\rho\hat{\eta}\ \mu\dot{\epsilon}\nu$$
$$\nu\epsilon\acute{\iota}\kappa\epsilon\alpha\ \kappa\alpha\grave{\iota}\ \chi\alpha\lambda\epsilon\pi\alpha\grave{\iota}\ \pi\rho\acute{\eta}\xi\iota\epsilon\varsigma$$

referred to the Law-courts seems to have been common in the sixteenth
and seventeenth centuries. Grotius' Latin version in Firmin-Didot's
edition of the Palatine Anthology opens thus:

Quod vitae sectemur iter? Fora plena molestis
Litibus:

The substitution of the King's Court for the courts of law originated

223

Bacon's poem—assuming it to be his—is well known, but I should like to quote it for the sake of comparison, and because there are some important differences of reading between the two printed authorities for the text, Farnaby's volume and the *Reliquiae Wottonianae*. Miss Law's chief reason for doubting Bacon's authorship was that in the first edition (1651) of the latter work the poem was marked, like others, *Ignoto*. From this she argued, with Dr. Grosart, that the copy found among Wotton's papers had been unsigned, and that either because Wotton did not know the author, or because he was himself the author. But this is a rash inference. Wotton may have known so well who was the author that he made no note of it. Collections of Donne's poems were frequently left thus nameless. Farnaby's ascription is not to be set aside lightly. He probably knew Bacon well. Moreover, in a collection preserved at Corpus Christi College, Oxford, of what seem to be papers that had been Wotton's (they include letters, printed from this source by Mr. Pearsall Smith in his *Life and Letters of Sir Henry Wotton*, and poems) there is a beautifully written copy of this poem signed "F. B.", which is the signature it would bear before it became proper to give it the more formal signature which it bears in the later editions of the *Reliquiae Wottonianae*, "Fra. Lord Bacon" or more correctly "Fra. Bacon, Lord Verulam", or as in a Trinity College, Dublin, MS. "Visc. St Albans". It is quite possible that in 1651 an editor would not recognize at once what "F. B." stood for.

apparently with Ronsard (1560). The first four lines of his version run:

> Quel train de vie est-il bon que je suive
> Afin, Muret, qu'heureusement je vive?
> Dans les palais il n'y a que procès,
> Noises, débats et querelleux excès;

but the Elzevirian edition gives as a variant of the last:

> Aux cours des Roys regne l'ambition,
> Les senateurs sont pleins de passion.

Of the further contents of this MS. collection I shall have something to say presently. Meantime this is the poem as printed by Farnaby (taken from Spedding, for I have not Farnaby's volume at hand) with the variants of the *Reliquiae Wottonianae,* one of which I have adopted.

The World

The World's a bubble: and the life of man
                    less than a span.
In his Conception wretched: from the womb
                    so to the Tomb:
Curst from the Cradle, and brought up to years,
                    with Cares and Fears.
Who then to frail Mortality shall trust
But limns on Water, or but writes in Dust.

Yet since with sorrow here we live opprest,
                    what life is best?
Courts are but only superficial Schools,
                    to dandle Fools:
The rural parts are turned into a Den
                    of savage Men:
And where's a City from all vice so free,
But may be term'd the worst of all the three?

Domestick Cares afflict the Husbands bed,
                    or pains his Head:
Those that live single, take it for a curse,
                    or do things worse:
These would have Children, those that have them none,
                    or wish them gone:
What is it then to have or have no Wife,
But single thraldom, or a double strife?

Our own Affections still at home to please
                    is a Disease.
To cross the Seas to any foreign soil,
                    peril and toil.

> Wars with their noise affright us: when they cease
>   we 'are worse in peace.
> What then remains, but that we still should cry
> Not to be born, or being born to die?

In Miss Law's version of this poem the first two stanzas are not given at all; but each of the last two is followed by what Miss Law printed as new and additional stanzas hitherto unknown. It is strange that she should not have noticed, what is evident at a glance, that these are not additional stanzas but replies, which the copyist has inserted, each after the stanza to which it refers. Probably the earlier stanzas with their replies have been torn away. I need not print Miss Law's stanzas for I have this summer found the whole poem from which they are taken, in the Corpus Christi College, Oxford MS. referred to already. That collection contains the following poems, all in the same handwriting: (1) Bacon's poem signed "F. B.", (2) a Latin verse rendering of the same signed "G. S. Equit. et Baronetti f. A. M.", (3) the reply to Bacon's poem, (4) a Latin verse rendering of this reply signed "H. B.", (5) (apparently in the same hand, but at a different part of the MS. volume) Sir Thomas Roe's lines "Upon the Glorious King of Sweden".

The reply to Bacon's poem runs as follows:

> The World's a Globe of State, our Life a Raigne,
>   Man Soueraigne:
> Begot with pleasure, and brought up in daies
>   With sports and playes:
> Courted while youthfull, and when Riper yeard
>   Honourd and feard.
> Who on this Rock doth stand, or Ocean steere,
> Rests in his Center, moues as in his Sphaere.
>
> Blessings so crowne each place, Tis hardly guesst
>   What Life is best:
> The Court is Honors wombe, transforming Clods
>   To Demigods:

The restfull Country Eden speakes, in all,
   Except the Fall:
And the trim Cities Plenty-horne imparts
Treasures to all, but above all, her Arts.

Wiues share our Cares by daie, wee their Delight
   Much more by night:
The Virgins like an Epicoene Phoenix shown,
   Both Twins in one;
The Childlesse are their own Heires; Sons give breath
   Even after Death:
The Mayden then, or Mariage state will bee
A Single Paire, or double Vnitie.

We dote on Home, as if that Mother Earth
   Gaue our Soules birth:
Trauaile descryes mens Customes, Habits, Parts;
   And these their harts:
Warre is a Kingdoms Physicke, Peace its Health,
   Their off-spring, Wealth:
What then remaines but that we choose of twaine,
Never to dye, or streight be born againe?

  This it will be seen is a very free expansion of the epigram
of Metrodorus, as Bacon's is of that of Posidonius. One of
the most interesting touches in the original, ἐν δ' ἀγροῖς φύσιος
χάρις, is delightfully and characteristically rendered:

   The restfull Country Eden speakes, in all,
     Except the Fall.

"I do not know", says Professor Mackail, "any other passage
in classical literature where 'the beauty of nature' in the
completely modern sense of the words is spoken of so explicitly." The Elizabethan rendering is not so "completely
modern" as the Greek.

  The MS. affords no clue to the authorship of the poem.
"Warre is a kingdoms Physick" echoes Bacon's essay *Of the*

true Greatnesse of Kingdomes and Estates: "And certainly, to a Kingdome or Estate, a Iust and Honourable Warre is the true Exercise. A Civill Warre, indeed, is like the Heat of a Feaver; But a Forraine Warre is like the Heat of Exercise, and serveth to keepe the Body in Health." It may be noted also that the "The World's a Globe of State" recalls the sentence in the essay *Of Great Place*, "For Imitation is a Globe of Precepts"; and that the line "Rests in his Center, moues as in his Sphaere" reminds us of the famous metaphor in the essay *Of Truth*, "Certainly, it is Heaven upon Earth, to have a Mans Minde move in Charitie, Rest in Providence, and Turne upon the Poles of Truth". What is said, too, about the married state is on the lines of the essay *Of Parents and Children*, children "increase the Cares of Life; but they mitigate the remembrance of Death". "The Childlesse are their own Heires" is, I suppose, a condensed manner of saying, "The Perpetuity by Generation is common to Beasts; but Memory, Merit, and Noble workes are proper to Men". Or does it rather mean that their wealth is more entirely their own? "There are some other that account Wife and Children but as Bills of changes. Nay more there are some foolish rich covetous Men, that take a pride in having no children, because they may be thought so much the richer" (*Of Marriage and Single Life*). Possibly Bacon wrote both poems but thought the first alone deserving of circulation as by himself.

But Bacon's verses called forth other poems on the theme of Court, Country, and Town. Miss Law points out in the article referred to that this is the subject of Donne's longest verse letter to Sir Henry Wotton, that beginning, "Sir, more than kisses, letters mingle soules, etc." As Donne's poem is well known, I need not quote more than a few lines, and I shall take some of those which Miss Law quoted "with a view to show that in writing thus Donne must have been acquainted with this particular poem", *i.e.* Bacon's *The World*. I quote from the 1633 text:

> Life is a voyage, and in our lifes wayes
> Countries, Courts, Towns are Rockes or Remoraes:
> They breake or stop all ships, yet our state's such,
> That though then pitch they staine worse, wee must touch.
>
> .   .   .   .
>
> Cities are Sepulchres, they who dwell there
> Are carcases, as if no such there were.
> And Courts are Theatres where some men play
> Princes, some slaves, all to one end, and of one clay.
> The Country is a desert where no good
> Gain'd (as habits not borne) is understood.
> There men become beasts, and prone to more evils;
> In cities blocks; and in a lewd Court devills.

Bacon's lines:

> And where's a City from all vice so free,
> But may be term'd the worst of all the three?

are clearly echoed in Donne's:

> Cities are worst of all three; of all three?
> (O knotty riddle) each is worst equally.

Donne's contribution brings us to the question of the date of the poems. Miss Law, assigning *The World* to Sir Henry Wotton, considered that the period when it was written was most probably some time between 1610 and 1615, when Wotton was out of favour with the king and when, to quote Miss Law's words, "Wotton's correspondence with his intimate friend and kinsman Sir Edward Bacon was characterized by a reckless bitterness of tone, astonishing in one usually so politic". In these letters he frequently burst into bitter invective against the Court: "This place of such servility in the getting, and such uncertainty in the holding of fortunes". Or again, in reference to the logicians of the Court and their fickle judgments he writes: "For yet I never in the Country, nor much less in the Court, see anything done of this kind that was not afterwards approved by those that had most opposed it". Miss Law finds a clue to the date in the mention of the Epicoene, which she takes to be a reference to Jonson's comedy. This is out of the question. Indeed the only argument for Miss Law's date is the parallel, in the new verses given above, with Bacon's essay *Of the true Greatnesse of Kingdomes and Estates*. This was not published till 1612. The argument has not much force, however, if Bacon himself wrote the poem. The essays, too, were known to his friends before publication.

If Donne's poem was written as a reply to or comment on Bacon's, this must be assigned an earlier date. It was only comparatively soon after Wotton's return from his first long residence abroad that Donne would have addressed him in the terms in which his letter closes:

> But, Sir, I advise not you, I rather doe
> Say o'r those lessons, which I learn'd of you:
> Whom free from Germane schismes, and lightnes
> Of France, and faire Italies faithlesnesse,
> Having from these suck'd all they had of worth,
> And brought home that faith which you carried forth
> I throughly love: But if my selfe I haue won
> To know my rules, I haue, and you haue Donne.

This is a suitable compliment to pay to a young man: it would not be quite so appropriately offered to one who had been for five years his country's ambassador at Venice.

But there is conclusive evidence that the poetic *débat* took place before 1598. On the "3 Aprilis" [1598] the following entry appears in the Stationers' Register: "Jone Brome Wydowe Entred for her copie under the handes of Master Kinge and Master Man, *Seven bookes of Epigrammes* wrytten by Thomas Bastard whereunto are added *Three Slepers* by the same Author vjd." In the course of the year appeared

"*Chrestoleros.*   Seuen Bookes of Epigrames written by T. B.

> Hunc novere modum nostri servare libelli,
> Parcere personis: dicere de vitiis.

Imprinted at London by Richard Bradock for I. B. and are to be sold at her shop in Paules Church-yard at the signe of the Bible.   1598."

This volume contains epigrams addressed to Essex, Egerton, and Wotton which suggest that Bastard was attached to the same group of adherents of Essex as Donne, Wotton, and Bacon.   The fourth epigram of Book II has been quoted more than once, but its exact significance becomes apparent when taken in connection with the poems I have given.   It runs thus:

> *Epigr.* 4.   *Ad Henricum Wottonum*
> Wotton, the country and the country swayne,
> How can they yeeld a Poet any sense?
> How can they stirre him up or heat his vaine?
> How can they feed him with intelligence?
> You have that fire which can a witt enflame
> In happy London Englands fayrest eye:
> Well may you Poets have of worthy name,
> Which have the foode and life of Poetry.
> And yet the Country or the towne may swaye,
> Or beare a part, as clownes do in a play.

What Bastard means by the "fire which can a witt enflame", "the foode and life of poetry", is the Court, otherwise the last two lines would lack point.   I have not got the *Chrestoleros* at hand (only some notes and extracts made in Professor Saintsbury's library) but Corser (*Collectanea*, ii, 211) says "there is little doubt that Bastard was well acquainted with the Greek Anthology".   It is worth noting that the *Chrestoleros*, like the Planudean Anthology, is divided into seven books.   The influence of the Anthology on Elizabethan and Jacobean epigrams deserves some attention.

If the poems in question were written before 1598, they must have been written after 1594, when Wotton returned to England. I incline to date their composition 1597-8, at some period between the return of the Islands' Expedition in October, and April 1598, when Bastard's volume was registered. There is no proof that Donne was a courtier before the Cadiz expedition (1596). His earliest verse-letters would seem to have been *The Storm* and *The Calm* (1597). On 20th July, 1598, he wrote to Wotton a letter referring to their joint expeditions and in the same vein as the poems in question:

> Here's no more newes then vertue: I may as well
> Tell you Cales or Saint Michaels tales for newes, as tell
> That vice doth here habitually dwell
>
> Yet as to get stomachs we walk up and down,
> And toyle to sweeten rest; so may God frown
> If but to loath both, I haunt Court, or Towne.

Bacon, Donne, and Wotton were all in 1597 in the unhappy position of suitors, kicking their heels, or toiling at ungrateful tasks, in the hope that Essex' influence might find them profitable employment; and Essex was playing his cards badly. On 30th October, 1597, Wotton writes to the Earl begging "that if there grow any actions between her Majesty and the Emperor wherein your Lordship may make any use of that time which I bestowed in these countries, and in this Court, it please you to employ me". A letter to Cecil also contemplates an embassy to Germany; but it was not till 1599 that Wotton found employment and went to Ireland with Essex, whither Donne sent him another verse-letter. For Bacon the year 1597, like so many before it, was a period of hope and disappointment and debt and suitorship and unprofitable labour. Donne too had apparently some months of waiting and suitorship before he entered Egerton's service:

THE WORLD

> What is hee
> Who officers rage and suitors misery
> Can write and jest?

are his words after he had found a haven.

If in their hours of enforced idleness Bacon and Donne and Wotton interchanged verses suggested by some Greek epigrams, it was not a purely literary exercise. Their verses reflected their feelings. Bastard's lines, indeed, are the utterance of a poet sighing in the country for the delights of London life; but the other poems strike a deeper note. Whoever wrote the reply to *The World*, based on Metrodorus' reply to Posidonius, it was clearly not so widely circulated, probably because it was more entirely a *tour de force*.

But satire of the Court, the Country, and the Town was not confined to the epigram. In *Every Man out of his Humour*, written in 1598 and acted in 1599, Jonson opens on the same scent. The characters whom he elaborates with such fierce scorn fall into the three groups,—the Court represented by Sir Puntarvolo, Carlo Buffone, Fastidious Brisk and Saviolina, the Town or City by Deliro, Fallace, Fungoso, the Country by Sordido. Sordido's character is a complete expression of that feeling about the Country to which Donne gives utterance:

> The Country is a desert, etc.

It is in a different spirit that Shakespeare contrasts Court and Country in *As You Like It*; but his satire of the Court in *Hamlet* is hardly less trenchant than Jonson's.

I have kept Wotton's own contribution to the last. Miss Law contended that *The World* was written by Wotton himself. I have not proved that Bacon is the author, but I think I have added to the probability that Farnaby's ascription was correct. And this probability is increased by the discovery that Wotton did write a poem which is much more

233

in the stoical but sweet-blooded vein of "How happy is he
born and taught" than Bacon's despondent lines.   The poem
has never hitherto been printed, so far as I know.   I have
met with it in two MSS.   In one of these it is erroneously
ascribed to Donne himself, but in the other it immediately
precedes Donne's own contribution to the *débat*,

> Sir, more than kisses, letters, etc.

and is headed and runs thus:

To J: D: from Mr. H: W:

Worthie Sir
Tis not a coate of gray or Shepherds life
   Tis not in feilds or woods remote to liue,
That adds or takes from one that peace or strife
   Which to our days such good or ill doth giue:
It is the mind that makes the mans estate
For euer happy or unfortunate.

Then first the mind of passions must be free
   Of him that would to happiness aspire;
Whether in Princes Pallaces he bee
   Or whether to his cottage he retire;
For our desires that on extremes are bent
Are frends to care and traitors to content.

Nor should wee blame our frends though false they bee
   Since there are thousands false for one that's true,
But our own blindness that we cannot see
   To chuse the best although they be but few:
For hee that every fained friend will trust
Proues true to frend but to himselfe vnjust.

The faults we haue are they that make our woe,
   Our virtues are the motiues of our ioye,
Then is it vaine if wee to deserts goe
   To seeke our bliss or shroud us from annoy:
Our place need not be changed but our will,
For everywhere wee may do good or ill.

But this I doe not dedicate to thee
  As one that holds himself fitt to advise,
Or that my lines to him should precepts bee
  That is less ill then I, and much more wise;
But 'tis no harme mortality to preach,
For men do often learne when they do teach.

What we may imagine to have happened is briefly this.
Bacon's attention was attracted either by the Greek epigrams
or (which I think is more probable) by the versions in *The
Arte of English Poesie*, a book which excited considerable
interest. It is referred to by Sir John Harington in 1591 and
was used just about the date of these poems by Meres in
preparing his *Palladis Tamia* (1598). Bacon tried his hand
at one or both of the epigrams, catching up and amplifying
Puttenham's division of Court, Town, Country. He sent
that which expressed his own feelings to Wotton, who, like
himself, was in the service of Essex. Wotton showed it to
Donne and Bastard, who wrote their comments; and to
Donne's weighty and eloquently complimentary letter Wotton
replied in a characteristic and equally eulogistic strain.

It may be worth noting that Sir John Beaumont, who
entered the Inner Temple in 1596, made a translation of
both the epigrams. There is no reference in them to the
main theme of Bacon's and Donne's meditations; but Beaumont, a young student, may have been tempted to make his
versions by the fact that the theme was in vogue during
these years.

Lastly, Bacon's poem in the *Reliquiae Wottonianae* is followed
immediately by this epigram:

De morte

Man's life's a tragedy: his Mothers Womb
(From which he enters) is the tiring Room;
The spacious Earth the Theater; and the Stage
The Country which he liues in: Passions, Rage,

Folly, and Vice are Actors: the first cry
The Prologue to th' ensuing Tragedy.
The former Act consisteth of dumb shows;
The second, he to more Perfection grows;
I'th' third he is a man, and doth begin
To nurture vice, and act the deeds of sin:
I'th' fourth declines: I'th' fifth Diseases clog
And trouble him; then Death's his Epilogue.

Ignoto

Is not this an expansion—in the same manner as Bacon's *The World* is an expansion of the epigram of Posidonius—of that other epigram in the Anthology attributed to Pallades:

Σκηνὴ πᾶς ὁ βίος καὶ παίγνιον.

"All life is a stage and a game: either learn to play it, laying by seriousness, or bear its pains". If this be so, is it not likely that it was composed about the same time, 1597–8, when Wotton and his circle were turning over the Anthology? If so, it would be earlier than *As You Like It* and may be the link between the Greek epigram and Shakespeare's brilliant expansion. It is difficult to believe that if subsequent to Shakespeare's version, it would not have profited by it. But I am wandering into the region of conjecture.

The chief interest of the few facts I have brought together is, that they throw a small pencil of light upon the lives of Bacon, Wotton, and Donne at a time when they must have been in close intercourse with one another. The death of Essex was soon to sunder them. Bacon made himself the chief instrument in procuring the condemnation of his patron; Wotton went into voluntary exile; and Donne digested his spleen in a fragment of sombre and enigmatical satire.

NOTE

Since I wrote this article Mr. James Hutton has shown, *Modern Language Review*, vol. xxi. No. 4, October 1926, that the version of the first epigram attributed to Drummond of Hawthornden is by Sir John Beaumont. He refers to other versions including Latin renderings by Dr. Johnson. Two in octosyllabic measure were printed in 1726 by a David Lewis in *Miscellaneous Poems by Several Hands*. London. Printed for J. Watts.

XII

A Review of *The Letters of Dorothy Osborne to William Temple* Edited by G. C. Moore Smith—1929

THIS is likely to be the final edition of these delightful letters. The chief drawback to their full enjoyment hitherto has been the want of a convincing arrangement, making it possible to follow the story of the last year of the long engagement through all the vicissitudes of fear and hope. Sir Edward Parry, in the *Everyman* edition, improved upon the order in which he had placed them in the edition of 1888. With the aid of further research, and the skilful use of the diary kept by Dorothy's brother Henry, and especially by a careful attention to allusions in one letter to what has been said in another, Professor Moore Smith has succeeded in giving a reader a heightened sense of the coherence of the series. Nothing has escaped his quick eye. For example, the thirteenth letter in the *Everyman* edition becomes the eleventh in this arrangement because, while both letters refer to Dorothy's taking steel, in the eleventh her "fellow servant", *i.e.* Jane, is with her:

> I make her play at Shuttlecock with mee, and she is the veryest bungler at it that ever you saw, then am I ready to beat her with the batledore and grow soe peevish as I grow sick, that I'le undertake she wishes there were noe steel in England.

But in the twelfth and thirteenth we learn that Jane is off to Guernsey. If Jane had gone off on 18th March, she could hardly be playing with Dorothy on 3rd April, or Dorothy still talking about the steel. In like manner the fourteenth letter here, which is the twelfth in the *Everyman* edition, obviously refers to the injunction for sending on *Cleopatra* given in the thirteenth (fifteenth in the *Everyman* edition), to say nothing of the reference to what Dorothy had said in that letter about the excusableness of a change in Temple's feelings. To take one more instance, the seventeenth and eighteenth letters in the *Everyman* edition are here reversed for the obvious reason that the opening words of 18 (*Everyman*, 17) "that you may be sure it was a dream that I writ that part of my letter in" refer to what Dorothy had said in 17 (*Everyman*, 18) of the half-asleep condition in which she was writing. But it would be invidious by any sustained comparison of Professor Moore Smith's arrangements of the letters with that of his predecessor to show how admirably he has done his work. It is sufficient, taking his edition by itself, to note the care and success with which he has divined the references to what has been said by Dorothy herself, or must have been said by Temple in one or other of his letters so unfortunately lost. The result is that the editor has given us an almost complete history of their intercourse during these years as well as a vivid picture of the character and mind of the writer. The introduction, notes, and appendices add to the completeness of the story and the picture.

What a valuable as well as delightful picture it is that accident and scholarship have preserved and restored! As a love-story it is worth all the romances of the century—which Dorothy read with so much sympathy—and worth most of the love-poetry too. Here is a real woman, passionately in love, who loves in her own words "passionatly and nobly", yet never loses sight either of the facts of life or of the claims of other interests and duties. Dorothy would have agreed with Dr. Johnson that Dryden by admitting the romantic omnipotence of love has recommended as laudable and worthy of imitation that conduct which through all ages the good have censured as vicious and the bad despised as foolish.

How passionately she loves comes out in the interesting series of letters following her visit to London in October to November, 1653 (46 to 53); but, acute as her suffering is, she is quite clear that to marry for love only, with no regard to fortune or friends, is a folly of which she will not be guilty:

> 'tis being masterd by that which Reason and Religion teach us to governe, and in that only gives us a Preheminence above Beasts. ˙ . . .
>
> Heer then I declare that you have still the same power in my heart that I gave you at our last parteing; that I will never marry any Other, and that iff ever our fortuns will allow us to marry you shall dispose of mee as you please. . . . You know 'tis not a fear of want that frights me . . . but I confess that I have a humor will not allow mee to Expose my self to Peoples Scorne, the name of Love is growne soe contemptible by the folly of such that have falcely pretended to it, and soe many Giddy People have maryed upon that score and repented soe shamefully afterwards that nobody can doe anything that tends towards it without being estemed a rediculous person. Now, as my Young Lord Holland says, I never pretended to witt in my life, but I cannot bee satisfyed that the world should think mee a foole.
>
> I believe there is nobody displeased that People speake well of them, and reputation is esteem'd by all of much greater Valew then life itself.

So might the best of Jane Austen's heroines have written, indeed there is not a little resemblance between Dorothy Osborne and the heroine of *Persuasion*. Ann Elliot too, one can believe, had been in her youth touched with a seriousness closely akin to melancholy:

> My mother, I remember, used to say I needed noe tears to Persuade my trouble, and that I had lookes so farr beyond

them that were all the friends that I had in the world dead more could not be expected then such a sadnesse in my Ey's.

Moreover, Dorothy's good sense and humour and wit are quite worthy of Jane Austen:

> Those that have fortunes have nothing else, and those that want it deserve to have it.

And again, of a friend's husband:

> 'tis the most troublesome, buisy, talkeing little thing that ever was borne, his Tongue goes like the Clack of the Mill, but to much less purpos, though if 'twere all Oracle my head would ake to hear that perpetuall noise. I admired her patience, and her resolution that can laugh at all his fooleries and love his fortune.

In more ways than one these letters illustrate the manners and spirit of the time. Dorothy "can never think of disposing myself without my father's consente". At his command, but on no other consideration, she would do more: "Sure the whole world would never perswade mee (unless a Parent commanded it) to marry one that I had no Esteem for". This, as Professor Schücking has emphasized in a recent book, was the accepted rule of conduct in England as it is in France at the present day. In marrying without her father's permission, Desdemona ceases to be her father's daughter. To Lady Anne Halkett (1622–99) whose mother had treated her very differently from Dorothy's father, to marry nevertheless "without the consent of parents is an act of the highest ingratitude and disobedience of which a child can be guilty". Ophelia's conduct in *Hamlet*, which has often been censured as showing her timidity, was that of which an Elizabethan audience entirely approved. There are indications, indeed, that to compel a daughter to marry against her will was felt to be harsh and unjust. Wither states it very clearly in the poem *Fidelia*; but that the father has the power to do so is taken for granted. In Dorothy's case, it may be noticed that before her father's death she had so far emancipated herself as to declare that she would not wed anyone if not permitted to marry Temple (see the quotation above from Letter 53). Like Clarissa in Richardson's novel, Dorothy was probably strengthened in this resolution by the too presumptuous interference of her brother, her quarrels with whom are an amusing item in the correspondence. But Richardson's novel is the first full statement of the position to which the Puritan was necessarily if not always willingly driven. If love implies marriage, marriage should imply love. The same logic, it may be noted, led Milton to write his pamphlets on divorce.

There are many other points on which one might dwell; for example, Dorothy's reading, her comments on the proper style for letter writing, or on the style of the English translators of French romances, or on the behaviour of the Cromwells in their exalted station, on the influence of a court upon morals, in which she anticipates Burke (see p. 143), on the new regulations for marriage, promulgated by Barebones Parliament, which, Carlyle tells us, was to have made Christianity at last the rule of life (p. 76). Dorothy thinks the old ways better. Poetry and fiction are a very partial and misleading guide to one who wishes to form an opinion of the life and manners of an age, though they are a very favourite court of appeal. There is much in the late Professor Robert Adamson's statement that he would prefer to rely on statistics rather than trust to the impression conveyed by novels and plays. The novelist and dramatist are prone to dwell upon the exceptional. Certainly these *Letters* afford invaluable help to anyone who wishes to judge of the mind of the seventeenth century. Dorothy is presented in her letters as vividly as the heroine of any novel, and has the advantage of being a real person. In her letters a dead century lives again.

There is little one could correct in or add to what Professor Moore Smith has done. I have noticed only one misprint—"May" for "Man" towards the foot of page 32. The opening of Letter 20 suggests, what is perhaps the case, that a fit of ague like a hiccough could be staved off by a sudden shock: "I doe not know that anybody has frighted mee or beaten mee, or putt mee into more Passion then what I usually carry about mee, but yesterday I missed my fit". Dorothy's opinions on married people kissing in public are not quite consistent. Compare pp. 67 and 95.

XIII

A Review of *La Jeunesse de Swinburne,* by Georges Lafourcade—1930

THIS is a remarkable piece of work, and, despite its bulk, of absorbing interest for any one who has ever felt the charm of *Poems and Ballads* or, which is more, can find pleasure in studying the development of a great poet's art, in the analysis of his thought and sensibility, of the phases through which his style and verse have passed in the formative period, of the influences which have coloured it in passing, all the more if in the end that art achieved complete independence and individuality. For such Mr. Lafourcade's thesis is invaluable, not alone as a study of Swinburne, but as applicable in its methods to the work of any poet great enough to reward so patient an analysis.

For the purpose of such an exhaustive study Mr. Lafourcade has been rarely fortunate in his access to unpublished or but partially published material allowed to him by Mr. T. J. Wise or unearthed in the British Museum. But he has made an excellent use of his opportunities and has been able to trace with a sure hand, if with some perhaps unavoidable repetition, the strange and complex evolution of the art that shaped, and the spirit that informs, *Atalanta in Calydon, Chastelard,* and the culminating and epoch-making *Poems and Ballads.* The study closes chronologically with a chapter on *A Song of Italy* and the *Ode on the Insurrection in Crete* as marking the transition from the purely aesthetic to the prophetic and rhetorical poet of the *Songs Before Sunrise.*

Of the two aspects in which one may consider the development of Swinburne's poetry, the spiritual and the formal, the first is the theme of the volume *La Vie*; but this is supplemented by the analysis of the thought and sensibility of each individual work in the second volume, *l'Œuvre*, of which the main subject is the complex evolution of the poet's art, his diction and versification. It is this minute analysis of each work in order that gives the impression of repetition. One hears not "once for all", as Mr. Lafourcade says, but more than once and again, of the poet's Sadism and of his, not atheism but rather anti-theism:

> Because thou art cruel, and men are piteous,
>   And our hands labour and thine hand scattereth;
> Lo, with heart rent and knees made tremulous,
>   Lo, with ephemeral lips and casual breath,
>   At least we witness of thee ere we die
> That these things are not otherwise, but thus;
>   That each man in his heart sigheth and saith,
>   That all men even as I,
> All we are against thee, against thee, O God most high.

It is difficult to avoid repetition on the subject of Swinburne's thought, because it is of so definite and limited a character, so devoid of all sense of the complexity of things, so abstract; even if that definiteness is a proof of the young poet's courage, his superiority to the shuffling compromises and apologetic invention of mysteries to disguise some obvious truth, which he criticizes in his contemporaries:

> Thus runs our wise men's song:
>   Being dark it must be light;
> And most things are so wrong
>   That all things must be right;
> God must mean well, he works so ill by human laws.
>   This, when our souls are drowning,
>   Falls on them like a benison;

LA JEUNESSE DE SWINBURNE

This satisfies our Browning,
And this delights our Tennyson;
And soothed Britannia simpers in serene applause.

Mr. Lafourcade's *Life* is an invaluable supplement to the late Sir Edmund Gosse's brilliant but guarded sketch. Intellectually, at any rate, it is a relief to have the whole truth at last about Swinburne as about Wordsworth and Byron, to be able to estimate aright the measure of actual experience that lies behind the poems. Say what one may, it would be interesting to know why and in what circumstances Shakespeare wrote the *Sonnets*. Nor is this the whole value of the *Life*. By the way in which the writer has presented the different periods, and sketched the personality of Swinburne's friends and acquaintances as they emerge, he has made an important contribution to the history of the Victorian age, the materials for which are accumulating but have not yet been fully exploited. Of the poet's own personality the picture is still a little incomplete, partly because the author has felt it necessary to emphasize, in opposition to the tendency to ignore, the sensuous and troubled element in Swinburne's passionate but thwarted nature. One gets only occasional glimpses of the more winning side, but there are some. I would select, as examples, three. The first is Birkbeck Hill's description of the young poet at Oxford:

> I wish you knew the little fellow. He is the most enthusiastic fellow I ever met and one of the cleverest. He wanted to read me some of the poems he had written, and have my opinion. They are really very good and he read them with such an earnestness, so truly feeling everything he had written that I for the first time in my life enjoyed hearing the poetry of an amateur.

The second is the account of Swinburne's relations with Christina Rossetti (i, pp. 174-6), and the third, Swinburne's own description of Elizabeth Siddal Rossetti and his

247

brotherly affection for "a wonderful as well as a most loveable creature". One can but regret with Swinburne that William Michael had not made fuller use of the young poet's reminiscences (i, pp. 191-3).

Morally Swinburne's evil genius would seem, as we learn for the first time, to have been Richard Monckton Milnes, whose

> erotic collection of books, engravings, etc., is unrivalled upon earth, unequalled, I should imagine, in heaven. Nothing low, nothing that is not good and genuine in the way of art and literature is admitted. There is every edition of every work of our dear and honoured Marquis. There is a Sapphic group by Pradier (i, p. 178, note).

That sentence from an unpublished letter of Swinburne's suggests the whole range of Milnes' influence—the erotic in art and literature, Sappho, and the Marquis de Sade with his combination of eroticism and a fierce anti-theistic philosophy. Nor should the guarding statement be overlooked, "nothing that is low, nothing that is not good and genuine in the way of art and literature". But on this subject we need not dilate. For the student of literature the interest and importance of Mr. Lafourcade's revelation is that it confirms and explains the impression of thwarted passion, desire and frustration, which a reading of *Poems and Ballads* leaves behind. Mr. Lafourcade has thought it important to stress this side of *Poems and Ballads* in order to correct the theory, to which Swinburne himself lent support, that their inspiration is purely literary. It corrects and qualifies this view but does not entirely negate it, because, as Lafourcade admits, Swinburne is always prone to "force the note". Three parts of Swinburne's inspiration, I would contend, is literary, the poet's delight in his own gift of song and his own power of dramatic ventriloquism. *Poems and Ballads* are in a measure, like Browning's, dramatic lyrics—and Browning's are but in part so. Whatever effect Swinburne's Sadism may have had on his personal experience and his poetry it prompted no such active cruelty to others as, witness the recent *Life of Lady Byron*, a similar vein, a certain perverse love of cruelty and of defying his own better impulses, did in Lord Byron, for Byron was a man, Swinburne remained an incomplete man if a great and wonderful lyrical poet.

And so we come back to Swinburne's art and Lafourcade's study of its evolution, its phases and ultimate character, which is the subject of his second volume. Mr. Bridges has distinguished between the young poet who thinks of poetry from the first as a means of self-expression, is more intent on what he wishes to say than on the art with which he says it, and him for whom poetry is primarily an art which he desires to master. It is the latter class apparently that produces the greater poets. This is, I think, the significance of Coleridge's remark that a proof of the poet in Shakespeare's early poems, *Venus and Adonis* and *Lucrece*, is the choice of a theme remote from the poet's personal interests. Even of the plays one might say that the earlier are expressions not of Shakespeare's mind only but of the mind of Marlowe and Lyly and Kyd and Peele, whereas *King Lear* and *Troilus* and *The Tempest* are all Shakespeare.

In Swinburne's early poems as now presented here from unpublished sources along with those which were issued, but passed unnoticed, before his final triumph, we can follow every phase of his experimental and complex evolution. Stevenson has spoken of "playing the sedulous ape" to different authors, and the imprint of Stevenson's models remains evident in his finished work. Swinburne did the same to a degree that far exceeded Stevenson's, but is the more astonishing because of the completeness with which he in the end detached himself from these shaping influences,

249

assimilated what he needed, and achieved a style individual and unmistakable. Mr. Lafourcade justly calls him a ventriloquist. Others have imitated. The peculiarity of Swinburne's pastiches is that they would do no discredit to the poet whom he is following, at his best. Morris, we are told, preferred Swinburne's *Queen Yseult* to his own poem or poems on the same or a similar subject, and, says Mr. Lafourcade, he was right: "For there is more of latent poetry in *Queen Yseult* than in the whole of the *Defence of Guinevere*". Dryden, Shelley, the Elizabethan dramatists, the Pre-Raphaelites both Morris and Rossetti, Ballads and Miracle Plays, Tennyson and Browning and Patmore—Mr. Lafourcade shows us Swinburne playing the ape to them all seriously or in the way of satirical parody.

The most enduring influences were the ballads, Shelley, Shakespeare, and Chapman, though of neither of the two last are there any examples of mere imitation. But probably the most interesting formative influences were the ballads metrically and the Pre-Raphaelites stylistically. Of the latter Mr. Lafourcade has much to say that is both fresh and valuable. The central principle of Pre-Raphaelitism has always seemed to the present writer to be the appreciation of the emotional effect of significant detail vividly rendered. But Pre-Raphaelite poetry and art were historically a complex phenomenon owing much of their effect to the deliberate reproduction of an earlier, simpler, more naive art which the poet and painter charged with a subtle blend of medieval and modern feeling. This has been always recognized in the painting of the school. Mr. Lafourcade has emphasized it in their poetry. The peculiar quality of Morris's *Defence of Guinevere* is due not only, as the late Mr. Dixon Scott contended, to the effect on his style of Morris's vivid pictorial imagination, but to the deliberate reproduction of the naive style and versification of the poetry of the thirteenth and fourteenth centuries, romances, lyrics, and Miracle Plays. These Swinburne read "under the impulsion and almost through the eyes of William Morris", and so he wrote verses like the following which might have come right out of the *Defence of Guinevere*:

> All the long white lines of sea,
> All the long white slope of lea,
> In the moonlight watched she.
>
> Then she pray'd if any heard,
> And the air about her stirr'd
> As the motions of a bird.

and:

> The night grows very old; almost
>   One feels the morning's feet move on;
> One lily glimmers like a ghost
>   On the black water, only one.
> I thought she was not dying; feel
>   How cold her naked feet are grown!
> I dare not either sit or kneel;
>   The flesh is stiffen'd to the bone.

and again:

> And stooped his face down close upon her head
>   And spake till his lips trembled with a smile . . .
> See now if there were left no Saracen
>   To stable in the city, and we ride
> We French knights, cross and lilies, two by two,
>   And the king midmost, with no man beside,
> Up slowly in the blood of all that crew
>   To find the place and worship—think our blood
> To drop and stain the tears we weep at prayer
>   On altar-stones—were this not very good?

Of this naive, vivid, imitative poetry the only survivor in poems published by Swinburne himself is the *Masque of Queen Bersabe*. What persisted from his discipleship and passed into his more individual work was not a few archaic words and turns of phrase, and the simple, frank sensuousness of description. For Swinburne's own taste in older literature was not for these medieval poets—neither Chaucer nor Spenser was quite a favourite of his—but the Elizabethan dramatists and the more frankly sensuous poetry of the Renaissance. Rossetti helped him here, *e.g.* in the *Ballad of Life* and the *Ballad of Death*. But he went, as with the popular ballads, more directly to the originals. One of the most interesting chapters in the second volume describes certain unpublished imitations of Boccaccio's *Decameron* and the French prose chroniclers, from which Lafourcade cites passages of amazing brilliance and sensuous quality as well as of ventriloquism. Certain parodies indeed of the French chroniclers in their own language, attached to *The Leper* and to the *Laus Veneris*, deceived his readers for years, even a scholar like Dr. Fiedler. Swinburne's blank verse shows the same progressive development through successive deliberate imitations—of Massinger and Fletcher, of Shakespeare and Chapman, of the Pre-Raphaelites, of the Greek tragedians— for to all the influences referred to must always be added, as by no means the least potent in their final effect, the English Bible and Greek poetry, dramatic and lyrical. Homer made no such appeal to Swinburne as he had to a greater poet and ventriloquist, Milton. It would be a nice study for a young student to consider Swinburne's lack of sympathy with certain supremely influential poets—Homer, Chaucer, Spenser, Keats. The influence of the last and the rejection of that influence Mr. Lafourcade has himself studied in an edition of Swinburne's *Hyperion*, an unpublished fragment after the manner of Keats. The first half of the second volume deals then mainly with this imitative period, illustrated from the chiefly unpublished work of the years 1849 to 1860, poems written at Eton and at Oxford. These include the fine poem *The Temple of Janus* with which Swinburne competed unsuccessfully—the prize went to John Nichol—for the New-digate, a poem which shows strongly the influence of Shelley, especially of the *Triumph of Life*; and also the poem on the death of Sir John Franklin, to which the classically educated taste of Dean Liddell preferred the unspeakable doggerel of some person unknown to fame, which had the honour of being read to the Royal Society. One can well understand Swinburne's antipathy for his University. As Chesterfield so often reminds his son, one forgives an injury, never a slight.

In the second part of the volume the author gives an exhaustive analysis of the sources, the form, and the thought and sensibility, of verse and prose, published and unpublished, of the years 1860 to 1867—*Rosamond, The Queen Mother, A Year's Letters, William Blake, Lesbia Brandon, Chastelard*, and finally *Atalanta in Calydon* and *Poems and Ballads*. Not the least interesting chapter—though lying somewhat apart from the study of the poetry—is that on the novel, published, with some modifications and omissions, in 1877 and again in 1905 as *A Year's Letters*. Mr. Lafourcade has been able to compare this with the original manuscript. It is a brilliant piece of work, revealing a surprising dramatic quality, and an ease and naturalness in the treatment of aristocratic life and character which Thackeray could not rival but which suggests Byron and Tolstoi. "The tragicomic catastrophe by which the young and inconsiderate 'hero' incautiously cuts himself out of a title and estate . . . by the simple and natural process of imprudently begetting a child on the wife of his hitherto childless kinsman" is claimed by Swinburne and accepted by Lafourcade as "original". Yet here too I suspect a source in the poet's multifarious reading. In the savage or humorous poem *The Curse* Donne writes:

> In early and long scarceness may he rot
> For lands which had been his, if he had not
> Himself incestuously an heir begot;

and a seventeenth-century note on a copy of Donne's poems points out that the conceit is also Marston's:

> Butt tell me Ned what may that gallant bee
> Who to obtain intemperate luxurie
> Cuckolds his older brother, gets an heire
> Whereby his hopes are turned to dispaire.

Swinburne was well acquainted with Marston and Donne too, and this is just the kind of joke which would make appeal to the mischief-loving humour he had indulged at the expense of Hutton.

But the keystone of Swinburne's early poetry and of Mr. Lafourcade's study is the *Atalanta* and *Poems and Ballads*. It is to the right understanding and appreciation of these that the whole work has been directed—to explain the spirit that informs them, a spirit of frustrated passion, love defeated and taking refuge in an apotheosis of lust, and a fierce anti-theism—and to analyse the subtle and varied lyric forms in which this troubled passion found expression. *Poems and Ballads*, he shows us, made clear to the British public what had disturbed them, even while they admired, in *Chastelard* and *Atalanta*, as *Don Juan* startled and shocked those who had admired the romantic strains of *The Giaour* and *The Corsair*. There had been nothing like the *Poems and Ballads* since the *Songs and Sonets* and *Elegies* of Donne. It is difficult for any one who has felt in his youth the charm of these poems:

> The passionate pages of his earlier years,
> Fraught with hot sighs, sad laughter, kisses, tears;
> Fresh-fluted notes, yet from a minstrel who
> Blew them not naively but as one who knew
> Full well why thus he blew,

as Hardy wrote; it is difficult to form a dispassionate estimate of them to-day, but a word or two must be attempted on Swinburne's poetry and Mr. Lafourcade's estimate.

Setting aside some survivals of his early ventriloquism such as *The Masque of Queen Bersabe*, there remain as the essential poems *Laus Veneris*, *The Triumph of Time*, *Anactoria*, *The Hymn to Proserpine*, *Faustine*, *The Leper*, *Dolores*, *Hesperia*, *Felise* and several shorter pieces, as *A Leave-Taking*, *Itylus*, *In the Orchard*, *Stage Love*, *Kissing her hair*, *The Garden of Proserpine*, and *Sapphics*. The first thought that arises on re-reading these is of the limited range of the experience which they record, and of the art they display with all its indubitable brilliance. It is with Swinburne's sensibility as with his thought. Just as he states with clearness and daring a few main thoughts on life and death, so his sensations are few but clear and sharp. Mr. Lafourcade has much to say of Swinburne's feeling for nature, and emphasizes this as a corrective to the contention that his inspiration was of a purely literary character (ii, 537 ff.). There is truth in his thesis that Swinburne's passion for sea and wind and sun was nourished, not on literature alone, but on his experiences in Northumberland and on the Sussex shores of the Channel. In a note on Tennyson's landscapes, which is not here cited, Swinburne declares he could not understand the line:

And white sails flying on a yellow sea

till he visited the coast of Lincolnshire and contrasted the colour of the sea there with the greyer and bluer seas of his own experience. That indicates observation, but his observation was very limited; and Mr. Lafourcade himself seems hardly to realize the significance of the descriptive vocabulary which he illustrates (ii, p. 538, note), namely, that for Swinburne sensations count mainly or only as they quicken the emotions, become emotions. Sun and wind and sea—these are emotional more than sensuous experiences. Hence his tendency, with Shelley rather than Keats, to personify these and all that he describes. "The white, wet flame of the breakers", "luminous face", "splendour of spears", "flame-like foam", "paler than young snow", "love wan as foam" (which might as well be "foam wan as love"), "waste white moon", these are emotional rather than sensuous descriptions. For truly sensuous description turn to Keats:

> I cannot see what flowers are at my feet,
>   Nor what soft incense hangs upon the boughs;
> But in embalmed darkness guess each sweet
>   Wherewith the seasonable month endows
>   The grass, the thicket, and the fruit-tree wild,
> White hawthorn and the pastoral eglantine,
>   Fast fading violets covered up in leaves,
>   And Mid-May's eldest child
> The coming musk-rose full of dewy wine,
>   The murmurous haunt of flies on summer eves.

Colour, temperature, scent, taste, sound—all are woven in. Compare Shelley and Swinburne:

> Swift as a spirit hastening to his task
>   Of glory and of good, the sun sprang forth
> Rejoicing in his splendour, and the mask
>
> Of darkness fell from the awakened earth.
>   The smokeless altars of the mountain snows
> Flamed above crimson clouds, and at the birth
>
> Of light the ocean's orison arose,
>   To which the birds tempered their matin lay.
> All flowers in field and forest which unclose
>
>   Their trembling eye-lids to the kiss of day,
> Swinging their censers in the element
>   With orient incense lit by the new ray
>
> Burnt slow and inconsumably and sent
>   Their odorous sighs up to the smiling air:
> And, in succession due, did continent,

Isle, ocean and all things that in them wear
The form and character of mortal mould
Rise as the sun their father rose to bear

Their portion of the toil which he of old
Took as his own and then imposed on them.

The sensations of light and sound and scent are merged in
the passionate emotion which Shelley lends to sun and
mountain and bird and flower. And so it is with Swinburne:

The low down leans to the sea; the stream
One loose, thin, pulseless, tremulous vein,
Rapid and vivid and dumb as a dream,
Works downward, sick of the sun and the rain;
No wind is rough with the rank, rare flowers;
The sweet sea, mother of loves and hours,
Shudders and shines as the grey winds gleam,
Turning her smile to a fugitive pain.

Not sense but sensibility, emotion, is the note of Swinburne's
temperament and poetry. *Poems and Ballads* is an amazing
explosion of emotion controlled and interpreted by the poet's
imagery and rhythm. Hence comes the most serious flaw in
Swinburne's art, an art which Mr. Lafourcade has analysed
with insight and justice, namely, the deficiency of archi-
tectonic power. This was to become more evident in later
odes and long lyrics (and no one has written more lengthy
lyrical poems), but it is evident here, too, in *The Triumph of
Time* and *Dolores*. Swinburne was never to be able to carry
a reader through an ode or rhapsody with the feeling that
the mood is developed through successive stages, as one is
carried through the *Epithalamion* of Spenser, the *Lycidas* of
Milton, or the *Odes* of Keats.

The keynote to *Poems and Ballads* Lafourcade finds in the
tragic experience of which the *Triumph of Time* is the record.

The failure to realize love in its normal entirety threw him back on the "roses and raptures of vice". "Comme il le dit lui-même, l'inspiration de *Dolores* est une réaction contre celle du *Triumph of Time*." But one must remember the poet's tendency to "force the note". It may be doubted whether, if "Boo" had been kinder, things would have gone very differently. The interest of this study is the light it throws on Swinburne's sensibility as expressed in his poems, for the interest of abnormality lies entirely in the light it throws on moods and instincts which are present in the normal also. Swinburne's sensibility, limited in range but intense, had two poles—passion and devotion. The counterpart to *Dolores* is not the *Triumph of Time* but the lines *In Memory of Walter Savage Landor*, and the second phase of his activity as a poet began with the worship of Mazzini in *A Song of Italy* and all that followed. But the passion which Swinburne sings is an experience in which pain and pleasure, attraction and repulsion, are strangely blended, as love and hate or contempt had been blended in the songs and elegies of Donne; and so it is a frustrated passion; and Swinburne's devotion, his purer passion, finds no adequate fulfilment, because it is always directed to a human subject and tends to disperse itself in a meaningless and disorderly rhapsody over Hugo or Mazzini or a baby's toes. He achieved neither great and satisfying love poetry nor the poetry of a satisfying devotion. Love and devotion are the only passions that justify and sustain ecstasy such as is the note of Crashaw's and Swinburne's poetry. In ancient literature, says Zielinsky, affection and passion were never united. The loves of Catullus and Propertius and Tibullus were one thing, the "amicitia" of which Cicero writes, the affection breathed in the lines of Catullus on his brother, were another. They were divided in Swinburne. The note of his poetry is "un accent douloureux et clairvoyant de passion inassouvie, de soif inextinguible"; and

Mr. Lafourcade closes his exhaustive study, to which I have done scant justice, with some lines from *Anactoria*:

> Alas, that neither moon nor snow nor dew,
> Nor all cold things can purge me wholly through,
> Assuage me, nor allay me, nor appease,
> Till supreme sleep shall bring me bloodless ease;
> Till time wax faint in all his periods;
> Till fate undo the bondage of the gods . . .
> And shed around and over and under me
> Thick darkness and the insuperable sea.

Still, one must not forget Swinburne's inclination to "force the note". He lived out his life to the end, if the poet gradually decayed, was indeed prematurely exhausted. It is some consolation for the early death of Keats and Shelley and Byron that they might have outlived their inspiration. Rome and the Bay of Spezia and Missolonghi are better than Putney.

XIV

A Review of *The Later Wordsworth*, by Edith C. Batho—1934

MISS BATHO has done in this interesting *apologia* something that very badly wanted doing. Since the revelation of the episode with Annette Vallon, Wordsworth's life and work have become a favourite field of investigation and theorizing for our younger critics who believe they have found in some of the phrases of modern psychology—inhibitions, sublimation, transference, etc.—a key that turns easily in every door and reveals what one wishes to find. Mr. Herbert Read's *Wordsworth, The Clark Lectures* (1929–30), and Mr. Fausset's *The Lost Leader* (1933) are the most recent and outspoken examples of this analytic treatment, this diagnosis psychological or metaphysical of a poet who after his early years in some way or other lost his soul. With the story of Annette as clue, Mr. Read can discover the beginning of the disintegration as early as 1797, that is, at the very date of the first emergence of Wordsworth's poetic genius in its full power, his recovery of happiness and the overflow of that happiness in song, in poems which have no equal as the expression of spiritual convalescence, returning health of body, mind, and soul. This is how Mr. Read describes it: "Wordsworth was recovering his stability, finding his ideal self, or personality, his philosophy of nature and his poetic genius; he was losing Annette, his faith in youth and change, his fundamental honesty". It is a strange combination of experiences which one would hardly expect to find in poems of such untroubled and rapturous joy as "It is the first mild day of March", "I heard a thousand blended notes",

> or:
>
> One morning thus by Esthwait lake
> When life was sweet, I knew not why,
>
> The sun, above the mountain's head,
> A freshening lustre mellow
> Through all the long green fields has spread,
> His first sweet evening yellow.
>
> Books! 'tis a dull and endless strife:
> Come, hear the woodland linnet,
> How sweet his music! on my life
> There's more of wisdom in it.

This great recovery was to be the central theme of *The Prelude*, and if with Mr. Read we are to accept the recovery as meaning an end of love, of faith in youth and change, a final breach with fundamental honesty, what *are* we to make of that poem? Mr. Read hints how we are to take it in his adjective "ideal". *The Prelude* is *not* a genuine record of Wordsworth's spiritual and poetic growth, but an ideal reconstruction of that life contemplated from a later point of view, from a time when he has repressed or denied some of his most poignant experiences and sublimated those he selected to cherish. Because in one of his early letters (written before he had recovered from the shattering experiences of his sympathy with the promises held out by the French Revolution) Wordsworth wrote: "I begin to wish much to be in town. Cataracts and mountains are good occasional society, but they will not do for constant companions"—a sentiment to the truth of which the whole tenor of Wordsworth's life bears witness—no poet felt more strongly than he the need of communication from time to time with his fellows, with understanding minds— Mr. Read declares that this statement "is a denial of the central doctrine of *The Prelude* and one of those minute fissures of reality that make us doubt the autobiographical validity of that idealistic structure". Annette is, Mr. Read and Mr. Fausset will have it, the clue to Wordsworth's life, and to the failure of his later poetry, the explanation of that last phase in "an atmosphere of domestic tyranny and provincial narrowness; of decaying sensibility and the slow growth of a thick shell of convention—conventional religion, conventional morality, and worst of all, conventional poetry".

What an untrue picture this is of Wordsworth's later life at home and in the world Miss Batho shows by an appeal to evidence, recorded evidence, not psychological and prejudiced interpretation. But before coming to Miss Batho's picture of the later man I must say a word on this reading of Wordsworth's earlier experience and its result in his greater poetry. In the absence of a full knowledge of the Annette incident we may, I suppose, read it in this manner, though I cannot myself find anywhere in Wordsworth's poetry any evidence of that troubled conscience, that sense of the loss of innocence, on which both the writers referred to lay stress so insistently—nothing remotely resembling the war between conscience and a perverse will of which Byron's later poetry is the record, or even of what one divines must be the accent of remorse in one or two of Shelley's lyrics, where certainly one might expect to hear such a note. No poetry breathes, as I have said, a more untroubled spirit of joy than that which flows from Wordsworth between the recovery of his peace of mind and the discovery of the gradual decay of his supernormal sensibility—a decay of a kind of which everyone who has had any acuteness of sensibility in youth becomes sooner or later aware. Wordsworth is not the only poet whose later work lacks inspiration.

Is it not possible to read the history of Wordsworth's life, including this episode, in quite another way and one more in harmony with the tone of the poetry written between 1797 and 1807, if it does not explain the gradual decline of his

263

poetic inspiration after that date, which is another question? That his love for Annette had been an exciting, absorbing incident Wordsworth's own description in *Vaudracour and Julia* is sufficient evidence:

> Earth lived in one great presence of the spring;
> Life turned the meanest of her implements,
> Before his eyes, to price above all gold—

and that Wordsworth could so write about it is evidence that in looking back he felt no inclination either to suppress or belie the experience. But the ferment which a passionate experience excites is not always a safe clue to its depth, its origin in the deeper levels of his personality. First love, especially for a young man who has not given himself away in cheaper "furtive lust", the discovery that a woman of his own class and upbringing can love him so well as to deny him nothing, is a tremendous experience; but it may be a misleading one. Witness Milton; or take the instance of Shelley again. The description of love in the lines quoted above is to my mind a truer one than that given in *Epipsychidion*; but it is not so ecstatic. Yet in what did Shelley's ecstatic passion eventuate? Nothing. Disillusionment. A state of "as you were", and an eager looking round for another woman with whom to renew the experience:

> The Serpent is shut out from paradise.

It is, of course, a compliment that Mr. Read and Mr. Fausset pay to Wordsworth in taking it for granted that he was not so "tickle o' the sere" as Shelley, that for his stronger, tougher nature such an experience meant more, would make a deeper and more enduring mark. Yes; but that mark may take another form than that of a troubled conscience. Anyone who has had occasion to make a sympathetic yet detached study of religious conversion will have observed certain differences in its effect—in some a violent fermentation which subsides and leaves no trace behind; in others a fermentation that does also subside without producing any profound alteration in character and life, yet leaves its mark, if only in the subject's better understanding of himself, of what is or is not for him. But there is a third effect produced more rarely, an effect not of fermentation but rather of crystallization. The religious appeal acts like the passing of an electric spark through a prepared solution; the character takes a shape it will never again lose. The reason is that in such a person the earlier, secular, careless life had not represented adequately the deeper strata of the soul; it was the religious awakening which revealed to the subject his own true self. So can love act in some, on the whole, one must admit, rare natures. Wordsworth's love for Annette was, like Shelley's, a violent fermentation, resembling in that his first passionate enthusiasm for the French Revolution. Both left their mark, but that mark is not to be deciphered as a deeply troubled conscience about Annette or a desertion of the cause of humanity. The issue of both was ultimately a deeper self-revelation. Just as it was impossible for Wordsworth, with his robuster mind, to continue with Shelley all his life to think that if Kings and Priests could all be hanged the world would run on wheels towards Elysium, so it was not possible for him to keep up a passion once he realized it had no roots in his deeper nature; nor, on the other hand, could he, like Shelley, simply forget it and pass on. He had a duty to Annette and, so far as one can discover, endeavoured to discharge it. The fact remains that the full flow of Wordsworth's stream of song began, not with the passion for Annette and the Rights of Man, but with his escape from them, his realization of the stratification of his own soul. Poetry as passion recollected in tranquillity—Mr. Read has justly corrected the misinterpretation of that phrase—is a description of Wordsworth's poetry as perhaps of no other poet's; for the theme of all the poems of his best years is the life he had lived from childhood to the year 1797, but that life as seen by one who had escaped from certain powerful but misleading influences, and can now read the whole in the light of a new revelation. That is his one great theme. Even if he draws from later details of experience he fits them into that picture and mood. From France and passion he reverted with all the force of a deep and passionate nature to England and affection. Dorothy and, supplying the intellectual element which she could not, Coleridge, provided the electric spark which crystallized Wordsworth's emotional and moral nature.

Miss Batho's book is of course not concerned with this earlier Wordsworth, and she has not found it necessary to add to the increasing number of analyses of *The Prelude,* analyses which tend too much to assume that it is a philosophical treatise rather than a poem. A poet utilizes philosophical ideas, whether derived with John Donne from Thomas Aquinas or with Wordsworth from Hartley, not to elaborate a complete philosophy, but as a help to define and articulate emotional experiences and convictions. Miss Batho's concern is with the later man and poet, "the Lost Leader" as Browning described him and as the complacent Liberalism of the nineteenth century naturally thought of him; the man who in the age of "unexampled progress", of the glorious expansion of Macaulay's panacea for all ills, *laissez-faire*, the doctrine that the duty of government was not to afford any paternal protection to the weak but to stand aside "leaving capital to find its more lucrative course, commodities their fair price, industry and intelligence their natural reward, idleness and folly their natural punishment" —the Wordsworth who felt that this was not what he had hoped for and was a progress, as Carlyle declared in much more violent language, towards a precipice, and so drew

back and apparently entrenched himself in a Tory resistance to change. That this did lead Wordsworth to oppose
changes that were imperative and have proved, if not in
their first yet in their ultimate workings, beneficial or capable
of being beneficial, need not be denied. But who to-day
will say that Wordsworth and Carlyle were wrong in their
distrust of democracy working merely by the counting of
noses, without regard to the complex structure of a social
organism, or in disliking an industrialism of "rugged individualism" which took no regard for the real inequalities
produced by wealth and poverty?

To prove that Wordsworth, despite his Toryism, was not
indifferent to the welfare of humanity and the poor, was not
a closed, hardened mind, Miss Batho appeals to the evidence
of those who knew him. A man has a right to be judged
by his equals, and those who admire him may rest in their
opinion. Miss Batho's witnesses are men of such high
authority and of such different shades of political thought
as John Stuart Mill, Thomas Carlyle, William Rowan
Hamilton, Thomas Cooper the Chartist, and others. The
more depreciatory descriptions of Wordsworth as an egotist
who could talk only of his own poetry proceeded, she has
shown, from a rather narrow circle in close touch with one
another, of whom Hazlitt, for special personal reasons, was
the most envenomed. If Wordsworth left on the minds of
some who heard him the impression of being self-centred,
he was in that like many other literary men who are good
talkers, Macaulay, Carlyle, Coleridge; and if Wordsworth
talked of his own poetry it was because in the circle he moved
in (to which Shelley and Keats hardly belonged) he was
almost alone in regarding poetry with entire seriousness, as
a thing of the first importance in the life of a country.

Miss Batho is on more difficult ground in dealing with
Wordsworth's religion and with his later poetry as poetry.

On the former subject she is, I think, essentially right. Whatever phases of thought on religion and morals he may have passed through in the years of fermentation, to say that in his great poetry Wordsworth writes as a pantheist seems to me a misapprehension alike of its underlying thought and of the feeling it communicates. In an interesting analysis of one of the rejected passages of *The Prelude* (which Mr. de Selincourt has printed) Mr. Read brings out very well the clearness with which Wordsworth had distinguished, yet interrelated, Nature, Man, and God: "So the great union of Man and Nature is consummated by a process of association which links up, at every stage, experience and the experiencing self, leading from sensation to feeling, from feeling to thought, and then creating a union of these faculties in God, who is the Whole of Being". If I understand this aright (which I am not sure) it is what Miss Batho means by Wordsworth's "panentheism". God is in Man and God is in Nature, and yet God transcends both, and the theme of Wordsworth's nature poetry is not so much the divine spirit manifested in Nature as the simpler and happier relation of natural things to God, to the inner law of their being. Henry Vaughan and Thomas Traherne had, in an earlier century, the same intuition of this happier, simpler relation of natural things to God. But Wordsworth reads the lesson of that intuition with a less obvious reference to the Christian doctrine of the Fall, more in the spirit of the age of Rousseau:

> The birds around me hopped and played,
> Their thoughts I cannot measure:—
> But the least motion that they made,
> It seemed a thrill of pleasure. . . .
>
> If this belief from Heaven be sent,
> If such is Nature's holy plan,
> Have I not reason to lament
> What Man has made of Man?

What is the contrast Wordsworth here emphasizes? I would venture to read it thus. The sources of happiness in all organic being—indeed, in all being, Wordsworth would say in moments of exaltation when he is lending life and personality to streams and winds and mountains—are impulse and law. Happiness is the consciousness, in Aristotle's phrase, of ἀνεμπόδιστος ἐνέργεια. The life of flowers and birds and animals is such a life. They are happy because their impulses flow freely along the channels prescribed by the law of their being by God. How this has been attained to by those who survive in the struggle for existence is a question which no Darwin had yet raised. The cause of man's peculiar trouble is twofold. He fetters his natural freedom by artificial laws of his own invention—social taboos, prudential maxims, traditional inhibitions. On the other hand he will continue to "kick against the pricks", to fight against the deeper laws of his nature which have their root in his social nature and his dependence on God. A Rob Roy achieves release from the first of these, and in so far is happy because free:

> The creatures, see, of flood and field,
> And those that travel on the wind!
> With them no strife can last; they live
> In peace, and peace of mind.
>
> For why?—because the grand old rule
> Sufficeth them, the simple plan,
> That they should take who have the power,
> And they should keep who can.

But this is a half truth expressed in a mood half humorous, half serious, for the law of man's nature is not that of the animals and flowers, but ultimately the law of love:

> by love subsists
> All lasting grandeur, by pervading love;
> That gone, we are as dust.

What Wordsworth learns from Nature is not naturalism, *fay ce que vouldras*, and Rabelais' doctrine of liberty rests itself on a faith in human nature. Rabelais is a humanist, as were Montaigne and Milton; and on the strength of the well-known lines written above Tintern Abbey Mr. Read makes Wordsworth, and justly, a humanist also. But the humanism of all these poets is not, as he thinks, and as it is the fashion now to declare, an entire contradiction of supernatural religion. Their humanism is the denial of a supernatural authority, or what claims to be so, commanding what is repellent to the deeper instincts of the human heart. If the Jewish prophets spoke the words of supernatural revelation, they spoke also in the language of the human heart, outraged by religious demands which involved passing their children through the fire to Moloch and sanctioning the orgies of fertility rites. To sacrifice and hecatombs they preferred a command to which the heart assented: "do justly and love mercy, and walk humbly with thy God".

I cannot, therefore, see that there was anything in the poetic creed of Wordsworth's years of great creative work that made it an apostasy to revert to the Christian and Anglican tradition in which, Miss Batho points out, he had been reared. Indeed Mr. Aldous Huxley has detected an Anglican flavour in the fine lines written before 1805:

> The unfettered clouds, and region of the heavens,
> Tumult and peace, the darkness and the light—
> Were all like workings of one mind, the features
> Of the same face, blossoms upon one tree,
> Characters of the great Apocalypse,
> The types and symbols of Eternity,
> Of first, and last, and midst, and without end.

"Something", says Mr. Huxley, "far more deeply interfused, had made its appearance in this Wordsworthian scene. The God of Anglicanism had crept under the skin of things"

(*Do What You Will*, p. 119). So Mr. Huxley in mockery says what Miss Batho seriously contends regarding Wordsworth's "panentheism" and the Catholic tradition in which he had been educated. If that tradition was at the back of Wordsworth's mind during all these years, it is not difficult to understand that he should retreat into the shelter of a more dogmatic and institutional religion when the ardour of his joyous and poetic faith in Nature began to give way with the decay of his sensibility and his encounter with the tragic facts of life. For every convert—and Wordsworth's crisis had been in the nature of a conversion—the problem arises sooner or later what is to be his support and guidance when the first fervour and glow of feeling has subsided. It is just here that, if he can accept them, dogmatic and institutional religion come to his aid, definitions and rites. They are not the expression of his own highest moments but are an evidence and reminder in moods of depression and dullness that such experiences have been and may be again.

The first severe shock to Wordsworth's recovered joy and faith was the death of his brother John in 1803. For Wordsworth affections were passions. His affection for his sister was so intense as inevitably to suggest to psychological critics of to-day an erotic interpretation. But the same interpretation would have in that case to be extended to his love for his children, for his daughter Dora especially, one might even say for his brother. The loss of each of these was as the tearing up of something from the very roots of his heart. To every man comes sooner or later a realization of the tragic character of life, and it could only come with the greater poignancy to one who, having passed through a violent fermentation in youth, had emerged into the sunlight again, and, with a force derived from a supernormal organic sensibility and a vivid creative imagination, renewed his joy and faith in life. What was he then to do? He might

271

yield like the Solitary in *The Excursion* to despondence, to the conviction that:

> Earth and high Heaven fail from the prime foundation;
> All things are here to rive the heart, and all are vain,
> Horror and scorn and hate and fear and indignation;
> Oh, why did I awake? When shall I sleep again?

He might, on the other hand, if I can follow Mr. Fausset, have attained to a mystical faith in life which would have made him "love good and evil", a strange creed which Mr. Middleton Murry apparently has evolved from a misprint in a poem of Keats. The artist indeed may find an equal aesthetic interest in good and evil. The saint may believe, and attain at moments to the conviction that in God these contradictions will find an ultimate solution. No living and suffering man, who is honest with himself, will ever feel or think that he is equally content with good and evil. Attaining to this mystical height Wordsworth would, I gather from the same source, have been indifferent to the hope of immortality, of another and better world beyond this. Historically it is only in some such faith and hope that men have ever, in the face of sorrow and death, risen beyond resignation to faith and peace of mind. It was the end of Jewish prophecy, after all its phases of earthly hope and expectation had passed. To Blake the only explanation of evil was that the vegetable world of the senses is an illusion, that truth lies beyond:

> The Grave is Heaven's golden Gate.

Wordsworth had too robust a mind to become a pseudo-mystic; too honest to affect ecstasies of religious conviction. In his later religion, as in his later politics, he fell back on a Christian Stoicism. He did not really cease to believe in human progress as Mr. Fausset asserts, though, like Carlyle, he did not swallow all the nostrums of current Whig

doctrine. "You were right," he said to Cooper the Chartist,
"I have always said the people were right in what they asked;
but you went the wrong way to ask it. . . . The people are
sure to have the franchise as knowledge increases; but you
will not get all you seek at once." For religious support,
as the glow of his sensibility and the confident faith which
it inspired faded, he looked round for the best he could find.
Unfortunately, institutional and dogmatic Christianity in
England was at a low ebb. He watched with sympathy the
early symptoms of its revival in the Oxford movement. All
this Miss Batho brings out in a clear and convincing way.

And what of the poetry of this last long phase? Miss
Batho has made a gallant effort to vindicate its merits, and
spoken justly of the difficulties with which Wordsworth had
to contend owing to the weakness and suffering of his eyes.
Much of it is certainly not great poetry. It is a pity that
Wordsworth continued to write Nature poems in the old
vein but without the old inspiration. But there are one or
two things to be said about this later poetry. First, no
one who realizes the narrow range within which Wordsworth's great and intense poetry moves should feel surprise
at its subsidence. Wordsworth never had the artistic range
of poets like Spenser and Milton, whether as regards form
or subject. He had but one great theme, his own early
experiences and their interpretation. His poetry is a product
of memories re-interpreted, comparable to Proust's great
novel. Secondly, as to the philosophical poem which
Wordsworth never wrote. With regard to this, Wordsworth
himself, Coleridge, and the critics seem to me to have fallen
into the same error as Wordsworth did once before when
he found to his dismay "*that we had crossed the Alps*". He
had, in *The Prelude*, written that great philosophical poem.
Thirdly, Wordsworth's later poetry should be read as something quite distinct from the earlier. It is poetry of a

different kind, poetry on a lower level certainly, but not at its best without interest, a poetry of reflection, of meditation, Christian and Stoical in tone. I am one of those, and there are others, who can read *The Excursion* with a quiet pleasure, this poetry of sober, meditative age, just as I find myself giving a higher value to *Paradise Regained* than I should once have thought possible. "Conventional" does not seem to me the right word to apply even to Wordsworth's later poetry. It is always too sincere to be merely conventional—awkward, if you like, even dull, but there are ever-recurring exceptions: sonnets like *Mutability* which Miss Batho quotes; the *Trossachs*; "There's not a nook within this solemn Pass"; "Such age, how beautiful"; "Ethereal minstrel! pilgrim of the sky"; the lines on the death of Hogg—and not a few others. *Dion* and *Laodamia* seem to me noble poems of this reflective, ethical kind, and are to be judged as such—breathing a noble Stoicism not untouched with a mysticism which his mystical critics have overlooked—the touch of mysticism which one feels when a poet carries a story of human life and character relentlessly to its end, so far as we can follow it, yet leaves the reader with a strange, elevated sense that this is not the ultimate end. In both these poems, Wordsworth traces with unwavering hand the inevitable working of justice, of moral law, yet leaves us with a sense of something mysterious and consoling in the final issue. He rejected the more sentimental close which he had given to *Laodamia* for one that seems more stern and has shocked his critics. The close of *Dion* is even more impressive in this way. Dion has fallen as the consequence of one moment's guilt, but

> in calm peace the appointed Victim slept,
> As he had fallen in magnanimity;
> Of spirit too capacious to require
> That Destiny her course should change; too just

To his own native greatness to desire
That wretched boon, days lengthened by distrust.
So were the hopeless troubles, that involved
The soul of Dion, instantly dissolved.

Miss Batho has written an excellent book. It is a piece of advocacy and will not convert all those to whom it is addressed, but it will give satisfaction to anyone who wishes to do justice to a great, if a limited, poet, and who dislikes seeing a great and complex spirit too easily interpreted by the application of a few formulae. It is a comfort to read a work which rests on evidence, not on conjecture and divination.

PRINTED IN GREAT BRITAIN
BY R. & R. CLARK, LIMITED
EDINBURGH